GOD'S PROMISE KEPT

VOLUME I

L. DALE REDLIN

Erben House, LLC
erbenhouse.com
info@erbenhouse.com
1521 N Argonne Rd, Suite C221
Spokane Valley, WA 99212

All scripture quotations, unless otherwise indicated, are taken from the New King James Version®. Copyright © 1982 by Thomas Nelson, Inc. Used by permission. All rights reserved.

Scripture quotations marked with (NIV®) are taken from the "Holy Bible, New International Version®. Copyright ©1978 by New York International Bible Society." Used by permission. All rights reserved.

Scripture quotations marked with (ESV®) are taken from "The Holy Bible, English Standard Version® (ESV®) Copyright © 2001 by Crossway, a publishing ministry of Good News Publishers." Used by permission. All rights reserved.

All hymn verses used are in the public domain.

Images used are in the public domain.

ISBN 979-8-9865934-1-8

Layout work for text and purchased cover designs was provided by Tim Schaser—Graphic Artist

Other books by this author:

God's Promise Kept, Volume II
It Takes Cow Chips to Make Dinner
My Father's Business
Poems of Prayer & Praise
Sheep & Shepherds

Printed in the United States of America
Second printing

ACKNOWLEDGEMENTS

My dear wife Hope: My God-sent partner, who is totally right for me, has put up with her husband's many hours of research, thinking, and computerizing. Besides, she was the first to faithfully read the manuscript of this book and offered valuable critique. Many are the blessings of our gracious and loving God. Among them is the loving guidance and corrections of a faithful, loving wife. Try as we might, we will never, ever be able to adequately fulfill the God-inspired words of the Apostle Paul: "Husbands, love your wives, just as Christ also loved the church and gave Himself for it . . . ." (Ephesians 1:25) Thank you, Hope.

Professor Emeritus Paul R. Koch: Paul has been a literary and theological asset to the Church of our Lord for many years. Many were the times that his expert advice on grammatical syntax was sought on the floor of conferences and conventions. His many years as professor and experience as the faithful Editor of the monthly periodical of the Church of the Lutheran Confession, *The Lutheran Spokesman*, has sharpened his editor skills beyond question. We are privileged to be able to make use of his vast experience and knowledge as Editor of *God's Promise Kept*. It is our heartfelt prayer that his literary and theological skills may be used in our Savior's kingdom for years to come. Thank you, Paul.

Mr. Timothy Schaser: Tim is the man who takes the ideas, suggestions, and writings of others and artistically turns them into an offering pleasing to the eyes of the beholder. He is the Graphic Artist who has been moved to use his God-given gifts and talents in the service of our Lord to produce a product that will grip the eyes of the potential reader. But more importantly, it is his hopeful desire that viewers will be moved to read the contents of this labor of love and, as a result, be drawn closer to the LORD God of heaven and earth. Tim is employed as a professional Graphic Artist with a full family life. He has joyfully taken on this project of love, doing the work in his spare time, for his and our Savior. Thank you, Tim.

AN UNBIASED WORD
FROM THE AUTHOR'S WIFE

When I was a Sunday School teacher, I was always searching for a book that would help me teach the story-lessons of the Bible to the little children who sat before me each Sunday. I wished for them to see how much their Savior loved them and that He was with them every day to guide and lead them. If I could teach the lessons of the Bible in such a way that they would be captured by how God moved the events, places and people, maybe they would remember how graciously God dealt with them and how He deals with us each day.

When I began reading this book, I didn't know what to expect, but as I read, I was pleasantly surprised. It seemed that the author was simply talking to me—he was right there speaking to me personally. As a result, I was drawn into the lessons and personally related to the messages as they unfolded before me. Bible passages and familiar hymn verses are used to help emphasize the life-issues taught. I liked that.

This book presents that wonderful God-designed journey from Eden to Bethlehem in a way that the reader just wants to keep on reading. I limited myself to one devotional or chapter each morning. However, at times I just had to cheat a bit and go on to the next chapter.

Not only is this writing interesting, it is up to date. That is, applications are continually made to today's life situations with which we are dealing every day. Then, as now, the LORD God has the answers for each of us as we face the trials of life.

Personally, I had the pleasure of being the first to read this work and, of course, offer suggestions on clarity, punctuation, and wording. So, I can personally recommend this writing with the promise that these Bible based devotions will brighten your life and bring you ever closer to the LORD our God.

The unbiased wife,
Hope

PREFACE

I thank the LORD God for the strength and stamina required to take this enjoyable Biblical journey with fellow believers from Eden to Bethlehem. As we take this trip, we observe the twists and turns, the ups and downs, the trials and adversities resulting in ultimate blessings for our fathers and mothers in the faith. Writing these pages has been a joy that reaches far beyond words. In fact, as I joined our fellow believers on this traveling experience, I felt at one with them. Their trials became my trials—their joys became my joys—their dreams became my dreams. And, of course, their blessings became my blessings. It is my prayer that each of you readers may have the same experience.

As we mosey along through God's Word, we find that a kind of mosaic takes shape before our very eyes. As we observe carefully, we will witness the LORD God of heaven and earth carefully weaving each episode into that amazing mosaic which we refer to as His Earthly Kingdom. Each piece is laid with care—each experience is part of the whole—every attempt of the Evil One to interfere with this godly endeavor of establishing His kingdom of life and salvation for all humanity is skillfully used by God for a resultant blessing for his people.

Furthermore, as we take this marvelous journey with God, we see how it becomes a template for each of our lives. With each episode the LORD God reaches out to each of us and before our very eyes demonstrates how He continues to work in our lives every single day. As a matter of fact, each of our lives is part of that divine mosaic created by hands of God. Each of us is a special piece in that divinely created product—His everlasting kingdom. His love for His people today is just as powerful. His miracles are just as prominent. His mercy is just as forgiving. His concern for each of us is just as real.

These writings are calculated to be devotional in format. They are designed in such a way that the reader will discover that each episode of God's mercy is like a link in a golden chain leading from promise to fulfillment. Yet, along the way we will be experiencing everyday life lessons as we witness God's interaction with sinful people, real like ourselves. It is my prayer that this will help us recognize more fully that the LORD God continues to function every day in each of our lives.

Added hymn verses have been carefully chosen to emphasize special points in each episode. From time to time extra information is included to help us get a full picture of God's design. To that end some relatively recent excavation discoveries are included.

Volume 1 will lead us from Eden through the God's Commandments which He graciously dictated at Mr. Sinai. Volume II will begin with entering the Land of Promise and conclude with the birth, life and crucifixion of the promised Messiah—Shiloh—the promised Seed of the woman—that One through Whom God's Promise Is Kept!

INI

TABLE OF CONTENTS

PROLOGUE 1

The Seventh Day 2

Angels 6

Trouble In Paradise 7

The Seditious, Sordid Scheme of Satan 9

The Disastrous Fall 11

The Aftermath 14

The Blame Game 16

God's Promise 18

GOD'S PROMISE KEPT **23**

The Devastation of Sin Hits Home 25

Satan at His Best—Working the Worst 31

An Ungodly Merger 41

God's Judgment Tempered with Grace 49

Honoring Self vs Honoring God 59

A Cradle for the Promised Seed 69

Sarai's "Solution" vs God's Promise 77

A Supreme Test of Faith 87

God's Promise via Isaac and Rebekah 97

Two Nations Are in Your Womb 105

Reason Overtakes Faith 113

The Deceiver Is Deceived 123

It Was Time to Go 131

Wrestling with God 141

First Things First 147

Joseph—God's Special Agent 157

God Prepares Joseph for His Ministry 167

Joseph's One-Line Sermon 177

The Blessing of Patient Endurance 183

From Prison to Palace 191

A (Kind of) Family Reunion .205

Identity of the "Man" Revealed 215

A Life-Changing Invitation Accepted 225

A Special Blessing for Judah .233

God Chooses Moses to Lead His People 243

Moses Called into God's Special Service 257

Excuses, Excuses, Excuses Galore 267

To the Promised Land with God's Blessing 281

I Am the LORD 291

Faith Put to the Ultimate Test 301

A Miraculous Lesson in Faith and Obedience 311

What Shall We Eat? What Shall We Drink? 323

Manna from Heaven 331

A Theocratic Government 343

Preparations for God's Once-and-Forever Sermon 353

God Requires Faithfulness to Him Alone. 359

God Requires that We Respect His Holy Name 369

God Requires that We Worship Him in Spirit and Truth 375

God Requires that Children Respect Their Parents 381

God Requires that We Respect Human Life 389

God Requires that We Respect Marriage 397

God Requires that We Respect Others' Property 403

God Requires that We Protect the Reputation of Others. 409

God Forbids Coveting Our Neighbor's Possessions 413

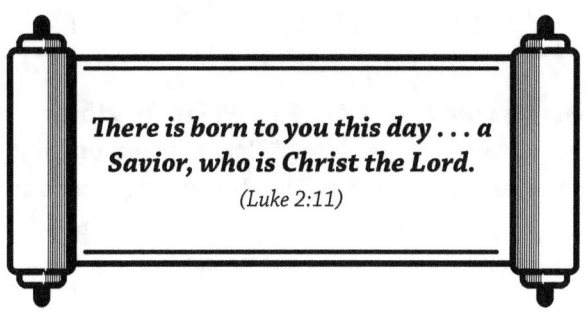

There is born to you this day . . . a Savior, who is Christ the Lord.
(Luke 2:11)

PROLOGUE

"Christmas Time." What a wonderfully precious time of the year! But maybe we should ask ourselves, *"Why is it so a popular; what makes it so wonder-filled? Why do we celebrate? What does that expression, 'Christmas Time' really mean to me?"* How would you answer that?

Well, here are a few possible responses: Family gatherings . . . we all enjoy them, don't we? And who among us doesn't take pleasure in hearing and/or singing Christmas songs and carols? Or maybe it's the buying and giving of gifts. And what about the decorations and Christmas lights adorning our homes and yards; they speak loudly and clearly, don't they? *"It's Christmas time!"*

And let's not forget that family trip to the hills—spending time searching for, finding, and cutting down our own special Christmas tree. Excitement rises as we transport our yearly find homeward, place it in its customary location, decorate it with ornaments from years gone by, and listen as it speaks in unmistakable clarity: "It's Christmas Time!"

Then again, some who have moved to a southern climate can only dream of that white Christmas like the ones they used to know as children. Yes, there are likely many recollections and mental scenes etched in each of our memories of that highly regarded time of the year, inviting us to reminisce with fondness.

But in the midst of all of our treasured memories of that joyful season, what about this: **"There is born to you this day . . . a Savior,**

1

who is Christ the LORD" (Luke 2:11). Where does that fit in? It fits in everywhere, doesn't it? Absolutely! That's the reason for it all! That's why we celebrate; that's the motivation for singing hymns and carols of joy; that's why we give gifts and decorate our homes and wish everyone a happy, blessed, and Christ-filled Christmas!

Indeed, many of us cannot imagine celebrating that joyous time of the year without Advent devotions, church services, the lighting of the Advent candles, hearing that simple and miraculous Christmas message expressed so wonderfully by our children. Yes, if we take time to give it some thought and listen to God's divinely inspired words, we surely realize that "Christmas Time" is really a celebration of what God has done and is doing for us constantly. Indeed, all of us are invited to listen carefully as the angels of God address each of us with these words: **"For there is born to you this day in the city of David a Savior, who is Christ the Lord"** (Luke 2:11).

Briefly put, the Savior of the world was born and came into this world for one reason and one reason only—because God loves us. The Christ Child was born to restore our life with God. In fact, that is exactly what our Savior tells us: **"I have come that they may have life, and that they may have it more abundantly"** (John 10:10).

Without a doubt, that's what Christmas is all about. It is a celebration of renewal and restoration of our lives with God. So, let's start at the beginning. As it has been said: "That's a very good place to start."

THE SEVENTH DAY

The heavens and the earth, and all the host of them, were finished . . . then . . . God . . . rested.
(Genesis 2:1–2)

The day after Creation—what a glorious day—we can only try to imagine it all. Before us stands the completed, pure and perfect Creation of all things. The brilliant stars of night have slowly slipped away and disappeared into the vast expanse of the firmament. The morning sun is slowly creeping over the horizon—the beginning of a new and glorious day of wonder, perfection, and breathtaking beauty welcomes us. As the fresh morning light sweeps away the final shadows of night, the seventh day has begun—the day following God's wondrous creative acts. **Thus the heavens and the earth, and all the host of them, were finished. And on the seventh day God ended His work which He had done, and He rested on the seventh day from all His work which He had done** (Genesis 2:1–2).

As Eve opened her eyes on that wonder-filled day, she glanced around a bit and could hardly believe it all. Adam, her God-created husband, had risen early and was doing some minor exploring of the grandeur and beauty of everything—everywhere. The entire world lay invitingly before them. It was breath-taking and beyond description. Here they would spend their lives discovering, enjoying, learning, raising their family, watching their children grow, and sharing the world with other creatures—forever.

In the distance were the God-created animals, large and small, of every shape and size, foraging amidst the lush vegetation. The crystal-blue skies were dotted with the early morning birds practicing their aviary skills and landing on the stage of welcoming trees to perform their morning concert. The soothing sounds of flowing water in a near-by creek created a superb background for the beauteous chorales of creation. It was all so excellent—so wonder-filled.

Cecil Frances Alexander (1818–1895) tried to capture the glories of creation with just a few poetic words:

All things bright and beautiful,
All creatures great and small,
All things wise and wonderful,
The LORD God made them all.

As Adam and Eve began their lives together in this marvelous paradise, their joy and peace were beyond description. Each time they lifted their eyes and surveyed the glories of creation, peace and tranquility filled their minds and hearts. The urge to discover, explore, and absorb it all captured their curiosity.

The grassy hills, the fruited plains, vegetation of every kind from the giant redwoods to the tiny buttercups to the microbes in the soil—rivers, streams, lakes, and seemingly endless seas teeming with an untold number of aquatic species—earth-bound creatures of every shape and size imaginable roaming about in the hills and valleys—the heavenly bodies beyond number, all created by the Maker of all things and placed in the heavens for beauty, light, and life—all creation welcomed and challenged the thoughts and faultless minds of Adam and Eve—the crowns of all creation. As a matter of fact, even after these many thousands of years, man has not come close to plumbing the depths of the mysterious challenges that await discovery in this incredible work of God.

But before we move on, we really should take a closer look at the sixth day of creation. Why the sixth day? Well, listen to God and you will understand why that day was so unique. We are invited to listen-in as God tells us all about the mind-boggling happenings of that day. **Then God said: "Let Us make man in Our image, according to Our likeness; let them have dominion over the fish of the sea, over the birds of the air, and over the cattle, over all the earth and over every creeping thing that creeps on the earth." So God created man in His own image; in the image of God He created him; male and female He created them** (Genesis 1:26–27).

These wonder-filled words are often rather hurriedly read and quickly passed over. Here let us pause for a bit to genuinely examine and spiritually absorb this mind-challenging revelation.

Notice first of all how the LORD God speaks of Himself in the plural: **"Let Us make man in Our image, according to Our likeness."** Here we are challenged with the concept of the plurality of God. Yes, His Triune nature is presented to us in the very first chapter of His Word. God the Father, the Son, and the Holy Spirit were all wondrously involved in this grand creative activity. As a matter of fact, we are informed by God that even before the six days of creation began, **the Spirit of God was hovering over the face of the waters** (Genesis 1:2). From that day forward, the Holy Spirit was involved in every aspect of the work of God. From creation of all things until the last second of this world's existence, the Holy Spirit is and will be continually involved with the work in God's kingdom of gracious love.

Secondly, the Apostle John was inspired by God to point out in the very first words of his Gospel: **In the beginning was the Word, and the Word was with God, and the Word was God. He was in the beginning with God. . . . And the Word became flesh and dwelt among us, and we beheld His glory, the glory as of the only begotten of the Father, full of grace and truth** (John 1:1&14). This truth of God stands absolute and undeniable: The very Christ, God's Son, our Savior, was there in the eternal presence of the Almighty from the very beginning. As a matter of fact, not only was He there, but **all things were made through Him, and without Him nothing was made that was made** (John 1:3).

But what really causes our heads to spin is when the LORD God clearly informs us that Adam and Eve were created in the **likeness** and **image** of Himself—the Triune God! Our first parents were created to be like Him! In other words, they were created holy, perfect, and pure. Indeed, they were created immortal! They were brought into being by God to

5

live forever in a state of everlasting perfection in that astoundingly glorious rulership of all of His grand creation.

Now, having been created in the image of God, Adam and Eve had a flawless relationship with God, with one another, and with all of creation. It might be difficult for us to wrap our faulty minds around that God-revealed truth—for having lived and experienced life under the grip of sin, we can hardly imagine living in a world with no wars, no disagreements, no worries, no sorrows, no sickness, no suffering, and no death! It's impossible for us to imagine pure and unadulterated peace . . . joy . . . love . . . unconditional happiness with God and with each other, every . . . single . . . day! But that's how it was until that never to be forgotten day when everything changed because of . . . SATAN!

ANGELS

He shall give His angels charge over you, to keep you in all your ways.
(Psalm 91:11)

So, why are we suddenly reading about angels? Well, all we can say is: *"Read on, and you will see."* To begin, what do we know about the origin of angels? Answer: Not very much. Yet this we can say—that besides the wonders of creation, angels were created by God, **who makes His angels spirits, His ministers** (servants) **a flame of fire** (Psalm 104:4). When did that happen? We don't know because God doesn't consider it necessary to tell us. However, it appears that these special creations of God were a happy and hearty lot. In fact, on the occasion of God's marvelous creation of the world they celebrated. On that special day we are told that **all the sons of God shouted for joy!** (Job 38:7)

To what can we liken these created beings? Well, in a way, they are like us. What? Like us? Yes, they are. Maybe we don't often think of ourselves as spirits, but that's exactly who we are—spirits with bodies. Angels, on the other hand, are spirits also—but without bodies. Yet we notice that on various occasions God does give them visible bodies in order to serve Him in some special capacity on Earth.

What do they do? There is one thing that is certain—the angels of God are very active. As we shall see, the Old Testament Scriptures are sprinkled with numerous appearances of angels when they are called upon by God to carry out some special work at critical times. We will notice this activity of angels regularly during our God-revealed journey that we are preparing to take to Bethlehem.

Besides serving God in various capacities, the angels had another very important work—the task of serving mankind on God's behalf. The Psalmist points directly to this everyday chore when he is moved by the Spirit to write: **He shall give His angels charge over you, to keep you in all your ways** (Psalm 91:11). God's benevolent watching over His children is constant and totally reliable. We're never out of His loving sight.

But then, into that wonderful picture of peace, love, joy, contentment and oneness with God . . . came a horrible catastrophe. There was a rebellion within the ranks of the angels. Yes, there was

TROUBLE IN PARADISE

The devil has sinned from the beginning.
(I John 3:8)

Many have asked the question: *"Why? What could have caused such a serious rupture in this wonderful, perfect creation and godly relationship?"* The bottom line is simply that we don't know. Besides, we don't need to know, for if we did . . . God would tell us. But He doesn't. With few details, God in His Word simply tells it like it was: **The devil has sinned from the beginning** (I John 3:8).

Besides, the Son of God, who was there from the beginning, saw it all. He makes no bones about it but clearly describes Satan for what he is: **"A murderer from the beginning, and does not stand in the truth, because there is no truth in him. When he speaks a lie, he speaks from his own resources, for he is a liar and the father of it"** (John 8:44).

This avowed opponent of God became the leader of this horrible insurrection against God, and there were those angels who followed. And in so doing they too opposed the living God! Then and there the darkness of evil entered the glorious design of God's flawless and wonder-filled creation.

As a result, Satan (sometimes referred to as the Devil) and his evil followers were no longer welcome in God's perfect domain of love, beauty, and perfection. So God cast them out of the glorious kingdom of God into Hell to suffer everlasting separation from God's gracious love. This was their eternal lot: **God did not spare the angels who sinned, but cast them down to hell and delivered them into chains of darkness, to be reserved for judgment** (II Peter 2:4).

From that time forward, the Devil and his followers were and will always be the arch-enemies of God. Likewise, they would forever be fierce opponents of God's children.

Satan's true nature came into full view when he cunningly schemed to foil the perfection of God's creation. The God-like persons of Adam and Eve, the very crown of the LORD God's miraculous work, would be his target. Why them? Well, think about it. They were the very masters, the overseers, the ultimate caretakers of God's creation. Everything that flowed from God's loving and creative hand was for them to enjoy eternally. They were living in pure bliss as complements of the Creator.

It appears that Satan, however, could not bear to observe the pure joy and happiness that filled the lives of Adam and Eve—but there they were before him every single day! Their holy relationship with their Creator-God was more than he could tolerate. As a result, this father of lies and deception fumed with resentment. He became absorbed with devising a plan to destroy this perfect harmony that existed in the kingdom of God. But he had to think this through carefully. So, let's listen in on the possible thought process of this evil spirit as it unfolded into

THE SEDITIOUS, SORDID SCHEME OF SATAN

Submit to God. Resist the devil and he will flee from you.
(James 4:7)

Satan's thinking likely went something like this: "Now, let's see: What is the link that ties God so closely to these masters of His creation? Of course! It is something very simple. The bond that firmly connects Adam and Eve to their Maker is . . . faith." He was right. Faith and trust in everything that God is, says, and does is what firmly tied His children to Him. That was true then and it is true today.

Therefore, Satan likely reasoned: *"If . . . if that cord of faith that rests in the hearts and lives of Adam and Eve were severed, their relationship with their Creator will be destroyed. That's it! Somehow, I've got to find a way to trick Adam and Eve into questioning the perfect and constant love God has for them."*

9

It was a difficult task that Satan assigned to himself. The reason for that was obvious, for the unfettered grace of God was everywhere to behold. It mattered not where one looked. The six days of creation unfolded countless examples of God's creative perfection and His endless love for the man and the woman. They were in perfect harmony with God, and everything in their lives was utterly flawless. How could Satan penetrate such a purely holy relationship? How could he create a scenario in which they would question God's holy and unadulterated love?

He studied the matter carefully. He noted that Adam and Eve were given the freedom to use and enjoy all of God's blessings—but there was one restriction. And what was that? God had spelled it out with unmistakable clarity to Adam:

"Of every tree of the garden you may freely eat; but of the tree of the knowledge of good and evil you shall not eat, for in the day that you eat of it you shall surely die" (Genesis 2:16–17).

Satan surveyed the matter carefully. As he observed the daily activity of the man and the woman, he recognized that their devoted faith, love, and trust in their Maker caused them to walk right past that **tree of the knowledge of good and evil**, hanging full with tantalizing, delicious fruit—and they did so without the slightest desire to eat from it. It was almost as though they were oblivious to its existence. Why? Because their trust in their Creator's words was perfect, pure, and holy. For God had said: **"Of the tree of the knowledge of good and evil you shall not eat"** (Genesis 2:17).

Those words of God settled it for them, so in complete trust and total love for God they simply took Him at His Word. No questions asked! Thus, the commitment of Adam and Eve to their Creator-God was proved every day as they gave no desirous attention to that tree.

This was the very untarnished faith that lay in Satan's sights. Absolute trust in the words of the LORD God was the golden cord that held God and man together in a perfectly harmonious bond. So Satan doubtlessly planned to somehow sever that connection. If he could plant the seed of doubt in their minds and hearts—if he could somehow break through that absolute faith and trust in their Creator-God . . . then the bonding cord would tear. That perfect relationship between God and man would be demolished.

So, how might the carefully laid plans of the Evil One proceed? *"Hmmm. Maybe I can deceive them by lying to them. Of course, that will involve some rather sly and tricky insinuations. But that's who I am. I'm good at that. For after all, am I not the father of lies? Let's see...how will I approach them? If I go to them directly, they will never listen. But . . . if I use one of God's created creatures as a front, they may not so easily be disturbed. As a spirit-being, I can easily occupy a creature's body and thus make my planned advances toward these unsuspecting children of God. But out of all the magnificent creatures of creation, which one should I choose to help carry out my subtle scheme—my dirty work? Ah-ha, what about the serpent? Yes! This cunning and crafty creature is perfect for the job."*

So the plan was set. Slyly the Devil slipped into the body of the serpent, and from there he would make his deceptive challenge, intending to create

THE DISASTROUS FALL

**"Of every tree of the garden you may freely eat;
but of the tree of the knowledge of good and evil you shall not eat,
for in the day that you eat of it you shall surely die."**
(Genesis 2:16–17)

What a joyful and happy life Adam and Eve possessed! Every day was a day of discovery, a day to experiment, a day for surprises. What wonders, beauties, and joys filled their lives! Eve was going about her activities, relishing the endless blessings of God's earthly kingdom in totally innocent thankfulness. Then suddenly, one of the created creatures spoke to her. This was rather unusual—but on the other hand, creation was full of unexpected surprises. The question coming from the serpent was also rather strange—yet it was very clear and simple:

"Has God indeed said, 'You shall not eat of every tree of the garden?'" (Genesis 3:1b)

What was Satan driving at? What was he suggesting? *"Yes, Eve. You may think everything is perfect. But do you not have the right to enjoy EVERYTHING? Isn't there something of which you may not partake?"*

Eve's answer was quick in coming. She was fully aware of God's instructions to her husband, Adam—so she answered with hardly a second thought:

"We may eat the fruit of the trees of the garden; but of the fruit of the tree which is in the midst of the garden, God has said, 'You shall not eat it, <u>nor shall you touch it</u>, lest you die'" (Genesis 3:2–3).

Indeed, someone might wonder: *"Why <u>did</u> God purposely plant that forbidden tree in the garden?"* Let's think about that for a moment. Loving obedience doesn't mean anything, does it, if one has no other choice? Remember, they were created with a free will, and they could eat of the forbidden fruit if they chose. But God had made it very clear that in the day they would eat from it, they would lose EVERYTHING! Their holy and perfect life with God would be over. They would die!

There is something else that we might wonder about. *"Eve, you fully understood what God had said—so why did you add the words, 'nor shall you touch it'? God didn't say that, did He? Of course not! Could this*

*exaggeration of what God had said indicate that you are beginning to think
that this prohibition of God was a bit harsh?"*

If so, that is exactly what Satan had hoped for. He saw an apparent
crack in her armor of faith. Immediately he verbally pounced on her
like a lion on its prey! Because of her apparent weakness, he felt that he
could go one step farther. So he openly contradicted what God had said,
added his lies, and questioned God's creative intentions. Listen to his
brazen, untrue accusation:

**"You will not surely die. For God knows that in the day you eat
of it your eyes will be opened, and you will be like God, knowing
good and evil"** (Genesis 3:4–5).

We want to cry out, *"Eve, stop! Think for a moment. You are already like
God. That's how He created you. Remember? You were created in His image.
Don't fall for this lie. The Devil is twisting God's words to make it appear
that God is withholding something from you. You know all about good; you
don't need to know evil. Evil is Satan's domain; that's his expertise; that's
his kingdom! No! No! No! Don't fall for his lies! Listen alone to what God has
said!"* But it was too late, and Eve was sucked into the Devil's black hole
of lies. Her faith in God and His words of love and care melted into a
puddle of unbelief!

There was the forbidden tree before her, hanging full with tantalizing
fruit. She was drawn to it. She became totally enraptured with the
desire to partake of the fruit from that forbidden tree. And besides,
she was enthralled with Satan's insinuation and the possibility of being
wise like God. The cord of faith and trust in God's words of guidance
snapped! **So when the woman saw that the tree was good for food.
That it was pleasant to the eyes, and a tree desirable to make one
wise, she took of its fruit and ate.** And if that wasn't bad enough,
she also gave to her husband with her, and . . . (what did he do?) **he
ate. Then the eyes of both of them were opened, and they knew**

that they were naked; and they sewed fig leaves together and made themselves coverings (Genesis 3:6–7).

Suddenly they were embarrassed because they were naked! Everything changed in a nanosecond. Why? Because their innocence was gone. Sin had entered their minds—their thinking—their hearts. From that instant on they were in bondage to Satan! The Evil One had them in his miserable grip and would not let them go! These faithless acts of godless disobedience resulted in

THE AFTERMATH

Adam and his wife hid themselves from the presence of the **LORD** *God.*
(Genesis 3:8)

What a change! What a transformation! Suddenly, from living in the midst of paradise and God's holy love to an existence in the dreadful, death-doomed domain of Satan. To demonstrate how Satan had taken control of their hearts and minds—when they **heard the sound of the LORD God walking in the garden in the cool of the day** (Genesis 3:8) what did they do? **Adam and his wife hid themselves from the presence of the LORD God among the trees of the garden** (Genesis 3:8).

Notice, only a short time earlier Adam and Eve had been perfectly comfortable with God. They completely understood His total love for them. They were surrounded by His goodness and His loving-kindness toward them. They were at one with Him in every way. But then suddenly they were afraid of Him! They were robbed of those wonderful, joyous, peaceful chats with God. Their hopeless and helpless condition was further revealed when **The LORD God called Adam and said to him:**

"Where are you?" (Genesis 3:9)

So typical of God, isn't it? Of course God knew where Adam was—but He was inviting a response. *"Talk to me, Adam! Come, speak with me."* And what a revealing response came from His disobedient child:

"I heard Your voice in the garden, and I was afraid because I was naked; and I hid myself" (Genesis 3:10).

Do you see how Adam had changed? We see it in his response, don't we? It was a sad and self-incriminating answer, to say the least. How far Adam had fallen! All of a sudden he was afraid of his Creator, and his nakedness caused him to feel shame. <u>The bottom line was simply that he no longer knew God!</u> He actually thought that he could hide from his Creator! The estrangement of Adam and Eve from God was total and clearly evident.

Of course, the LORD God was fully aware of what had happened, but he wanted Adam to own up to his transgression. So God probed further, wanting Adam to make a clear, repentant confession.

"Who told you that you were naked? Have you eaten from the tree of which I commanded you that you should not eat?" (Genesis 3:11)

"Adam, you have changed. Why do you feel shame for your nakedness? You have disobeyed Me, haven't you? Tell me. Have you eaten of the forbidden fruit?" But there was no answer—no response—not a single word of repentance. Instead, what else? Of course, the blame-game began.

THE BLAME GAME

"The woman whom You gave to be with me, she gave me of the tree, and I ate"
(Genesis 3:12).

The depth of Adam and Eve's sin and their alienation from God was clearly revealed as the blame game began. But there were not many other choices, were there? Adam thought that he would simply blame his wife, so he blurted out this terribly lame excuse for his sin. Just listen to this:

"The woman whom You gave to be with me, she gave me of the tree, and I ate" (Genesis 3:12).

"Adam, did you really say that? 'The woman whom You gave to be with me'—she made me do it! Really? Of course! It's all her fault! Right? And if blaming your God-given companion isn't bad enough, what else are you saying, Adam? Are you actually assigning to God some of the blame for your predicament? Are you really so crass as to accuse God of being instrumental in your sin by giving you the blessed gift of a wife?"

And what about the woman? Where was she going to hang the blame? It had to be the serpent. Right?

"The serpent deceived me, and I ate" (Genesis 3:13).

Here we go again: *"One of Your created creatures. He's to blame!"* Everybody has their scapegoats, don't they? Nobody wishes to own up to their own sinful thoughts, words, and actions against the will of the LORD God of heaven and Earth.

Has anything changed in this regard to this very day? Not really! And it never will as long as this world stands. Why? Because every human being is born as sinful flesh from sinful flesh. And our corrupt nature today functions exactly like that of Adam and Eve, doesn't it? *"Others are to blame . . . but I'm innocent!"* And besides that, we hear God getting blamed all the time. When something seems to go wrong in one's life, what do we hear? We hear, "Why did God let that happen to me?"

We need to remember, God does not play such useless, silly, destructive, and soul destroying games. He didn't play them with the first humans and He doesn't play them with His children today. God's words were clear then, and they are clear today. Adam and Eve knew exactly what God had said, for His words were simple and crystal-clear:

"Of the tree of the knowledge of good and evil you shall not eat, for in the day that you eat of it <u>you shall surely die</u>" (Genesis 3:3).

They did eat, and they did die! It's as simple as that. And it shall always be true . . . then . . . today . . . and as long as this world exists, **the wages of sin is death** (Romans 6:23). They severed their life line to God through their disobedience to Him—and as a result, spiritually they became stone dead!

What does that mean, exactly? It means that they had no spiritual strength, no spiritual rights, no spiritual hope. Their holiness was gone—their immortality was gone—their life with God was gone—their free will was gone. EVERYTHING THAT WAS REALLY IMPORTANT WAS GONE! They were lost and adrift in a world that had suddenly fallen under the curse of sin. Satan had stolen them away from God, and they were his prisoners! They belonged to him! And he wanted to keep it that way. He wanted to hold them in spiritual captivity in his godless kingdom of evil forever!

Was there any hope? Was there any chance for redemption? Was there any light at the end of this terrible tunnel of spiritual death and destruction? My friends, because of God's merciful love for us, it is my pleasure to announce: <u>Yes, through God's inestimable love for every single human being ever to be born upon the face of this Earth, there was and is hope for all mankind.</u>

Please, permit an explanation: God has His way of counteracting Satan, and how He did so has been recorded in the Bible for the whole world to enjoy! By God's undeserved goodness, the following inimitable words spoken by God have by His mercy echoed down through the centuries and throughout all of the world. They are, first of all, <u>God's words of condemnation spoken against Satan and his evil kingdom.</u> Secondly, <u>they are God's absolute pledge to provide salvation for every human being on the face of this Earth.</u> Here is God's promise in all of its majestic beauty and simplicity:

GOD'S PROMISE

"I will put enmity between you and the woman,
And between your seed and <u>her Seed</u>;
<u>He</u> shall bruise (crush) your head,
And you shall bruise (crush) <u>His</u> heel."
(Genesis 3:15)

Let's spend a little time digesting those all-important words from God. It is as though God is saying, *"Satan, you have managed, through your vicious conniving, to successfully attack My perfect creation and drag it into your kingdom of death. You stealthily arranged to lure the woman and her husband away from Me. Now, I wish to make something perfectly clear to you. Listen carefully, for this is how it is going to be: You and My faithful children will be at spiritual war during all the years that follow. Then one day this struggle will come to a head. That day is when you face My special and chosen unique Seed, a descendant of the woman. As a result of that struggle, your evil head will be crushed—your evil power over My created beings will be destroyed, once and for all time. In the process, that special Seed of the woman will be significantly wounded. His wound will heal, but your head will be crushed once and for all time. Your horrific, hellish hold upon mankind will be forever destroyed."*

In other words, the assurance of our LORD God, spoken by His Apostle shall be forever true: The **wages of sin is death, but the gift of God is eternal life in Christ Jesus our Lord** (the designated Seed of the woman) (Romans 6:23).

That, my friends in Christ, is what Christmas is all about! This Christmas **gift of God—this eternal life in Christ Jesus our Lord** is at the center of all of the happenings described throughout His precious Word. This emphatic basis for expectation was the reason why God planned and carried out the happenings described throughout His Proclamation. That is the reason why those who opposed God and His people were cursed. That is why God's people, who lived a life of faith and trust in Him, were blessed.

That God-appointed Seed would come to extinguish the works of the Devil and rescue humanity from his evil clutches. Through this Savior of the world, all who trust in His redeeming love are delivered into His kingdom of grace. And finally, one day, this God-produced faith in the hearts of His redeemed children will melt into the reality of His eternal kingdom of glory. In that blessed kingdom **new heavens and a new earth in which righteousness dwells** (II Peter 3:13) will last forever.

Restoration! Everything that was lost will be restored through the God-ordained Seed of the Woman. And that, my friends, is the message of Christmas! Those words of the God-appointed Seed of the woman sum it all up very well:

"I have come that they may have life, and that they may have it more abundantly" (John 10:10).

And that is why we joyously sing with Martin Luther and proclaim with heart and soul:

> *Dear Christians, one and all, rejoice,*
> *With exultation springing,*
> *And with united heart and voice*
> *And holy rapture singing,*
> *Proclaim the wonders God has done,*
> *How His Right Arm the vict'ry won;*
> *Right dearly it has cost Him!*
>
> *He spoke to His beloved Son:*
> *"'Tis time to have compassion.*
> *Then go, bright Jewel of My crown,*
> *And bring to man salvation.*
> *From sin and sorrow set them free;*
> *Slay bitter death for them that they*
> *May live with You forever."*
>
> *The Son obeyed his Father's will,*
> *Was born of virgin mother,*
> *And, God's good pleasure to fulfill,*
> *He came to be my brother,*
> *No garb of pomp or pow'r he wore;*
> *A servant's form like mine he bore*
> *To lead the devil captive. (CW 377:1,5&6)*

PRAYER

LORD, our God, Your faithfulness has been the one abiding strength of Your people down through the generations. Satan is conquered—his head is crushed—we have become Your dear children through faith in Your redeeming love in Your Son, the Seed of the woman, our Savior.

But to this day the Evil One does his best to stifle the blessed words of Your promise of redemption. Still today his efforts are everywhere present to soften the seriousness of the spiritual warfare that exists between Your people of faith and his legions of evil. Therefore I pray, O LORD, that You will forever keep me close to You, by the power of Your Spirit. Strengthen me by Your gifts of grace in Word and the Sacraments. Fill me with Your spiritual power that I may readily confess You and Your gracious love for all people. And, LORD God, help me always to confess Your name before others, in love and compassion for their souls, just as You have had compassion for me through the promised Seed of the woman, Jesus Christ, my Savior and Lord. In His holy name I pray. Amen.

GOD'S
PROMISE
KEPT

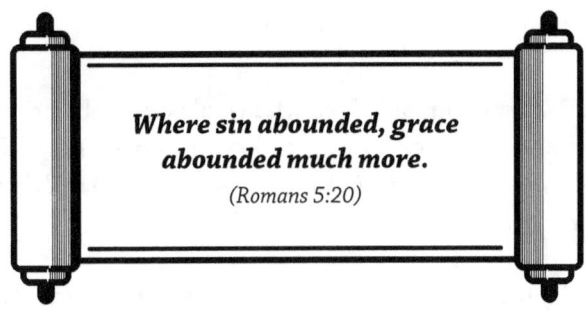

Where sin abounded, grace
abounded much more.
(Romans 5:20)

THE DEVASTATION OF SIN HITS HOME

How could Eve forget? How could Adam not make comparisons with the days gone by and the drastic change that had suddenly shattered their lives? The perfection, the joy, the excitement, the inviting future—these all lay dead under the curse of their disobedience to God.

Yet in the midst of all of the darkness of death that shrouded every day, there was one amazing shaft of light shining into their lives. And what was that constant glow that encompassed their everyday living? Their hearts and minds were firmly fixed upon that one grand promise of God: Redemption through the woman's Seed. That was the one beam of glory in the midst of a world captivated by satanic darkness.

It might seem contradictory, yet it was God's will to directly involve the woman in His promised restoration and redemption of mankind. After all, Eve was instrumental in plunging mankind into estrangement from God and spiritual death. Yet God gave the woman the privilege of producing the Child of Hope—the God-ordained cure for this plague of sin, death, and hell.

So, what could be the best possible happening in the lives of Adam and Eve? You guessed it! By God's grace, Eve became pregnant with her first child! That's a good reason for delight for any married couple. But besides the natural excitement of giving birth to a child, Eve had another expectation in her mind. She remembered God's words. She knew that it was the woman's Seed who would crush the head of Satan. So, what was she thinking? *"Could I be carrying that promised Seed? Could this child, growing in my womb, be the promised One who will deliver us from this awful scourge of sin?"*

We can well understand how Eve might have been ecstatic and joyfully overwhelmed with such a possibility, so when her first male child was born, she happily cried out:

"I have gotten a man from the LORD" (Genesis 4:1).

Indeed, the Savior, the Crusher of Satan's head, was designated by God to be a male. In her mind, everything seemed to be falling into place. She had given birth to a man-child! So, what did she and Adam name him? Naming a child, as well as the meaning of the name, was very significant. Hopes and expectations were often carefully considered when placing a chosen moniker upon a new-born child. His name would be Cain, which simply means "gotten." Indeed, she may well have thought that she had "gotten" the Savior—the One promised by God who would conquer Satan and restore their perfect relationship with their Creator.

But if that was her blossoming expectation, it died on the branch of reality. In God's plan of grace, it was far too early for Christmas—far too early for the birth of the Savior, the Seed of the woman. Yes, Adam and Eve and their offspring would eventually learn and gradually realize that it would be a long and often difficult journey for the believers of God's promise as they traveled that long and challenging road from Eden to Bethlehem.

Abel was the name given to her second son. His name means "nothingness" or "emptiness." That given name might very well signify that Eve had become terribly distraught. Our heart aches for her as she must have finally come to realize how sin with all of its terrible consequences had cruelly overtaken everything. There was likely a feeling of guilt—an emptiness—a nothingness that hung over their lives like a death pall.

The awful truth of their LORD's words spoken to them shortly after their tragic fall into sin must have finally hit home: **To the woman He said: "I will greatly multiply your sorrow and your conception; in pain you shall bring forth children; your desire shall be for your husband, and he shall rule over you"** (Genesis 3:16).

The vileness of sin had cast its ugly shadow over everything. Even the very unique privilege of childbirth, granted by God only to women, would become a painful experience. Then also, because of sin, the headship principle of the man had to be emphasized for the sake of an orderly family life. Unquestionably, the man would be the dominant individual in their relationship. He would be the God-ordained head of the wife and the family. His responsibility would be huge since he would be ultimately responsible for the welfare of his wife and children. The woman would carry on her life with a genuine respect as well as a strong inclination toward her husband and as a **helper suitable for him** (Genesis 2:18).

And to Adam He said: "Because you have heeded the voice of your wife, and have eaten from the tree of which I commanded you, saying, 'You shall not eat of it': "Cursed is the ground for your sake; in toil you shall eat of it all the days of your life. Both thorns and thistles it shall bring forth for you, and you shall eat the herb of the field. In the sweat of your face you shall eat bread till you return to the ground, for out of it you were taken; for dust you are, and to dust you shall return" (Genesis 3:16–19).

Can we imagine the shocking difference in their lives? Likely not. But let's try. We must remember, Adam and Eve were created holy and righteous, like God. They lived as a god and a goddess with all the joys, beauties, and perfection of God's created nature all about them. No needs, no cravings, no cares, no worries. Everything was totally flawless and certainly far beyond our fondest imagination. Their relationship with each other was pure, unadulterated, loving devotion. They enjoyed a perfect relationship with each other in every way. There were no disagreements, no quarrels, no frustrations. They understood each other perfectly.

Without a doubt, as we spend each day in this sin-corrupted world, it is impossible to describe and far beyond our mental capacity to grasp their pure and holy life. We can only try to imagine; right? One minute everything was perfect and without flaw. Then, all of a sudden everything was totally opposite. As a result of sin, their lives would be filled with challenging and difficult tasks. Thorns and thistles reared their ugly heads and competed with everything desirable. What had been automatic and pure joy became burdensome, back-breaking-toil. Just to eke out a day to day living was filled with sweaty labor and mind boggling decisions.

And if that wasn't bad enough, their lives would one day come to an end. Physically, they would die! Remember? God had not created them to die. They were created immortal. They were designed to live in perfect happiness with their family and God forever. But because of sin, a separation from God had occurred, and their everlasting life with God was no more. After a life of intense and difficult labor, their bodies would return to the earth from whence they had come.

Briefly stated, everything that God had intended for His perfect creation was gone—but we must be reminded, the one thing that remained and gave them hope and joy every day of their lives was the promise of redemption in the woman's Seed. God's promise was the one and only glorious spiritual light in the midst of a world of spiritual darkness. And that light spelled restoration. Everything that had been lost would one day be restored through God's gracious, merciful love for mankind. It was to that blessed promise of God that His believing children clung by faith. Without that wondrous assurance from God, life would have been meaningless and pointless. Living would have been nothing but totally hopeless drudgery in this world—and then perishing in hell for eternity.

So it is to this very day, my friends: Without God and His compassionate promises in our lives, what is the point of it all? Without the LORD God one's life is like a broken pencil—where's the point? Indeed, the questions have to be asked by every unbelieving soul: "What is my life all about? Why am I here? What is my purpose?" Without the promise of God's love in the Messiah, the Savior of all the world, one's life becomes nothing but an aimless existence.

And so with sadness we recognize that throughout the world there are poor souls everywhere wandering about in chaotic emptiness. They are trying to make some sense out of a life without God and His merciful love in our Savior. But they find that it is all a dead-end street. Emptiness prevails. A bit of truthful wisdom comes down to us from centuries ago, and shall ever be true:

> *"Our hearts for Thee, O God, were made.*
> *And will not rest until they rest in Thee." (Augustine)*

PRAYER

O, my God: As I walk through this world that You have created out of nothing, I am amazed. In spite of sin, the beauty, the intricacies, and wonders on every hand to this very day cause me to view with amazement all that You have created . . . and wonder with heartfelt faith at what it was like in the beginning. Yet I am content and filled with a heart of praise and thanksgiving, for You have opened my naturally blind eyes by Your Spirit to experience the intense joy of knowing Your love for me in the Messiah, the Seed of the woman. By faith in Him I am at peace, for I know that what we now see is but a small reflection of the glory that shall be revealed to us when all is restored in eternity. As the Apostle Paul was moved by the Spirit to remind us: **Now we see in a mirror, dimly, but then face to face. Now I know in part, but then I shall know just as I also am known** (I Corinthians 13:12)— and so we sing with hearts and minds:

*Seek where you may
To find a way that leads to your salvation.
My heart is stilled;
On Christ I build—He is the one foundation.
His Word is sure;
His works endure. He will o'erthrow my ev'ry foe;
Through Him I more than conquer.*

*Seek Him alone,
Who did atone, Who did your soul deliver;
Oh, seek Him first,
All you who thirst for grace that fails you never.
In ev'ry need;
Seek Him indeed. To ev'ry heart He will impart
His blessings without measure. Amen. (CW 395:1,3)*

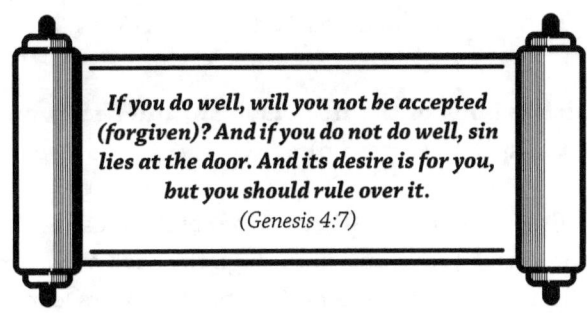

If you do well, will you not be accepted (forgiven)? And if you do not do well, sin lies at the door. And its desire is for you, but you should rule over it.
(Genesis 4:7)

SATAN AT HIS BEST— WORKING THE WORST

It might seem that things could not get any worse in the lives of Adam and Eve—but they could . . . and did. The full impact of defying God and His words suddenly blotted their family life in a horrendous way. Besides the traumatic effect of sin upon their lives in general, a glaring problem was becoming evident. And what might that be? Well, as parents who loved their children, they observed something that caused them great concern. To put it bluntly, there were obvious signs that Cain's relationship with God was purely outward. Yes, it was another reminder of the devastating result of Satan's work.

Adam and Eve had to come to grips with the fact that the very core of their natures had been corrupted by sin. As a result, their offspring would be sinful flesh born of sinful flesh! As our Savior points out in His conversation with Nicodemus:

"Most assuredly, I say to you, unless one is born again, he cannot see the kingdom of God" (John 3:3).

And when Nicodemus didn't get it, the Lord went on to explain:

"That which is born of the flesh is flesh, and that which is born of the Spirit is spirit" (John 3:6).

Adam and Eve had to learn—they had to come to realize that their faith in the promise of redemption through the Seed of the woman <u>did not automatically transfer to their offspring</u>. They were learning the hard way that raising children in the toxic environment of a world lost in sin would not be easy. It would require constant spiritual vigilance and work!

Without question, forgiveness, redemption, and restoration through the Seed of the woman was and is for everyone—yet not all would accept it simply by faith. The reason? The corrupted world surrounding Adam and Eve as well as ourselves is filled with ways and ideas that appeal to the sinful nature of all of us. Godlessness can easily become the way of life. Besides, Satan doesn't quit, for he knows his days are numbered. He has nothing to lose. He will try anything, use everything, tempt with whatever means possible in order to turn us and our children's minds away from God and His blessings to the things and ways that appeal to the sinfully corrupted minds and hearts of every one of us.

So we can well understand how it must have been a deep, worrisome concern for Adam and Eve when they saw evidences that Cain's corrupt nature, with which he was born, was controlling his life. It appeared that he was heartlessly going through the expected motions of dedication to God but without genuine, thankful love for the LORD God and His promise of salvation in the woman's Seed.

One day the whole problem became clearly and agonizingly obvious. Here's what happened: Both Cain and Abel brought offerings to the LORD. Offerings? Why bring offerings to the LORD? That's a good question. Why was and is that important for every child of God? Well, let's stop and think about that for a moment. In their state of bliss,

Adam and Eve gave all glory and praise to their Creator continually, showing their heartfelt appreciation and thankfulness to God for His love for them every day. They were fully aware that their life and everything that they enjoyed were blessings from God. So in their joyfully perfect love, they demonstrated their oneness with God by talking with Him and walking according to His will every single day.

But sin changed all of that. There they were: Adam and Eve with trials and troubles on every hand. Daily laborious toil was all around them. In the place of automatic blessings on every hand, suddenly their minds, hands, and backs were stretched to the limit to produce a living. It was very, very easy to become so caught up in the everyday work-a-day-world and the challenges with which they were confronted daily that they could easily forget about God and His blessings of love and mercy.

Especially, the challenges of everyday life competed forcefully with God's promise of the Seed of the woman who would one day free them from all of this. Therefore, it was tremendously important that they take a break, now and then, and make a conscious effort, in the midst of their trials and burdens, to lift their hearts and minds in thankfulness to God.

So, this is what happened: Abel was a shepherd, while Cain was a tiller of the soil. Both were honorable labors. We should be careful to not automatically attribute some special significance to the fact that Abel was a shepherd. That's easy to do, for since the **"LORD is my Shepherd,"** (Psalm 23:1) one might easily sanctify shepherds. We must remember that their occupations were of no consequence in their relationship with God. What each lad offered to God was naturally dictated by his chosen field of labor.

Cain's offering came from the fruits of the field, while Abel's offering came from the firstlings of his flock. Before God, one offering was as acceptable as the other. However, what do you think made a major and decisive difference before God? You guessed it—it was the attitude of the heart. The inspired writer of the book of Hebrews clearly spells it out: **By <u>faith</u> Abel offered to God a more excellent sacrifice than Cain, through which be obtained witness that he was righteous, God testifying of his gifts; and through it he being dead still speaks** (Hebrews 11:4). As a result, **the LORD respected Abel and his offering, but He did not respect Cain and his offering** (Genesis 4–5).

Now what? Cain might have recognized that his bad attitude was an open book before God and repent—but he didn't care. What probably was his intention? *"Make Mom and Dad happy. Even though my 'worship' is nothing but sterile ritual, I'll just go through the expected motions."* That was all that Cain was inclined to do . . . he felt that was good enough.

So what should Adam and Eve do? Many God-loving parents with a similar problem have asked that same question: "What should we do?" The answer might be: Do not threaten; try not to argue or lecture but rather lovingly encourage. Show them your concerned care—set aside time for family devotions—pray . . . and pray continually. Moses says it best:

"You shall love the LORD your God with all your heart, with all your soul, and with all your might. And these words which I command you today shall be in your heart; you shall teach them diligently to your children, and shall talk of them when you sit in your house, when you walk by the way, when you lie down, and when you rise up (Deuteronomy 6:5–7).

So what do you think happened with Cain? Well, for one thing, we can assume that Satan was carefully prompting Cain's attitude and actions. He never misses an opportunity. So then, one day the Evil One saw the door for his evil work open wide. He jumped right in. Cain was ripe for picking, and Satan was ready to harvest. With Satan's prodding, Cain became very angry with God and fiercely jealous of his brother. He was falling deeper and deeper into the trap of Satan. Rather than looking at himself and his own godless actions—rather than heartily repenting and pleading for God's forgiveness, he remained resentful toward God and hateful against his brother.

So, what happened next? Well, the LORD God saw it all. He always sees it all! God spoke directly to Cain. He came right to the point:

"If you do well, will you not be accepted (forgiven)? And if you do not do well, sin lies at the door. And its desire is for you, but you should rule over it" (Genesis 4:7).

Indeed, God was pleading with Cain *"Repent! Turn away from your jealous resentfulness. I will forgive you. Come, walk with Me in the paths of righteousness. Satan and sin are on your very door-step, desiring to rob you of your life with Me. Say 'NO' to Satan! Say 'YES' to Me, your loving LORD. Rule over this life-threatening anger that rages in your heart and soul."*

Sad to say, Cain brushed aside that merciful warning of the LORD God, and Satan drew Cain deeper and deeper into his trap. He tightened his grip on Cain's heart like a boa constrictor. Finally, the Evil One moved in and utterly dominated Cain's mind and soul. Satan had him! Cain's life was in the hands of the Evil One.

We all need to pay attention! It is a very vivid and sad lesson for us all: When the Devil is given an inch, he takes a mile! He is never satisfied with "a little." He wants all! He wants our mind, our heart, our body—and above all, our soul!

However, Abel was a bright and shining light in the family of Adam and Eve. He believed God's promise of redemption with all his heart. His worship, his offerings, and his faith-life were pleasing to God. Did Abel's example impress Cain? Apparently it did . . . but negatively!

Indeed, it caused Cain's heart of jealous rage to burn with even more intensity. Ultimately, it was Abel's faith and love for his LORD, as well as his obvious devoted attitude in worship, that finally threw Cain into a mind-consuming, jealous rage. Satan had him in his evil clutches. As such, Cain acted as the Devil's puppet.

Finally, Cain's unchecked hatred boiled over. He was alone with his brother in a field. Satan prodded him on, *"Now is your chance to, once and for all, rid yourself of this menace. Get him out of your life once and for all."* The Evil One took control of Cain's mind and heart and . . . he did it! He murdered his own brother! There it was: Sin, in all of its terrible monstrosity most vividly manifested! There it was: Satan at his best accomplishing the worst. There it was: The wretched result of impenitence and disobedience to God playing itself out in stark, bold and satanic reality!

From that horrible day to this, murder of people by other people is a constant Satan-guided threat in humanity. It's a continuing pattern all across this created world. At this writing, it is reported that besides the individual murderous acts reported <u>every day</u>, there is a total of forty-two wars going on within this sin-dominated world . . . people slaughtering their neighbors everywhere across the face of the Earth—

crowds fleeing everywhere and anywhere from the gross and devilish schemes of those in the Devil's grip. And Satan loves it.

Governments, law enforcement, and armies try to control the vile infestation of bloodshed and murder. Through threats and punishment people are somewhat constrained—but the genuine God-ordained solution is found where most refuse to look. It is discovered in one place alone—namely, in the love of God for lost sinners. When that love of God dominates the heart of man, he is moved to compassion rather than hatred and murder. **Beloved, let us love one another, for love is of God; and everyone who loves is born of God and knows God. He who does not love does not know God, for God is love. In this the love of God was manifested toward us, that God has sent His only begotten Son into the world, that we might live through Him** (I John 4:7–9).

What sorrow must have filled the hearts and minds of Adam and Eve as they witnessed this coarse, brutal action of unbelief carried out by their very own son! Where could they go for comfort? How could they find peace in their hearts and minds in the face of such hateful, Satan-provoked sin? In the midst of it all, there was one sacred blessing, one light of hope which brightened their day. To that they could cling by faith—the promise of God's merciful and gracious love in the coming Seed of the woman. Finally, one day, the crushing of Satan's head—the redemption of humanity from the evil grip of Satan's murderous hands would be realized. To this promise of God they could and would cling, even in the face of such a hideous, satanic crime.

Adam and Eve could find peace in the fact that Abel was the first soul carried by the angels of God to his eternal home to be with the LORD God. The holy writer of the Book of Hebrews writes this epitaph: **By faith Abel offered to God a more excellent sacrifice than Cain, through which he obtained witness that he was righteous, God**

testifying of his gifts; and through it he being dead still speaks
(Hebrews 11:4).

Indeed, it is a long way from Eden to Bethlehem—and we have only
just begun the journey. When would that promise be fulfilled? When
would that promised Seed of the woman come? When would the head
of Satan finally be crushed? Well, the way from Eden to Bethlehem was
not far in miles and not such a long distance in God's calculations, for as
the Apostle Peter is inspired to remind us, **Beloved, do not forget this
one thing, that with the Lord one day is as a thousand years, and
a thousand years as one day** (2 Peter 3:8). For the longing, hoping,
yearning, faithful children of the heavenly Father, it was a very, very
long way, yet believing children of God did not lose heart but continued
to pray:

Come, O precious Ransom, come,
Only Hope for sinful mortals!
Come, O Savior of the world!
Open are to You all portals.
Come, Your beauty let us view;
Anxiously we wait for You. (CW 8:1)

PRAYER

LORD God, my Savior and my Guardian, sin against You and
Your guiding and gracious words of love always leads to misery and
heartache. I pray, Lord, fill me with Your Spirit that I may always
recognize the lure of Satan, the enticements of the unbelieving world
around me, and the beguilement of my sinful nature. Cause me always
to remember that You are the center of my life, who always leads me
in the right paths and the good ways. And when I forget, forgive my
faltering ways for the sake of my Savior, the promised Seed of the
woman. By Your Spirit renew me through Your forgiving love and grant

me Your peace in mind and heart. Without a doubt, through the merits of Jesus Christ, Your Son and my Savior, I know that I will have Your every blessing. In Your name of gracious love, I pray. Amen.

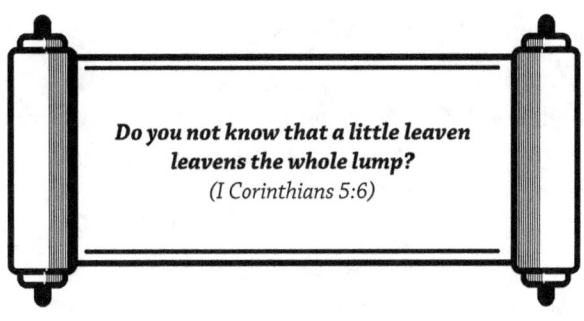

AN UNGODLY MERGER

Some of the most sad and heart-rending words in the Holy Scriptures are these: **Cain went out from the presence of the LORD** (Genesis 4:16). In his satanic hatred for everyone and everything godly, Cain cut himself off from every shred of spiritual life. Truly living for time and eternity means embracing God and everything that He is, says, and does. So, by faith in the promise of the Seed of the woman, spiritual life with the LORD God for time and eternity was assured. In fact, when our Savior came, He clearly described His purpose for coming into this world with these precious words:

"I have come that they may have <u>life</u>, and that they may have it more abundantly" (John 10:10).

The perfect life with God that was lost in the Garden would be restored completely and entirely by the promised Seed of the woman—but Cain walked away from it all. In his angry hatred he severed himself from the LORD God entirely. It must have been a day sad beyond description as Adam and Eve watched their first-born son and his family depart from the moorings of godliness.

As we might expect, the children of Cain were a godless family. How could it be otherwise? The offspring were carbon copies of their father, Cain. As such, they functioned not in the fear of God but according to their own natural fleshly desires and lusts. Did they have a god? Did they have a religion? Maybe! Remember, since mankind was created to worship and love God what is clearly written in the sands of time is this: When people have forsaken the true God, they naturally try to fill that void in some other way. So what do they do? Out of the imagination of their own godless minds and hearts they produce a substitute—someone or something else to cling to, to trust in. It becomes their god!

Observe mankind. There it is exemplified in bold relief. Everybody believes in, trusts in someone or something. It might be themselves. Maybe it's wealth, possessions, prestige, a created image, etc. etc. And that is fine with Satan. The Devil cares not at all that people worship whatever they create as a god, <u>as long as they don't give their heart and mind to the holy, true LORD God of heaven and Earth</u>. The fire of Satan's passionate hatred for God will never diminish for a second, and those who follow him will walk lock-step in his godless ways. On the other hand, the family of the LORD God worshiped their Creator and looked with believing anticipation toward the day that the Seed of the woman would come and annihilate Satan.

Likely, Adam and Eve gave birth to a number of children, but the one who is mentioned in particular is Seth. Why Seth? Well, he and his offspring became the God-appointed family from the lineage of Adam and Eve who were to carry the promise of redemption in the woman's Seed to its fulfillment. As such, Seth was the forefather of many of our Biblical patriarchs such as Noah, Abraham, Isaac, Jacob, Judah, and David, as well as Joseph and Mary. They all came from the family of Seth.

So there we have it. The world was being populated on one hand by the children of Seth—those who were faithful to God and His promise. On the other hand, there were the children of Cain, who grew up and lived without knowing the blessings of God and His promise of the Savior. Their lives were directed by the ways of Satan and their natural lusts and desires. If they had a god, it was one of their own making or created in their own image. But, sad to say, they knew not the LORD God and were totally oblivious to His promise of salvation.

Briefly said, they were lost in this world of sin, as so many poor, searching and seeking souls are lost yet today. The enduring truth of the inspired words of the Apostle Paul are written for all to hear and take to heart: **Do not be deceived, God is not mocked; for whatever a man sows, that he will also reap. For he who sows to the flesh will of the flesh reap corruption, but he who sows to the Spirit will of the Spirit reap everlasting life** (Galatians 6:7–8).

And so it was: Time passed—many years passed—centuries passed; children were born, and populations grew. Would the children of Seth attempt to spread the Word of salvation in the Seed of the woman beyond their borders? Would God's people let the light of the LORD God and His forgiving love in the promised Seed shine with unmistakable brightness? Might they at least have attempted to penetrate the gates of the children of Cain with the gospel of God's love and salvation? Unfortunately, there is no indication that they did. As a matter of fact, the very opposite took place.

The sad commentary that is played out again and again throughout the ages is on one hand the <u>faithlessness</u> of mankind, and on the other hand the <u>faithfulness</u> of God. Before us is one example of that heart-rending truth as the people of God began to lose their spiritual bearings! They began to drift away from their Shepherd and LORD—and Satan was ever present to urge them on in their spiritual folly. What? Again? Could God's family fall from faithfulness again? Yes! Indeed they could, and they did!

This depressing episode goes like this: The believers, the children of God, who were the offspring of Seth, became infatuated with what they saw down the road, so to speak. The children of Cain deeply impressed the Sethites. Of particular interest to the sons of God were the daughters of the Cainites. Listen to the God-inspired details: **The sons of God saw the daughters of men, that they were beautiful; and they took wives for themselves of all whom they chose. There were giants on the earth in those days, and also afterward, when the sons of God came in to the daughters of men and they bore children to them. Those were the mighty men who were of old, men of renown** (Genesis 6:2 & 4).

My, Oh my, Oh my! There it is . . . in all its shameful, sordid, and sad details! Well, it didn't happen overnight, but it happened nevertheless! Rather than doing mission work—rather than striving to do everything possible to share with the Cainites the wonderful love of God for all mankind—rather than spreading the blessings of God's promise of forgiveness and spiritual restoration in the Seed of the woman—instead of giving to others the most precious gift ever possessed by mankind, unfortunately and disgustingly, the hearts and the minds of the Sethites were overwhelmed by the fleshly, worldly ways of the Cainites!

More and more regularly, the Sethites took wives from their unbelieving neighbors. And with what principles did they raise their children? Apparently not with the knowledge and love of the one true God of heaven and Earth, but in godlessness and spiritual depravity.

To many this may appear to have been a success story. Old differences were being forgotten. The "out-of-date" ways of their godly fore-parents were no longer important and therefore not heeded. We can clearly hear them arrogantly boast: *"Things are different now! We are tired of the attitudes of the past. It's time that we all learn to get along and adopt some of the ways of our neighbors. Besides, those Cainite women are pretty easy on the eyes."*

Well, what happened next was as sure to happen as the sun rising in the east—it was bound to occur. A gradual merger took place. The Sethites and the Cainites not only "got along"—but many of the worldly, fleshly, godless ways of the Cainites were adopted by the Sethites! The outcome of this godless merger? **Giants** on the Earth resulted—not necessarily giants in stature but "**mighty men . . . men of renown**" (Genesis 6:4). They made a name for themselves! They were wealthy! They established kingdoms and ruled! How impressive! It was all good, right? Not a chance! It was all WRONG!

Stop for a minute! What was missing in this whole picture of "progress?" More and more, God's people were forgetting the LORD God and deleting Him from their lives. They were forgetting that they were the carriers of the promise of the Seed of the woman. As such, they were the only hope for all of sinful mankind! Satan was having a ball! God's people were being spiritually devoured by the lies of Satan's henchmen! The archenemy of God was destroying their faith in the LORD God little by little—inch by inch—fraction by fraction. He was managing this by his sly fabrications and through the people's fleshly appetites.

We can clearly hear the chant: *"You only go around once in life, so live it up! Let your flesh have its desired fling. Why not? The here and now is all that is important. Let yourself go and gorge yourself on the things of this world and what you want—now! Me, me, me is what life is all about."* (Sound familiar?)

The sad outcome of it all soon became apparent! As so often happens (and is happening even in this our day), God's believers succumbed to the godlessness and immorality of the unbelievers among whom they lived.

The rhetorical question penned by the apostle Paul is applicable for all time: **Do you not know that a little leaven leavens the whole lump** (I Corinthians 5:6)? The leaven of godlessness did its job. The entire **lump**, with the exception of merely one family, was spiritually devoured by Satan and his horde! The result of this deplorable, doleful drama was a disaster! A world of unbelief and godlessness was spawned. The ugly tentacles of Satan and sin burrowed their evil way into and through every crevice of humanity.

AND GOD SAW IT ALL! He always sees it all. God's conclusive decision? **The LORD saw that the wickedness of man was great in the earth, and that every intent of the thoughts of his heart was only evil continually. . . . So the LORD said, "I will destroy man whom I have created from the face of the earth, both man and beast, creeping thing and birds of the air, for I am sorry that I have made them"** (Genesis 6:5,7).

Sad—Sad—Sad! God's patience was tried to the limit. Finally it was over. IT WAS OVER! It utterly depresses our mind and overwhelms our heart. How could the mercy and love of our Creator and Savior ONCE AGAIN be cast aside and treated as though it were nothing? Was there any hope? Was there a glimmer of light somewhere in this dreadful day of doom? Yes! Yes! Yes! Praise the LORD, there was: **Noah found grace in the eyes of the LORD** (Genesis 6:8). Only ONE FAMILY out of the millions of people on the earth—one family alone remained faithful to the LORD God and trusted in His promises!

My friends, without a doubt it is a long way from Eden to Bethlehem. What is so amazing is that in spite of the gross unbelief of mankind, the LORD God, our Savior and Shepherd, remained absolutely true and faithful to His Word and promises every inch of the way! From Eden to Bethlehem, GOD NEVER BLINKED. Regardless of the faithlessness of man, the faithfulness of God stood absolute, firm, and solid!

This should be a soul-strengthening assurance for every faithful child of God even in this our day. In the midst of a whole world of godless unbelief, one family faithfully stood with God. And so it is to this very day, my friends in Christ. The dark threatening clouds of evil may cover the Earth—yet in the midst of the gloom and doom, <u>God's believers will</u>

continue to bathe in the bright sun of the love of God as it continues to shine with remarkable brightness through the dread darkness.

And so, to this very day, and even unto the end of life, we will confidently continue to confess with the Apostle Paul: **I am persuaded that neither death nor life, nor angels nor principalities nor powers, nor things present nor things to come, nor height nor depth, nor any other created thing, shall be able to separate us from the love of God which is in Christ Jesus our Lord** (Romans 8:38–39).

And so may we ever sing with heart and voice:

There's nothing that can sever
Me from the love of God,
No want, no pain whatever,
No famine, danger, sword.
Though thousand foes surround me,
For slaughter mark their sheep,
They never shall confound me—
The vict'ry I shall keep! (CW 445:2)

PRAYER

Oh LORD, how devastating, how frightful are the tentacles of sin! How obvious are the activities of Satan all around me, even in this our day. But in defiance of every obstacle thrown in my path by Satan and unbelieving mankind, Your steadfast love for me supersedes them all. LORD, You have graciously taught me that when the devil and his lying ways are permitted to hang around in my life, they gradually become more and more dominant. It is just so easy, because of my sinful nature, to gradually become accustomed to and finally embrace Satan's sordid schemes. Yes, I may even begin to defend them. How do I know this? Because I too am guilty, LORD. I know that I have a spiritual struggle, a fight of faith that goes on regularly. LORD, I need You every minute of every day. I am in desperate need of the constant power of Your Spirit in my life, for with You in my life, I will be able to fight the fight of faith successfully each day. And when I falter, for the sake of the Seed of the woman, Jesus Christ, my Savior and Lord, forgive me and renew me with Your strength in the Spirit to live with You and for You each day. In my Savior's name I pray and furthermore earnestly entreat:

Renew me, O eternal Light,
And let my heart and soul be bright,
Illumined with the light of grace
That issues from Your holy face.

Destroy in me the lust of sin;
From all impureness make me clean.
Oh, grant me pow'r and strength, my God,
To strive against my flesh and blood.

Create in me a new heart, Lord,
That gladly I obey Your Word.
Oh, let Your will be my desire
And with new life my soul inspire.

Grant that I only You may love
And seek those things which are above
Till I behold You face to face,
O Light eternal, through Your grace. Amen. (CW 471)

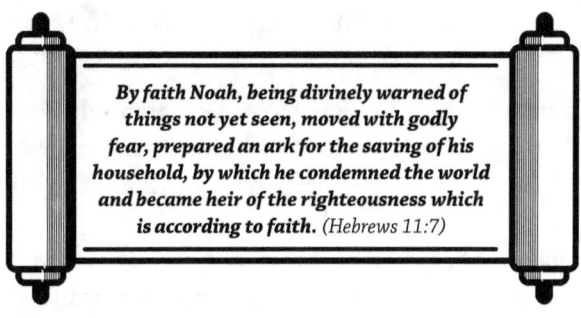

By faith Noah, being divinely warned of things not yet seen, moved with godly fear, prepared an ark for the saving of his household, by which he condemned the world and became heir of the righteousness which is according to faith. (Hebrews 11:7)

GOD'S JUDGMENT TEMPERED WITH GRACE

God's righteous judgment was about to fall upon a wicked and perverse mankind.

"And behold, I Myself am bringing the flood of waters on the earth, to destroy from under heaven all flesh in which is the breath of life; and everything that is on the earth shall die. But I will establish My covenant with you (Noah); and you shall go into the ark—you, your sons, your wife, and your sons' wives with you. And of every living thing of all flesh you shall bring two of every sort into the ark, to keep them alive with you; they shall be male and female" (Genesis 6:17–19).

Noah was entrusted with the awesome, solemn duty of building a huge floating barge. God laid out the dimensions precisely so that this mighty craft would house a pair of every breathing creature that God had created to occupy the Earth, together with Noah and his family.

It's all so utterly amazing, isn't it? And what is more astonishing is this: In the midst of all of the unbelief, the wickedness, and the rejection of God by mankind, yet a time of grace was permitted. Really?

Even then, a time of gracious mercy? Yes, God granted 120 years for Noah to build the ark—120 years of merciful kindness for a world devastated by sin—120 years of grace for repentance and faith.

What a scene; what a picture; what a continuous sermon! I have heard that people sometimes complain that our Sunday morning sermons are occasionally too long. Well, nothing compares to this one! This was without question the longest sermon ever preached! We have many ways to communicate the Word of our LORD God today. We have radio, television, computer, skyping, streaming etc., but frankly, there doesn't appear to be anything that can top this!

For 120 years this sermon continued before their very eyes as board by board—fastener by fastener—wall by wall—from stem to stern—a God-designed boat was being crafted. And everyone knew the reason why. With that mighty sermon Noah was calling everyone to turn from their godless ways, and in repentance and faith receive the promises and love of their gracious Creator and Savior!

Can you imagine the ridicule and scorn that Noah and his family must have endured? Here they were, out on the "west forty," so to speak, building a huge vessel on perfectly dry ground! Talk about faith! Talk about resolution! Talk about absolute confidence in God's Word! Can you hear the scornful mocking and derision of the crowds? *"Hey, Noah, think it might rain one of these days? That flood you're always talking about—it's clouding up, Noah. What do you think? Do you think maybe this is it? How about it? Do you suppose we can hitch a ride, Noah? It might be fun!"*

But Noah kept on building—Noah kept on preaching. With every hammer blow and with every hoisted timber, both law and gospel were being declared with unmistakable clarity. **By faith Noah, being divinely warned of things not yet seen, moved with godly fear, prepared an ark for the saving of his household, by which he**

condemned the world and became heir of the righteousness which is according to faith (Hebrews 11:7). Without question, it's a very long way from Eden to Bethlehem—but with each golden link in this God-ordained chain of events, we draw ever closer to the God-promised salvation in the Seed of the woman.

However, at this particular juncture in time even God's mercy had finally run its course. Yes, even 120 years of God's long-suffering was over—the amazing grace of God finally reached its end. Sooner or later, it always does! The ark was finished. No hitch-hikers were allowed. But, oh, what precious cargo was carried by that Ark! The entire Church, the faithful, Noah and his family were there. Two of every God-created creature that walked the earth or flew in the air were collected and housed on that huge floating craft of God.

But there was far more than that. Above all, that vessel carried the most blessed and precious treasure ever to be possessed by humanity. Not jewels like pearls or diamonds—not gold or silver or some such precious metals. The treasure carried by the Church aboard that veritable vessel of victory was the grandest wealth ever possessed by fallen mankind—namely, THE PROMISES OF GOD, ESPECIALLY THE PROMISE OF REDEMPTION AND RESTORATION OF HUMANITY RECEIVED THROUGH FAITH IN THE SEED OF THE WOMAN! Praise the LORD God!

Then, when all creatures that God wished to preserve on the Ark had arrived and were housed aboard that ship of salvation, God triggered the Flood. **All the fountains of the great deep were broken up, and the windows of heaven were opened. And the rain was on the earth forty days and forty nights** (Genesis 7:11b–12). Such a few words to describe those unimaginable, tumultuous happenings that followed. God pulled back the retaining wall of the firmament, and water gushed forth from the windows of heaven. Torrential rain literally poured from the sky. As a result, the world became engulfed with an avalanche of water never before experienced and never to be encountered again.

We can only try to imagine: For forty days and nights the waters flooded from the heavens like giant waterfalls. People, animals, and even birds clawed and pressed through the frantic crowds to gain access to the highest elevations available. Families tried to stay together. Children were held tightly and feverishly led. Everywhere there was jostling and pushing among the frenzied creatures trying to gain what was thought to be the safest places possible.

Those who were physically handicapped and the elderly were likely unable to keep up and inevitably were trampled under the feet of the hysterical masses. The calling out to loved ones—screaming and yelling were everywhere! But all was in vain. The relentless flood of water from heaven together with oceanic tsunamis pushed upward foot by foot and yard by yard. Terrified creatures—from giant dinosaurs to the tiniest insects—from people of position and status to the lowliest peasants—pregnant women and little children . . . all were swallowed up in this world-wide, watery grave. The final gasp of life was extinguished as the waters rose more than twenty feet above the highest mountain peaks.

And that's not all. To add to the intensive horror, convulsive volcanic actions rumbled within the bowels of the earth. In the midst of this torrential flood, geysers shot up. Scorching lava spewed forth, sizzling and boiling as it rose to the surface from within the depths of the earth. The crust of the world literally opened wide, swallowing all manner of plant, animal, and human matter. Every last bird could no longer stay aloft. Robbed of sustenance and a place to plant their feet, one by one they plunged head-long into the churning sea. Giant tsunamic eruptions pounded on the sides of the ark, tossing it about like a tiny toy. We can hardly imagine the horrific nature of it all!

Then, finally, after forty days and forty nights of this world-wide terror, all became quiet and still. An eerie quietness settled upon the flooded planet as the ark of God floated serenely and safely upon the earth-covering sea. How long? God tells us. For one-hundred-and-fifty-days—for five months the waters remained! A rather trite expression seems to fit here amazingly well: It was "the calm <u>after</u> the storm."

Do you suppose that Noah and his family might have wondered: *"What just happened? What is next? Where is all of this water going to go?"* Apparently, God did not fill them in on any of the details about post-flood action. This seems to be common practice for God. If you have noticed, in the happenings in our lives, God spares us the details. That opens the door for simple trusting faith in Him and His words to us. He is simply saying, *"Don't sweat the details. Leave them to Me. I'll take care of them all in due time."*

And so it was, after days of patiently watching and waiting . . . God's solution became evident. The giant world-wide sea began to recede. First slowly, then more noticeably the waters began to shift with obvious direction and then began to rush vigorously. Torrential currents began to slice deep valleys into the earth's surface. Numerous, huge river beds were created. In some cases canyons resulted as the rushing waters tore through the jagged terrain left by the hemorrhaging of the deep. Layers upon layers of soil and molten lava were laid down, forming huge, spectacular mountain ranges. Hills, valleys and plains were gradually exposed as the waters receded to lower levels, forming enormous as well as smaller bodies of water.

Look at our world today. What do you see? If we pay attention, we will still see the deep scars of that judgment of God upon a world that had sinfully rejected Him. Every quiet riverbed, every towering mountain range, every seemingly endless ocean, every serene lake, every layered and jagged earth formation—they all speak to us. They are constant reminders of the anger of God against mankind which had cast aside His merciful love and care as though it were nothing!

The countless monuments carved on the face of our planet are chilling testimonies of that horrendous time of world-wide-death. These graphic illustrations everywhere in the world are still preaching a mighty sermon to everyone every day! They are calling upon every one of us, every day, to repent of our sins of thanklessness. They are screaming out in a world that too often and too readily walks with Satan and refuses to honor the one true God of heaven and Earth and His Word of Truth. These graphic reminders are calling on all of us to open our hearts and minds to Him and cling steadfastly in faith to our Shepherd's pleadings and His redemptive love for each of us in the Seed of the woman, the God appointed Redeemer and Savior of all mankind.

As we look upon the ruptured face of the planet on which we live, surely we see the result of the wrath of God against a world of people who had rejected Him. But we also see the evidence of the healing hand of the LORD God, our ever-loving Creator and Savior, resting upon this torn world. He has brought about nature's awe-inspiring beauty and pleasantness that present us with breathtaking scenery, far and wide, across the face of this planet. We join the poet, who invites all of creation to unite in praise of the LORD God, as all of us today enjoy the beauties of the healing hand of God upon His marvelous creation:

> *Oh, forest leaves so green and tender,*
> *That dance for joy in summer air;*
> *Oh, meadow grasses, bright and slender,*
> *And flow'rs, so wondrous sweet and fair,*
> *You live to show His praise alone;*
> *With me now make His glory known.*
>
> *All creatures that have breath and motion,*
> *That fill the earth, the sea, and sky,*
> *Now join me in my heart's devotion;*
> *Help me to raise His praises high.*
> *My utmost pow'rs can never quite*
> *Express the wonders of His might. (CW 242:2–3)*

Indeed, God has given us the awe-inspiring mountain ranges—the deep forests with a multitude of plant and animal varieties—the blooming vegetation that colors the landscape—the open plains with golden grain waving in the soft breeze of a sunny day—the fruit trees and bushes hanging full with delicious, bountiful, and mouth-watering produce—pasture-lands with myriads of wild and domesticated animals grazing and loafing on a summer day—the numerous winged creatures, large and small, decorating the skies with their practiced flying skills and their colorful markings—the rivers, the falls, the lakes, and seas teeming with living creatures beyond number—and each time we see that colorful rainbow arching the sky we hear our LORD promising:

"I will never again curse the ground for man's sake, although the imagination of man's heart is evil from his youth; nor will I again destroy every living thing as I have done.
While the earth remains,
Seedtime and harvest,
And cold and heat,
And winter and summer,

**And day and night
Shall not cease"** (Genesis 8:21–22).

Without a doubt, it is a long way from Eden to Bethlehem. Yet the gracious love and mercy of God are ever present—they never fail. His limitless kindness is typified to this very day by His "writing" in the sky for all to see and remember.

"I set My rainbow in the cloud, and it shall be for the sign of the covenant between Me and the earth. It shall be, when I bring a cloud over the earth, that the rainbow shall be seen in the cloud; and I will remember My covenant which is between Me and you and every living creature of all flesh; the waters shall never again become a flood to destroy all flesh" (Genesis 9:13).

Yes, God's merciful love endures and rests upon us all in His creation and in His living promise. So, as we continue on our journey to Bethlehem, He constantly reminds us: Watch and wait, Christmas is coming.

However, that day of spiritual liberty was still a long way off after the Flood. We are reminded of the impatience of our children when we are taking a rather lengthy trip. Time and again along the way they will restlessly ask: "Are we there yet?" The answer then and now is "No, we are not there yet. It's still a long way off. But relax. We'll soon be there. You can count on that." In spite of the unfaithfulness of mankind and the constant opposition of Satan, God always remains faithful to His believing people and His promises.

"For the mountains shall depart and the hills be removed, but My kindness shall not depart from you, nor shall My covenant of peace be removed," says the LORD, who has mercy on you (Isaiah 54:10).

Faithful children of God continue on, with a prayer in heart and mind:

Oh, come, Oh, come, Emmanuel,
And ransom captive Israel
That mourns in lonely exile here
Until the Son of God appear.
And our gracious God always answers:
Rejoice! Rejoice! Emmanuel
Shall come to you, O Israel. (CW 23:1)

PRAYER

Thank you, LORD, my Creator and my Savior, for Your steadfast love. How merciful, faithful, and kind You are in the face of man's thoughtless and faithless actions. Before me every day stand the reminders of my sins in my thoughts, words, and deeds. In the world around me Your gracious love is refused and Your long-suffering abused, but by Your loving grace I also see the works of Your gracious, healing hand. Above all, I hear Your words of merciful kindness in Your gospel of forgiveness that is granted to me and to all people, through the merits of Jesus Christ my Savior and Lord. I beg You, Lord, my ever-faithful Shepherd, stay close to me. Lead me and guide me in righteous paths that Your name may be glorified and that Your kingdom of love and life may come to many. For the sake of Your merciful kindness in the Seed of the woman, my Savior, I pray. Amen.

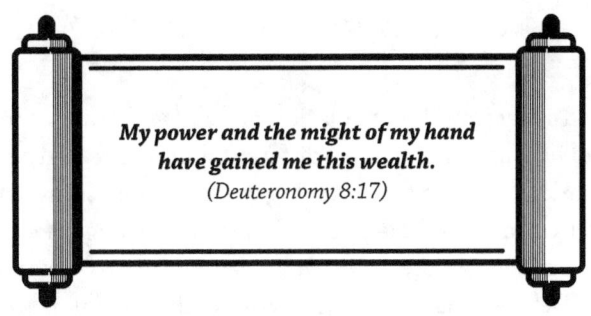

*My power and the might of my hand
have gained me this wealth.*
(Deuteronomy 8:17)

HONORING SELF VS HONORING GOD

So God blessed Noah and his sons, and said to them, "Be fruitful and multiply, and fill the earth" (Genesis 9:1).

So, here we are at a fresh beginning. As one would expect, after the world-wide Flood, the Earth was gradually re-populated by the children of Noah—Shem, Ham and Japheth. What an opportunity! What a challenge! The whole world lay at their feet. It was theirs to repopulate and enjoy. As we have observed, the torrential evidences of the Flood were extensively carved everywhere on the surface of the Earth. These consequential reminders stood as constant testimonies to the generations that followed. They preached an on-going sermon, reminding all of the repercussions that resulted from rejecting God and His Word.

But at the same time, as has been noted, the proofs of the LORD's healing hands were everywhere before their eyes. In fact, we might say that the preaching of God's Law and Gospel was being declared every day in the world. His curse because of sin was obvious, but also His love and mercy for mankind were clearly portrayed with the greening of the fields and the blossoming of nature. Trees of various varieties were springing up; fruits, nuts, and vegetables were becoming available! In short, there was plenty to eat and much beauty to enjoy.

Under God's blessing the population of birds and animals multiplied by leaps and bounds. Things were different, but under God's constant favor the world took on a beauty and special grandeur. But Satan never takes a vacation, does he? He wasn't done with his ongoing pursuit to foil God's promises and prevent—or at least postpone—his own final demise. The Devil's constant activity was clearly evident as we observe the growing population and their priorities.

For example: From the family of Ham came a son who was particularly well known. His name was Nimrod. He is described for us in God's Word like this: **He began to be a mighty one on the earth. He was a mighty hunter before the LORD; therefore it is said, "Like Nimrod the mighty hunter before the LORD."**

And what kind of hunting did he do? Here is a brief peek at his "hunting" escapades. **And the beginning of his kingdom was Babel, Erech, Accad, and Calneh, in the land of Shinar** (Genesis 10:8–10).

Quite a resume for this well-known "hunter"—wouldn't you say? It appears that Nimrod was a very industrious person. He was instrumental in gathering people together and establishing communities and cities. Actually, many believe that Nimrod was not a hunter of game at all. Rather, they see him primarily as a hunter of people. Why was that? Well, it's obvious that he needed a huge labor force to carry out his construction projects. As a result, he likely searched far and wide throughout the growing population for men to work in his extensive building programs, which appear to have been huge and far-reaching, to say the least. Together with Babel in Mesopotamia (which became Babylonia and the present-day Iraq), such well-known cities as Nineveh in Assyria were being built and were growing.

What kind of materials did they generally use for construction? Well, it appears that through experimentation they soon became knowledgeable in construction with brick and mortar. As a result, plans were made to build nothing less than a metropolis on the plains of Shinar—between the Tigris and Euphrates rivers.

Now, maybe this all sounds good. It might even be seen as healthy progress—but we must remember the LORD's will. What was God's instruction again? **God blessed Noah and his sons, and said to them:**

"Be fruitful and multiply, and fill the earth" (Genesis 9:1).

Now, that doesn't sound like a difficult bit of instruction to follow, does it? In fact, without question it was a totally exciting, God-ordained directive. Since it was the LORD's will and therefore carried with it His blessing, how could one go wrong? It was as though God were saying: *"Just go ahead with faith in My blessing and a confident song in your heart. Get on with it! Repopulate and fill the earth. You will experience a tremendously blessed result. I will see to it."*

But what was actually happening—also very prominent in our world today—was that God's simple words of direction as well as the blessing of the LORD are only too often forgotten about and most times never sought. Rather than taking God's simple words to heart and prayerfully attempting to do everything possible to walk that way, mankind only too often looks to himself rather than to God. His sinfully corrupted ego prods him on to do whatever it takes to accomplish certain goals. Why? Well, of course, he wants the credit—he desires the glory. And so, by his own schemes and self-indulgence, he ventures to accomplish great things. Above all else, he wishes to be able to say:

"My power and the might of my hand have gained me this wealth" (Deuteronomy 8:17).

That is exactly what was happening to the people of Nimrod's day: **"Come, let us build ourselves a city, and a tower whose top is in the heavens;<u> let us make a name for ourselves, lest we be scattered abroad over the face of the whole earth</u>"** (Genesis 11:4).

Now, just a minute here! What was that again that God had clearly spoken?

"Be fruitful and multiply and <u>fill the earth</u>" (Genesis 9:1).

Do you see what was happening? In direct contradiction to the will of God, they really didn't want to extend their reach over the whole planet! Rather, they wanted to concentrate on themselves and what they desired. It was their goal to make a name for themselves. They wanted the credit—the prestige—the glory for becoming such intelligent people who could construct beautiful buildings and impressive cities. Indeed, they envisioned constructing a tower that would reach into the heavens—a skyscraper of all skyscrapers—the infamous Tower of Babel!

Listen to their ego talking: *"This will be such a colossal building that everyone will come and see how unique and how grand it is. They will recognize what geniuses we are. Forget God and His blessings. We've got better things to do. Look! Observe the result of our creative minds. We've got the know-how. We have the ability. And, of course, we want all the glory for ourselves! Besides, we don't want to be scattered all over the face of the Earth. We want to stay here and become a great nation, a huge kingdom with power and strength to match. We need to look to ourselves and do what is best for us. Don't give another thought to what God has said. It's all about us. We deserve the praise!"*

Satan never takes a break, does he? No, he doesn't. And after the disastrous fall into sin, he has his foot in the door of everyone's life. To accomplish his evil purposes, he squeezes through the door left ajar by our sinful nature, and from there he attempts to move, ever so gradually, into the hearts and minds of people. Having done this, he then strives to shift them away from God's Word and will.

Listen to his spiel: *"Disregard repopulating the Earth. Pay no attention to God's will. You have made yourselves into what you are. Cast aside His promise of the Messiah. That's a pipe dream, anyway. Unite, become strong and powerful. Look at the spectacular world you can make for yourselves. For, after all, this life is all about you, you, you—what you want—what you can be—how great you can become!"*

Satan knows just how to do it, doesn't he? One would think that we would all catch on—that we would all learn how he operates and therefore recognize his lies and where they lead and therefore refuse to follow him—cut him off and out of our lives! The trouble is, <u>our sinful nature agrees with him</u>. He doesn't need to change his tactics, for they work so well. Look around in the world. His strategy is accomplishing his evil purposes pretty well, every day . . . don't you think?

The people of that day were in Satan's pocket. Everything was going his way during the centuries since the Flood. The population was rather formidable. The results of the anger of God against a rebellious people in the world-wide flood were clearly before them to see and remember—yet that judgment of God against an ungrateful people was becoming rather vague in their memory. And it appears that Nimrod, who **began to be a mighty one on the earth** (Genesis 10:8), had a huge following. And those who followed in his footsteps were on their way . . . with Satan in the driver's seat.

Well, the LORD saw it all. He always sees it all! And He, of course, recognized that the people were making a huge mistake. How could He remedy such a prideful, arrogant attitude? It is interesting to watch as God to use what we might consider to be a rather mild form of correction.

Here it is in all of its simplicity: God observed that one of their obvious traits that enabled them to carry on their selfish work efficiently was that they had no language barrier. They all could easily communicate with each other. This drew them together in the unity of their godless endeavors. What could be done about that? God had the answer. Actually it was a rather obvious solution: **Confuse their language, that they may not understand one another's speech** (Genesis 11:7). It was simple and effective.

As we all know, even when we are speaking the same language, sometimes we have a difficult time understanding someone else's point of view. But when someone is speaking a language totally foreign to us, we become utterly lost in our attempt to communicate. It's rather frustrating, wouldn't you say? Sometimes it's even comical—but not this time.

They were totally baffled in their attempt to carry on their labors with each other. We can imagine the impact that this had on their work.

They were thwarted in their attempt to accomplish their goals. Tempers flared. Accusations resulted. They couldn't get anything done! Gradually, the fruit of their prideful ambitions withered on the vine.

As a result, their selfish desires in their joint endeavors came to a screeching halt. What could they do? Since they found it impossible to work together, many moved to other areas. Gradually the LORD's purpose was accomplished as the inhabitants were dispersed far and wide. **The LORD scattered them abroad from there over the face of all the earth, and they ceased building the city** (Genesis 11:8). That's how God's mission was very gently and effectively completed. Satan's evil guidance came to naught. The sinfully devised plans of man were scuttled.

Now, you might ask, *"What in the world does this have to do with the birth of the promised Seed of the woman? What does it have to do with the Promise of salvation and restoration?"* Good question! Answer: It has much to do with the God-planned salvation in the promised Messiah. You see, as people became introverted and self-centered, God and His promises and blessings became less and less important in their lives. They were very successful outwardly . . . but spiritually they were bankrupt. Their relationship with God and His promises had been replaced with a love for themselves, things, and self-indulgence.

Yes, indeed, Satan had managed to turn their interest, their mind, their attention, their heart away from God and His will. What did they need? They needed trials—they needed difficulties. What? Who needs that? Answer: They did! It's a tough lesson to learn, but we all need to learn it. The Apostle Paul had learned it very well, and he was moved by the Spirit of God to teach us: **We also glory in tribulations, knowing that tribulation produces perseverance; and perseverance, character; and character, hope. Now hope** (confident expectation) **does not disappoint, because the love of God has been poured**

out in our hearts by the Holy Spirit who was given to us (Romans 5:3–5).

What is the LORD God teaching us through His apostle? He is urging us to dig beneath the surface of our trials and suffering and discover God's blessing in it all. We can do this by talking it over with Him. For our gracious God, loves us with an everlasting love and promises to hear and answer every prayer brought to Him in faith. Through our heartfelt prayers and hearing Him speak to us through His Word, He draws ever closer to Himself. This exercising of our faith is good for us and leads to the many blessings of which His apostle speaks.

When all is said and done, this is simply a description of a healthy Christian life. The Apostle Paul is moved to put it like this: **If we live, we live to the Lord; and if we die, we die to the Lord. Therefore, whether we live or die, we are the Lord's** (Romans 14:8).

So, to sum it up, the people of Nimrod's day had all but banished the idea of the absolute need of the LORD God in their lives. God was becoming less and less important to them while their own personal pride in themselves and their ingenuity grew with every passing day. The promise of the Messiah, the grandest blessing that mankind would ever receive, had diminished in favor of their wants, their desires, and their vain glory. With His gentle solution God called attention to their serious spiritual need! **Confuse their language, that they may not understand one another's speech** (Genesis 11:7).

This had the benevolent effect of giving their hearts and minds some spiritual breathing room, so to speak. This caused them to have to struggle each day with everyday labors. As a result, maybe some would be drawn closer to their LORD. Perhaps some would recognize the absolute necessity of a constant living relationship with their Creator and Savior every day. Besides, the directive of the LORD God would also finally be accomplished: **"Be fruitful and multiply and fill the earth"** (Genesis 9:1).

Without question, it is a long way from Eden to Bethlehem—but we will get there! God will see to it in spite of the stumbling blocks that Satan lays in the way! In the face of the self-centered, self-indulgent sinfulness of mankind, God will do what He has promised. He doesn't have much to work with—namely, sinfully corrupted people. Nevertheless, He is determined to see to it that His promise is kept and we are delivered, saved, and restored. And all of this simply because He loves us and wishes to keep us as His very own for time and for all eternity. Therefore God's faithful people are moved by His ever-living Spirit to continue to pray:

> Come, oh, come, life-giving Spirit,
> God from all eternity!
> May Your power never fail us;
> Dwell within us constantly.
> Then shall truth and life and light
> Banish all the gloom of night.
>
> Show us, Lord, the path of blessing;
> When we trespass on our way,
> Cast, O Lord, our sins behind You
> And be with us day by day.
> Should we stray, O Lord, recall;
> Work repentance when we fall.
>
> Grant our hearts in fullest measure
> Wisdom, counsel, purity,
> That we always strive to please You,
> Working for You willingly,
> Let the Gospel spread and grow,
> Bringing Satan's overthrow. (CW181:1,2,5)

PRAYER

LORD God, my merciful and ever faithful Creator, Sanctifier, and Savior: You have faithfully been with Your people every day, watching and providing creative ways by which You keep all of us close to You. Sometimes we falter in our appreciation of Your ever-gracious activities in our lives. Sometimes we complain. Sometimes we trust too much in our own selves—our own ingenuity—rather than realizing that it is You who finally makes all things work for our good. I pray, O LORD, that by the strength of Your Spirit I and all Your dear children will realize that You are all-important in our lives. Your blessing is all that we really need to accomplish major things according to Your will. Strengthen us by Your Spirit through Your infallible Word. May we ever walk in Your grace, staying close to You as we carry on in this world of sin. Move us always to give You the deserved praise for the good in our lives. Finally, lead us to repent of all the selfish and self-centered actions that detract from Your deserved glory. I pray, always and alone, through the merits of Your promised Seed of the woman, Jesus Christ, our Savior and Lord. Amen.

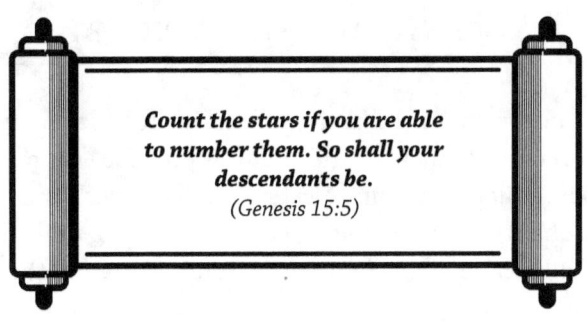

A CRADLE FOR THE PROMISED SEED

God made the following declaration to <u>Satan</u> . . . and the following promise to all humanity:

"I will put enmity between you and the woman,
And between your seed and her Seed;
He shall bruise (crush) **your head,**
And you shall bruise (crush) **His heel"** (Genesis 3:15).

God made the following declaration to <u>Abraham</u> . . . and the following promise to all humanity:

"In your seed all the nations of the earth shall be blessed"
(Genesis 22:18).

God inspired the Apostle Paul to explain:

Now to Abraham and his Seed were the promises made. He does not say, "And to seeds," as of many, but as of one. "And to your Seed," who is Christ (Galatians 3:16).

During our journey from Eden to Bethlehem, we will continually witness God's faithfulness to His promises. His covenant, which He made in the Garden of Eden, never abated for a single second. Rather, it was confirmed in His promise to Abraham. That's our next step in our onward journey toward that day of blessing for all mankind. As we march on toward fulfillment of the grandest promise ever made, we recognize something rather unexpected. We watch with anticipation and a heart of faith as we are told of God's next move. And here it is before us: God creates a "cradle" for the promised Seed of the woman.

A cradle? Yes, a cradle. But not the manger in Bethlehem—not yet! That comes much later. No, the cradle for producing this holy Child would be none other than . . . the creation of a special people—the nation of Israel. The nation of Israel, a cradle? Yes, indeed! And it is very important that we remember this one recurring truth: The one and only purpose for establishing the special theocratic nation of Israel was to produce the most precious blessing that this world would ever know.

My friends in Christ, nations come and nations go. Governments will rise and governments will fall. Historians try to evaluate the accomplishments that a nation might have contributed to the welfare of the world. But name any country that has ever existed and point to any achievement or contribution that it might have made to life and living here in this world, and you will find that without exception, there is no nation that has ever existed or ever will exist on the face of this Earth that has had a more profound impact or produced a greater gift for the world than the nation of ancient Israel.

Of course, it was all done under the providence of God. In keeping with God's promise in the Garden of Eden, our LORD gave to the offspring of Abraham one singular and all-important godly mission: Produce the Seed of the woman! This Individual—this veritable God-Man would crush the head of Satan, deliver mankind from the Devil's tyranny, and restore God's crowns of creation to life and immortality—to live with Him forever.

To accomplish this monumental phenomenon, God chose Shem from Noah's family, and from Shem's family God chose Abraham. To Abraham

God made a simple yet far-reaching pledge—a promise that God repeated at numerous times:

"I will make you a great nation; I will bless you and make your name great; and you shall be a blessing. I will bless those who bless you, and I will curse him who curses you; and <u>in you all the families of the earth shall be blessed</u>" (Genesis 12:2–3).

What other person—what other people on the face of all the Earth has ever been given such a promise from God? The answer is easy—NONE! The offspring of Abraham would become a great nation. Why? Because of what God planned for it. It bears repeating: From that nation the Seed of the woman, the Savior of all the world, would be born. As a result, that nation would be a blessing to everyone, everywhere. Therefore it was God's will that all people throughout the ancient world were destined to hold that nation in high regard and do everything necessary to protect it.

This was the will of God not because the people of Israel were morally better or more socially important than any other people, for they were sinners like everyone else. The reason why Israel was to be held in high regard and protected at all costs was for one justifiable reason and one reason only—that nation was called to carry out God's mission of restoring all mankind to once again become the original holy and perfect beings which they were created to be in the first place. Because of that, all who would bless this nation would be blessed by God, while those who would do harm to His people would fall under His curse.

What a promise of God! It must have seemed a daunting and unreasonable revelation in the ears of Abraham. Let's think about that for a bit. God had directed him to leave his homeland and the idolatrous influences that were all around him and to migrate approximately 400 miles south-west to, of all places, Canaan, <u>a land saturated with idolatry</u>. With the exception of Sarah's grave site, he never owned an inch of that territory. Besides, he and his wife did not have any children. Nevertheless, God promised that Abraham would become a great nation. Now, if that isn't mind boggling, I'd like to know what is!

Nevertheless, according to God's promise, the offspring of Abraham would be known far and wide throughout the ancient world, for his descendants would become the "cradle" for the Seed of the woman, the world's Savior. It cannot be emphasized too much—this unique nation of God was to be known as the single God-created light in the midst of this sin-darkened world. <u>Everyone</u> was to look to this nation for God's redemption, salvation, and restoration. That is exactly what our Savior Jesus Christ meant when He pointed out to the Samaritan woman at Jacob's well:

"Salvation is of the Jews" (John 4:22).

So also Simeon, a priest of God, after thousands of years had passed, was moved by the Spirit to proclaim, as he held and beheld that precious baby—the Christ Child in his arms:

"My eyes have seen Your salvation which You have prepared before the face of all peoples, <u>a light to bring revelation to the Gentiles, and the glory of Your people Israel</u> (Luke 2:30–32).

However, back at the time of Abraham, this was not so clear. As a result, he had a problem with this promise of God. What could possibly be his difficulty with such a singular, God-proclaimed honor? Well, it was an obvious question, and any of us might have had similar concerns. Briefly said, here it is: Abraham's corrupted reason was overcoming his faith. As it has been well said, "Reason is never more unreasonable than when it insists upon reasoning in things beyond the realm of reason." (Dr. Norman Madsen) And this matter with which Abraham was struggling was definitely beyond his reasoning capabilities. As a result, he was beginning to lose confidence in that monumental proclamation of God.

Simply put, here was Abraham's problem: How could he become a great nation when he and Sarai had not been blessed with even a single child? Indeed, how could his offspring bring forth the Seed of the woman when he had no children? He talked with God many times about this. In fact, he cried out in anguish: **"Look, You have given me no offspring!"** (Genesis 15:3)

So, how did God help Abraham deal with this? As He does with us even to this day, God patiently comforted Abraham with His Word. He repeated His promise to Abraham again and again and again. On one occasion God even invited Abraham to step outside his tent and lift his eyes to the heavens. What did he see? There, in the cool, refreshing darkness of a cloudless night, he beheld the beauty of the heavens filled with twinkling stars beyond number. It was a sight that never grows old even to this very day. But what had this to do with God's promise?

Listen to God's challenging words to Abraham and you will see. **"Count the stars if you are able to number them. So shall your descendants be"** (Genesis 15:5).

Have you ever tried that? Counting the stars, I mean. It's virtually impossible! Even to this day we are discovering heavenly bodies that we never knew existed. So God wanted Abraham to understand that he was dealing with God here. He was in direct communication with the Almighty, whose will and ways are not subject to man's abilities or reasoning.

What happened? Praise the LORD, Abraham got it! He **believed in the LORD, and He accounted it to him for righteousness** (Genesis 15:6). Faith—faith—faith in the promises of God was and always will be the link that ties God and man together. Indeed, it is faith that simply takes God at His Word and connects us to our gracious LORD, in spite of our reasonable calculations or understanding to the contrary.

The inspired writer of Proverbs expresses it all very simply: **Trust in the LORD with all your heart, and lean not on your own understanding; In all your ways acknowledge Him, and He shall direct your paths** (Proverbs 3:5–6). There it is in a nutshell. We all must learn this lesson and relearn it over and over again—sometimes every day—sometimes many times in a day. But what a blessed state in which to be—functioning every day with faith in the Almighty.

Indeed, our future rests securely in the hands of our changeless, miracle-working God. Let's all just relax a bit in His grace. Let's just face each day without knowing what we do not know. With the LORD God in our lives, we can and should face each day with confidence, knowing that our loving LORD <u>does</u> know the future and <u>can and will</u> do what is good and right for His believing children. Acknowledge, trust Him, and He will guide us through the challenging obstacles that lie in our paths.

So let's listen to those words again, spoken about Abraham: **He believed in the LORD, and He accounted it to him for righteousness**. It might be presumptuous to designate a verse or two from God's living Word as being the most significant among everything God has spoken. However, some have done exactly that. These simple words, spoken about Abraham, have been named by some to be the most significant of all the verses in the Bible.

Why do you think such huge importance is assigned to these words? Could it be that in a few syllables a huge division is established—a clear gulf is thereby fixed between all man-made religions of the world and the one true religion of the LORD God of heaven and Earth? For with these words the miracle of the righteousness and salvation of God is fully portrayed in a nutshell.

Abraham was counted a righteous man before God not because of anything he himself was or did. Abraham was righteous and the recipient of forgiveness and salvation simply because <u>he believed the promises of God</u>.

The Apostle Paul emphasizes this point when he was inspired to write: **If Abraham was justified by works, he has something of which to boast, but not before God. For what does the Scripture say? "Abraham <u>believed</u> God and <u>it</u> was accounted to him for righteousness"** (Romans 4:2–3).

Was Abraham always a pillar of faith-filled strength? No he was not! Did he not have struggles with his reason and his sinful nature? We have seen that he clearly did. Because he was a child of God, did Satan leave him alone? Not a chance! The faithful children of God are Satan's most prominent and favorite targets. And there is a reason for that. He was and is very well aware that one day the Seed of the woman would crush his evil head. Therefore he works feverishly and constantly to accomplish his goals. And you remember what those are—right? Very simply, to convince God's people to follow him in his godless pursuits—to drive a wedge between believers and the promises of God. And Abraham was a key element in God's plan. So although Abraham was righteous by faith in God's promises, his struggles never abated— and of course, Satan took advantage of every opportunity to foil God's benevolent mercy.

So it is with each of us. As we make our way through this world, we can be absolutely certain that the Devil is very active every day. Whether we are at work or at play—at home or away, each of us needs to recognize:

> *I walk in danger all the way;*
> *The thought shall never leave me*
> *That Satan, who has marked his prey,*

Is plotting to deceive me.
This foe with hidden snares
May seize me unawares
If e'er I fail to watch and pray;
I walk in danger all the way. (CW 431:1)

Nevertheless, we can and should also be certain that our good and gracious, almighty God is also walking with us every second of every day. For that reason we can and should pray with faithful confidence, together with David:

"The LORD is my rock, my fortress and my deliverer; the God of my strength, in Him I will trust, my shield and horn of my salvation, my stronghold and my refuge" (II Samuel 22:2–3).

PRAYER

I thank and praise You, LORD, for the blessing of Abraham, the father of the faithful. Through him and his offspring You have provided a cradle for the Christ, my Lord and the Savior of all mankind. So it will ever be true that through Abraham all the families of the Earth are blessed. As a matter of fact, I too, together with all of the faithful children of God the world over, have become Abraham's children. For as the Apostle Paul is moved by God to assure us: **"For as many of you as were baptized into Christ have put on Christ. There is neither Jew nor Greek, there is neither slave nor free, there is neither male nor female; for you are all one in Christ Jesus. And if you are Christ's, then you are Abraham's seed, and heirs according to the promise"** (Galatians 3:27–29). LORD, my God, I pray, by the power of Your Spirit, keep Your truth continually before me through Your Word and Sacraments. For then, strengthened in my faith, I can rest in peace, knowing that I am in Your merciful hands for time and forever. In the name of my Savior and Lord I pray. Amen.

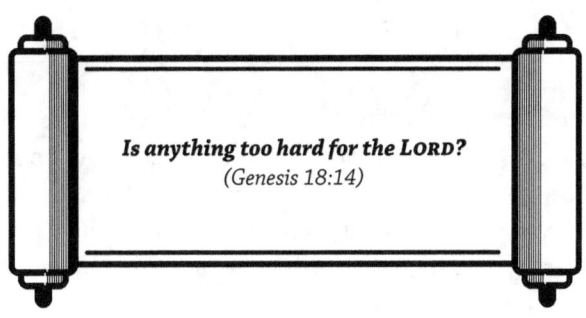

Is anything too hard for the LORD?
(Genesis 18:14)

SARAI'S "SOLUTION" VS GOD'S PROMISE

Sarai, Abraham's wife, was beside herself. Why was that so? Well, to put it bluntly, Sarai was getting up in years . . . but still no child! As it was with Abraham, so it was with Sarai—her reason overtook her faith. In her weakness of faith, Sarai conjured up what she fully believed to be a reasonable solution.

And what a "solution" it was! Did the Devil have anything to do with it? Of course he did. He is a genius at planting logical ideas and reasonable methods into the hearts and minds of God's people to <u>replace</u> a directive from God. Of course, we must quickly add that rational thought is certainly a precious gift from God. However, it should always be used in conjunction with faith in the instructions of God . . . not in opposition to them.

Well, here was Sarai's faulty analysis and "solution." Her warped thinking went like this: *"I have an Egyptian maidservant named Hagar. Maybe Hagar can conceive on my behalf. If Abraham will cooperate, he might take Hagar as his concubine and possibly have a child with her. This child, then, would be a seed of Abraham which would be in keeping with God's plan, wouldn't it?* What an ingenious solution...Sarai thought! That will solve the problem. Right?" Wrong! (Note: The custom of the day permitted a concubine arrangement though it was not in keeping with God's creative plan in the beginning.)

The question that Sarai failed to ask was this: Will this proposal be acceptable to God? The answer to that unasked question is easy: Of course not! Nevertheless, Sarai convinced Abraham that this was the only way to accomplish God's directive. As with Adam of old, in weakness of faith Abraham succumbed to his wife's request. And, indeed, Hagar did conceive and bore a son.

My, Oh my, Sarai! What have you done? And Abraham . . . to what have you agreed? The result of that faithless action reached far beyond that generation. It is sad but true. That sordid life-decision produced a catastrophic result. In fact, it has had a lasting effect upon humanity even to our day. What most people fail to realize is this: The Angel of the LORD (Note: Many believe that this special designation refers to the very Son of God Himself) clearly outlined the disastrous outcome of Sarai's and Abraham's faithless action when He appeared to Hagar and proclaimed:

"I will multiply your descendants exceedingly, so that they shall not be counted for multitude. Behold, you are with child, and you shall bear a son. You shall call his name Ishmael (God hears)**, because the LORD has heard your affliction.** (Now, take special note of the following description of Hagar's offspring.) **He shall be a wild man; his hand shall be against every man, and every man's hand against him. And He shall dwell in the presence of all his brethren"** (Genesis 16:10–12).

So what is the fall-out from this godless act coached by Satan and devised by Sarai? First off, who are the descendants of Ishmael? Well, it appears that all Arabs claim descent from Ishmael. As a result, they consider themselves to be children of Abraham. And of course they are correct according to their genetics—but the rest of their story, as it was foretold by none other than the Angel of the LORD, is clearly documented in ancient history.

These descendants of Ishmael have generally espoused the teachings and guidance of a man by the name of Mohammed. As a result, their total rejection of God and His Word continues even in this 21st century A.D. Who is Mohammed? Briefly, he lived from 570 to 632 A.D., was well aware of the Word of God but wished to initiate his own ideas of a moral philosophy for life. As a result, another man-created religion was born.

What again is typical of every man-made religion? You remember, don't you? In every case the abilities of sinful man are promoted. As a result, followers of Mohammed are required to follow his "rules" to gain the blessing of Allah—their designated supreme being. Furthermore, the teachings of Mohammed require that all those who do not recognize him as the one true prophet of Allah are declared to be infidels. Some within their ranks have concluded that murdering such "infidels" in the name of Allah earns for them a special blessing in the after-life.

It might be shocking to learn that Mohammed was actually illiterate. He could neither read nor write. Nevertheless, his ideas for life and living were recorded by others. Eventually, these writings were processed and became the holy book of the Muslims—the Quran.

According to the predictions of The Angel of the LORD, Ishmael's descendants would be, and indeed are, exceedingly great in number. They were destined to, and obviously have, spread over vast territories on the face of the Earth. Furthermore, it is worthwhile noting that God's Angel further described them as wild and fierce—constantly feuding among themselves and with everyone else!

As always, the future belongs to God, so His predictions regarding the offspring of Hagar and Abraham have proven to be totally and historically accurate. Down through the generations, political solutions have been proposed to somehow appease these warring factions of

Ishmaelites, but no lasting peace has been achieved. This curse upon humanity will, no doubt, be experienced until the last day of this world.

There is only one cure for this insufferable situation: The gospel of God's love in the Seed of the woman is the only hope for them and for every one of us. Only the LORD God, through the blessing of redemption and salvation in the promised Savior, Jesus Christ, can change their spirit. As long as the LORD and His redemptive blessing in the one and only Messiah of God are rejected, the children of Ishmael will continue in their Satanic driven, murderous, and godless pursuits.

But enough of that! Let's get back to the joy and blessing of God's promises to Abraham. This man of faith was not getting any younger. In fact, Abraham had arrived at the ripe, old age of 100 years. And Sarai?... Well, she had reached the great-grandmotherly time in life. She was 90 years old and still childless! It appears that the LORD was pushing this matter of faith-building to the limit. But fear not, it was all done in God's wisdom with His ultimate, saving purpose in mind.

On the other hand, Satan must have felt that everything was going his way. *"No child—no seed—therefore no worries!"* The promise of salvation and the crushing of His evil head, as promised in the Garden of Eden, would have come to an abrupt halt if Abraham and Sarai had gone childless. What could make Satan happier?

"But wait just a minute, Satan. Not so fast. Pay close attention as the LORD God goes about His miraculous working with Abraham and Sarai." Notice the way by which the LORD God does this. He simply repeats His promises and adds some new features. First of all,

"As for Sarai your wife, you shall not call her name Sarai, but Sarah (Princess) **shall be her name"** (Genesis 17:15). Sarah was to be recognized for the princess that she truly was. Faults? Yes! At times lacking in faith? Without question! But she remained a true, faithful daughter of God who continued to look for the promised Messiah. As such, she was a princess in God's eyes.

Every Christian woman should find a great deal of comfort and peace in these words from God. Each may look at her own life and find many shortcomings, failings, faults, and guilt. But then, stop for a moment and think of God's love for Sarai. In God's eyes she was nothing less than a princess as she looked with repentance and faith to the coming Savior of us all.

Secondly, God simply reiterated His promise to Abraham: **"I will bless her and also give you a son by her; then I will bless her, and she shall be a mother of nations; kings of peoples shall be from her"** (Genesis 17:16).

The entire future of the earthly kingdom of the living God was laid out before Abraham and Sarah in just a few simple, well-chosen words. Abram and Sarah will be the forbearers of a kingdom that will encompass the entire world, and kings (in the eyes of God) will labor among His people with the "authority" of God's Word. What a promise! What a revelation!

But did Abraham understand? No, he did not! What? Why not? Because he couldn't get past the first few words. What are they again? **"I will . . . give you a son by her."**

Abraham's faith was slipping badly. As a matter of fact, God's promise was growing somewhat ridiculous to him. **Abraham fell on his face and laughed, and said in his heart, "Shall a child be born to a man who is one hundred years old? And shall Sarah, who is ninety years old, bear a child?"** (Genesis 17:17)

There we go again! Same song! Which verse is it, anyway? Reason says, *"It can't be done. It can't happen. Therefore it will not happen!"* Ever have that happen to you? It has to me! So we need to pay attention. What did God do to support Abraham's sinking faith? Again, He simply repeated nothing other than His words of promise: **"Sarah your wife shall bear you a son, and you shall call his name Isaac"** (Genesis 17:19).

That's it: God's straight forward, unambiguous answer. What was God saying? *"Abraham, you are so filled with worry and concern. And without a doubt, what you are saying and thinking makes reasonable sense. But you are forgetting something. You are dealing with God! And what God has promised, He will do!"* Simple faith in His words relieves a great deal of tension and misery. So it is with us, every single day of our lives. Need we say more?

Yes, Isaac would be the carrier of that gracious promise of the coming Messiah. Of this, God left no doubt: **"I will establish My covenant with him for an everlasting covenant, and with his descendants after him"** (Genesis 17:19).

The covenant! The Covenant! The COVENANT ! That precious promise—that unalterable contract made by God already in the Garden of Eden and carried through in His repeated promises to Abraham, was being developed according to God's will in His own good time. But remember, He chose to bring it about by using people whom He had created—though He knew very well that after the fall into sin **the imagination of man's heart is evil from his youth** (Genesis 8:21).

Would they often stumble in their faith? Yes! We all know what that's like! But when all was said and done, not only did Abraham believe that God would one day bless him with a son from his God-given wife, but finally the whole world would be blessed through this Son. Yes, as that promised Seed, the Lord Jesus Christ Himself declared, **"Abraham rejoiced to see My day, and he saw it and was glad"** (John 8:56).

We must be reminded constantly: Faith in God's never-failing promises is at the center of the religion of the one true God and the divine force in every Christian's life. Abraham had to learn and relearn this, again and again, by the power of the Spirit of God. As a matter of fact, this had to be learned and relearned, through the power of God's Spirit, by Adam and Eve, Noah, Jacob, Moses, David, Elijah, Daniel—and indeed by Joseph and Mary and all the rest of His people. They all had to learn and relearn this through repentance and renewed faith . . . and so do we!

Let's not forget about you and me! Together with all the saints of God down through the ages, we must relearn this lesson many times in our lives. Our faith in the promises of God needs to be strengthened continually. How? By the Spirit-laced power of God's Word. For that reason, those words of promise were repeated to Abraham again and again and again:

"In your seed all the nations of the earth shall be blessed" (Genesis 22:18).

"In your seed all the nations of the earth shall be blessed" (Genesis 26:4).

"In your seed all the families of the earth shall be blessed" (Genesis 28:14).

What a way to teach a lesson in faith! The LORD permitted Abraham and Sarah to get far beyond child-bearing age before He granted them a son. The reason? God wanted them to clearly see that their son was not merely a son produced by natural reproduction, (*Though that in itself was absolutely a miracle of God.*) but this son would be the long-awaited child of promise. With this beautiful lesson in faith, we are reminded that God fulfills His promises even though human reason declares it impossible! As a result, together with Abraham, we need to be reminded time after time:

"Is anything too hard for the LORD? At the appointed time I will return to you, according to the time of life, and Sarah shall have a son" (Genesis 18:14).

Though her body was old and withered—though her faith was weak and faltering, yet **by faith, Sarah herself also received strength to conceive seed, and she bore a child when she was past the age, because she judged Him faithful who had promised. Therefore from one man, and him as good as dead, were born as many as the stars of the sky in multitude—innumerable as the sand which is by the seashore** (Hebrews 11:11–12).

Indeed, it is a long way from Eden to Bethlehem, yet God's promises and the power of the Spirit through His Word continue every inch of the journey. God's faithful instructions carried blessings far beyond anything that Abraham and Sarah could have imagined—for not only did Abraham receive the promise that he would be blessed as the father of the physical nation of Israel, but as the forefather of the Christ he would also be the father of every faithful child of God down through the generations. The Apostle Paul is inspired to clearly explain: **Now to Abraham and his Seed were the promises made. He does not say, "And to your seeds," as of many, but as of one, "And to your Seed," who is Christ"** (Galatians 3:16).

As a result, we are all children of God **through faith in Christ Jesus**. And so it bears repeating again and again and again: **For as many of you as were baptized into Christ have put on Christ. There is neither Jew nor Greek, there is neither slave nor free, there is neither male nor female; for you are all one in Christ Jesus. And if you are Christ's, then you are Abraham's seed, and heirs according to the promise** (Galatians 3:26–29).

What a blessing! Believers in the promised Seed, down through the generations are children of Abraham and, above all, are children of the living God through faith in God's promise. The <u>fulfillment</u> of that glorious promise of God is where we are headed. Although it is a long way from Eden to Bethlehem, it is well worth traveling as we see God's guiding hand and His steadfast and gracious love every inch of the way. May we learn to pray with heart and mind, as we make our way to the predicted completion of God's journey of love:

Oh, how great is Thy compassion,
Faithful Father, God of grace,
That with all our fallen race
And in our deep degradation
Thou wast merciful that we
Might be saved eternally!

LORD, Thy mercy will not leave me—
Truth doth evermore abide—
Then in Thee I will confide.
Since Thy Word cannot deceive me,
My salvation is to me
Well assured eternally. (TLH 384:1&4)

PRAYER

LORD God, as I meditate upon Your words and see how patient and long-suffering You have been with our forefathers in the faith, I pray for Your patient loving-kindness, also toward me. Often I am weak and lacking in the kind of constant faith that ought to be mine. Therefore, I pray that the power of Your Spirit will rest upon me as I face the various trials of this life. LORD, please remind me of Your continual love and undeserved mercy displayed in Your Word. Assure me again and again that I am Your dear child by faith in Your salvation in the Seed of the woman, my Messiah and my Savior. Help me always to see Your unfailing love and guidance in the midst of the most trying circumstances with which I am confronted. And move me always to patiently turn my life over to You to bless as You will, according to Your perfect timing and merciful kindness. For after all, is anything too hard for the LORD? (Genesis 18:14) In the name of our blessed Savior and Lord I pray. Amen.

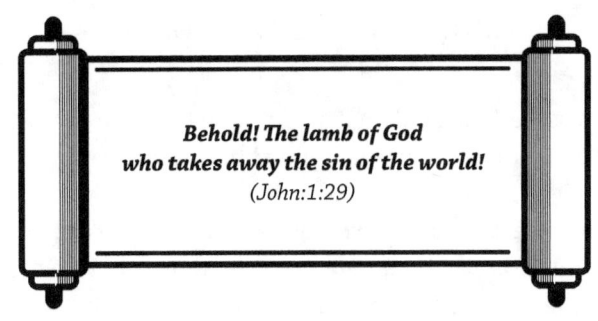

Behold! The lamb of God
who takes away the sin of the world!
(John:1:29)

A SUPREME TEST
OF FAITH

And the LORD visited Sarah as He had said, and the LORD did for Sarah as He had spoken. For Sarah conceived and bore Abraham a son in his old age, at the set time of which God had spoken to him. And Abraham called the name of his son who was born to him—whom Sarah bore to him—Isaac (Genesis 21:1–3).

It finally happened. Maybe it does not all add up reasonably, for after all, Abraham was 100 years old and Sarah was 90! But when we insert the miraculous workings of the Almighty into the equation, it all "adds up" very well and makes perfect sense. Indeed, it would appear that the LORD stretched this faith strengthening exercise with Abraham and Sarah for twenty-five long and trying years—and for very good reason. Although they were elderly and far past the normal time for begetting a child, yet it was the right time in the providence of God to fulfill His promise to these two chosen vessels.

The long-awaited son became a reality. What a precious miracle-child this was! Yes, precious to God—precious to Abraham and Sarah—and precious to all of humanity! For their baby would carry the promise of the Messiah, the Seed of the woman, and through this child's offspring the whole world would be blessed. For from Isaac's descendants the promised Messiah would be born, and Satan's head would be crushed once and for all. All people would be freed from his evil tyranny, and those who trusted God's redemptive work of salvation in the Messiah would find peace in God's kingdom for time and forever.

As God had directed, and as we well remember, they called his name *Isaac*. Yes, God chose that name for very good reason. Why the name *Isaac*? Well, there was a particular reason for that choice, for it means: "one laughs." Not a day would go by for Abraham and Sarah without their being reminded: *"You laughed. You just couldn't believe it, could you?"* Each time they called their son by name, they must have recalled how they had laughingly scorned the possibility of this miraculous birth taking place.

Time passed. Abraham turned 130 years of age, and his son Isaac was a strapping adult of thirty years. As we know, the faith of Abraham and Sarah had been tested severely as they waited for God's promise of a son to be fulfilled—and beyond a doubt, with that faith-challenging trial, their trust in the LORD grew much stronger.

That's the way it is with us also, isn't it? We all need to recognize that faith needs exercise. A "couch potato" faith simply gets weaker with every passing day. We are generally aware that muscles grow stronger through exercise, but when they are allowed to remain unused, they deteriorate. Why do doctors encourage their patients to *"get up"* and walk as soon as possible after surgery? *"Get those muscles working in order to strengthen them!"* So it is with faith. Spiritually speaking, your "muscle" of faith needs to be exercised in order for it to grow stronger.

We may complain about certain challenges and difficulties in our lives, but we need to be reminded that every one of them serves a God-given purpose. How does that work? Well, when we are faced with and struggle through various problems in life as children of God, where do we turn? We turn to our heavenly Father, don't we? We converse with the One who can really help—the LORD, our God. We talk it over with Him.

Sometimes we fall on our knees in tears begging our gracious God to help us. In so doing, we draw closer to our LORD as we place such matters into His very capable hands and urge Him to help us—show us the way—guide us in our decisions—comfort us in moments of distress. As we do this, we are "exercising" our faith. As a result, our faith in our divine Physician grows stronger. Our faith is strengthened even more as we watch our merciful LORD graciously answer our prayers according to His will and make all things work for our good.

Now observe as God takes this lesson in faith-building to another level. The faith of God's servants Abraham and Sarah had grown stronger through many years of exercise. But suddenly Abraham was faced with such a heart-rending test of his faith that in our comparative weakness we stumble and falter as we try to wrap our minds around it and put ourselves into Abraham's sandals.

In order for us to assimilate the full thrust of this episode into our hearts and minds, we must hear this entire lesson in faith from the Spirit Himself. Are you ready for this? Here it is: **Now it came to pass after these things that God tested Abraham, and said to him: "Abraham!" And he said, "Here I am."**

And He said, "Take now your son, your only son Isaac, whom you love, and go to the land of Moriah, and offer him there as a burnt offering on one of the mountains of which I shall tell you" (Genesis 22:1–2).

What is happening? Is this for real? Are you as astonished as I am? Each time I read these words from God, I gasp in horror. How could this be? For a father to be called upon to offer his only son as a sacrifice upon an altar takes our breath away. But it even goes beyond that, doesn't it?

Think about it: God's promise to Abraham down through many decades involved this specific child. Isaac was the promised seed from whom the ultimate Promise of promises would finally be fulfilled. It was through him that all the nations of the Earth would be blessed. He was the miracle child for whom Abraham and Sarah had hoped—prayed for—waited for so very long. We cower in our faltering faith when we think of the absolute confidence in God that was required to fulfill such a request as this! We ask ourselves, *"What would I have done? How would I have reacted?"*

We who have been blessed with children are petrified at the thought of being asked by God to perform such an act of absolute, faithful obedience to God's clear and unmistakable command. Yet, as horrified as we are, it is all part of the wonder-filled journey to that blessed Christmas day that we all enjoy with thankful and devoted hearts. It is faith-strengthening for us to see the steadfast devotion of our fathers and mothers as they confidently kept their eyes fixed firmly upon the promises of their heavenly Father.

And how about Satan's reaction? Well, Satan was ecstatic. How could he lose? If Abraham would refuse God's instructions, he might thereby prove to be unfit for God's ultimate purpose. On the other hand, if Abraham would carry out God's command and sacrifice his son, the entire plan of salvation for the world and Satan's ultimate destruction would be nullified. Yes, the bearer of the Promise would be dead, and Satan would have won the victory! Would this be the end of the Promise of salvation for mankind and the crushing of Satan's head?

Listen carefully to the faith-filled response of Abraham to this ultimate test of his faith. Let us read slowly as we go together with Abraham and Isaac, attentively measuring Abraham's resolute and Spirit-filled reaction to God's instructions: **So Abraham rose early in the morning and saddled his donkey, and took two of his young men with him, and Isaac his son; and he split the wood for the** burnt offering, and arose and went to the place of which God had told him. Then on the third day, Abraham lifted his eyes and saw the place afar off.

And Abraham said to his young men, "Stay here with the donkey; the lad and I will go yonder and worship, and we will come back to you." What an interesting statement, **"We will come back to you."**

What was Abraham thinking? What was he saying? **"We will come back to you."** Did he confidently believe that God would, somehow, someway intervene? The reality of the moment is mind boggling. But we remember, **"Is anything too hard for the LORD?"** Faith, faith, faith—remember?

Well now, let's not get ahead of ourselves. The matter of the word **"We"** will be resolved a bit later—but as for now, without hesitation **Abraham took the wood of the burnt offering and laid it on Isaac his son, and took the fire in his hand, and a knife, and the two of them went together. But Isaac spoke to Abraham his father and said,**

"My Father!" And he said, "Here I am, my son." And he said, "Look, the fire and the wood, but where is the lamb for a burnt offering?"

The innocent, trusting words of Isaac tug at our heart strings as we listen to the confident, faith-filled and loving response of Abraham. And Abraham said, **"My son, God will provide for Himself the lamb for a burnt offering."** In other words, *"Leave it all in the hands of God. He will take care of it."*

And the two of them went together. Then they came to the place of which God had told him. And Abraham built an altar

there and placed the wood in order; and he bound Isaac his son and laid him on the altar, upon the wood. And Abraham stretched out his hand and took the knife to slay his son. But the <u>Angel of the LORD</u> called to him from heaven and said,

"Abraham, Abraham!" And he said, "Here I am." And He said, "Do not lay your hand on the lad, or do anything to him; for now I know that you fear God, since you have not withheld your son, your only son, from Me."

Then Abraham lifted his eyes and looked, and there behind him was a ram caught in a thicket by its horns. So Abraham went and took the ram, and offered it up for a burnt offering instead of his son. And Abraham called the name of the place, The-LORD-Will-Provide; as it is said to this day,

"In the Mount of the LORD it shall be provided."

Then the <u>Angel of the LORD</u> called to Abraham a second time out of heaven, and said: "By Myself I have sworn, says the LORD, because you have done this thing, and have not withheld your son, your only son, in blessing I will bless you, and in multiplying I will multiply your descendants as the stars of the heaven and as the sand which is on the seashore; and your descendants shall possess the gate of their enemies. <u>In your seed all the nations of the earth shall be blessed, because you have obeyed My voice</u>" (Genesis 22:3–18).

Take a deep breath, dear reader. What a tremendously marvelous lesson to teach us about absolute faith and trust in the promises of God! It was Abraham's Spirit-given faith that God was vigorously exercising for the challenges that lay ahead. And what an exercise it was—as the holy writer of Hebrews spells it out: **By faith Abraham, when he was tested, offered up Isaac, and he who had received the promises offered up his only begotten son, of whom it is said,** *"In Isaac your seed shall be called"* (Hebrews 11:17–18).

So the question that we had at the beginning of this lesson in faith is answered. Remember? Abraham had instructed his servants to wait, and he had promised, **"We will come back to you"** (Genesis 22:5).

Yes, Abraham spoke those words with total confidence, **accounting that God was able to raise him up, even from the dead** (Hebrews 11:19). This episode revealed the absolute and amazing Spirit-filled strength of Abraham's faith. Indeed, even the resurrection of his son from death by the hand of God was part of this faith-equation. O, LORD, give us such a faith as this!

Besides that, we cannot help but make the comparison of Abraham and Isaac with our heavenly Father and His only Son, Jesus the Messiah. For example: Compare the total obedience of our Savior to his heavenly Father's will: **"Not My will, but Yours, be done"** (Luke 22:42).

Each carried the wood for the sacrifice: **And He, bearing His cross went out to a place called the Place of a Skull** (John 19:17).

Each was the only son of his father: **"This is my beloved Son in whom I am well pleased"** (Matthew 3:17).

Furthermore, **The Angel of the LORD**, who spoke to Abraham and halted the sacrifice of Isaac, is a designation which is used throughout the Old Testament on only a few very rare and special occasions. It is presumed by many to be a specific reference to the pre-incarnate Son of God. If it is, [and I share that understanding], our Lord and Savior is here visually pre-living what would eventually happen to Him when the fullness of the time had come for His crucifixion and resurrection.

Yes, He Himself, the Son of the living God, would be sacrificed on a different altar—the altar of the cross for the sins of the world. However, there is one huge difference: In the case of our Messiah, there would be no substitute to take His place. He, the designated Seed of the woman, <u>was</u> the Lamb of God who took <u>our</u> place and became the ultimate sacrifice for the sins of all mankind. As John the Baptizer, the forerunner of the Christ, clearly pointed out:

"Behold! The lamb of God who takes away the sin of the world!" (John:1:29)

Furthermore, as we well remember: the Father, the LORD God of heaven and Earth, did raise up His Son from the dead to reign over His kingdom here and forever in eternity. **And He shall reign forever and ever!** (Revelation 11:15)

Yes, my friends in Christ, does anyone still need to ask: "What do these words of Holy Scripture have to do with Christmas—the ultimate fulfillment of God's promise proclaimed in the Garden of Eden?" Unmistakably, we see that this marvelous lesson points directly to Christmas—the fulfillment of the promise of the LORD God in the Garden.

As we catch our breath, after meditating on these soul-stirring words from our LORD, we see clearly that Satan's hopes were again dashed into a thousand pieces! The ultimate test of Abraham had been given. His unquestioning faith in God's goodness and promises was unwavering.

Abraham's children were, beyond a shadow of doubt, the designated cradle for the Messiah.

The offspring of Abraham, the nation of Israel, was the nation in which spiritual salvation was to be found by every individual on the face of all the Earth. That is why Abraham is such a central figure in the Bible. That is why God put him through such challenging tests. His faith had to be tried to the limit in the purifying fire of God's furnace to produce a people worthy of such a unique, world-saving honor.

We thank our LORD God for producing in Abraham such a steadfast faith. In spite of his and Sarah's weaknesses and in the face of Satan's constant maneuvering, the promise of the Seed of the woman was preserved, and fulfillment was a certainty. By God's grace Christmas was promised and Christmas would come. No doubt about it!

When we consider the constant workings of God carried on continuously for us and for our salvation—when we witness Him painstakingly working with our fathers and mothers in the faith in order to rescue us from Satan's evil clutches, we fall on our knees in heartfelt prayer:

PRAYER

O LORD, my gracious and loving God, I am well-nigh speechless when I hear of the steadfast faith that You gave, strengthened, and preserved in Abraham. Yes, I too pass through various difficulties of life. I, too, am confronted with mind boggling decisions which bring me to my knees in tearful prayer for Your help and guidance—yet nothing in my life comes close to the test of faith to which You placed my faithful father, Abraham. I realize how necessary this was for our salvation which You planned for me and for all people, in the promised Messiah, for it was to be the Seed of a woman, from the very offspring of Abraham, who would crush the head of Satan for us and deliver us into Your kingdom of life, liberty, and happiness, for time and forever. I thank and praise You, my LORD, for laying these things out so clearly for me to grasp by my simple faith. As a result, I may live in peace and joy in the midst of this world of sin and finally inherit the blessings of my eternal home because of Your love for me in Jesus Christ, Your Son and my Lord. It is in His name that I pray with a thankful heart:

> *Oh, for a faith that will not shrink*
> *Tho' pressed by many a foe,*
> *That will not tremble on the brink*
> *Of poverty or woe,*
>
> *That will not murmur nor complain*
> *Beneath the chast'ning rod,*
> *But in the hour of grief or pain*
> *Can lean upon its God,*
>
> *A faith that shines more bright and clear*
> *When tempests rage without,*
> *That, when in danger, knows no fear,*
> *In darkness feels no doubt,*
>
> *That bears unmoved the world's dread frown*
> *Nor heeds its scornful smile,*
> *That sin's wild ocean cannot drown*
> *Nor Satan's arts beguile,*
>
> *A faith that keeps the narrow way*
> *Till life's last spark is fled*
> *And with a pure and heav'nly ray*
> *Lights up the dying bed.*
>
> *Lord, give us such a faith as this,*
> *And then, whate'er may come,*
> *We'll taste e'en now the hallowed bliss*
> *Of an eternal home. (CW 405)*

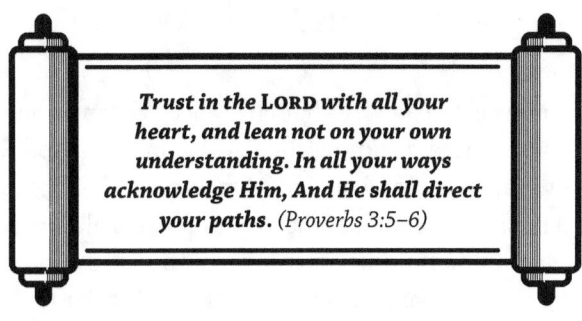

Trust in the LORD with all your heart, and lean not on your own understanding. In all your ways acknowledge Him, And He shall direct your paths. (*Proverbs 3:5–6*)

GOD'S PROMISE VIA ISAAC AND REBEKAH

"Isaac, maybe you should be thinking about marriage. After all, you are the carrier of the sacred promise of God. Yes, that promise rests upon you and your offspring, for as the LORD God promised your father on many occasions: **'In your seed all the nations of the earth shall be blessed . . . '** (Genesis 22:18).

"No marriage—no seed—no blessing. Get it? Humanly speaking, the promise of Christmas for the whole world is in your hands."

But Isaac had a problem. There was no young lady in the area where Isaac lived who was of interest to him. Now, why was that? Did Isaac simply consider himself to be just "too good a catch" for any of the girls in the neighborhood? Well, that was not the case at all. It was not that Isaac was so difficult to please—it was just that . . . well, all the girls "in the neighborhood" were avid idol worshipers! Sort of deflating for a faithful child of the LORD God . . . isn't it?

You likely remember that Abraham was called by God to dwell in Canaan. Yes, he and his family dwelt among the Canaanites who were totally given to the worship of man-invented gods. Every idolatrous and inhumane practice imaginable was carried on everywhere in that godless land. I suppose one might wonder: *Of all possible places, why did God call Abraham to move to such a God-forsaking country as Canaan?*

Certainly, God was fully aware that His called servant would be dwelling in a land where the knowledge of the one true God was non-existent. But we must remember that Abraham was being groomed for a very special mission for God. Preparations for this all-important work required absolute and unquestioning faith in the LORD God of heaven and Earth. There in Canaan, Abraham's faith was "under the gun" every minute of every day. As has been mentioned repeatedly—this served to exercise his faith daily, and as a result his trust in the LORD God would be strengthened day by day.

So that was God's plan. It was His will for Abraham to move smack-dab, directly into the midst of idolaters. Such a place was not difficult to find, for during the centuries following the Flood, the world once again was populated by gross idolaters. Godless practices and idol facilities were everywhere. So there they were—Abraham and Sarah, together with their miracle son Isaac—one family living with faith in the one true God—strangers in an unfamiliar land.

So what should they do? They knew it was totally out of the question for Isaac to marry an idolater. Consider what was at stake! Salvation for the entire world rested in the hands of Abraham, Sarah, and Isaac. And the solution to this problem was certainly not obvious—at least not immediately. Did God intervene quickly? No, He did not. Remember? Struggling in faith is good for faith! We should remember that! So, what should they do?

Well, Abraham had a plan. He usually did! As with all of us, some plans are good, some are not so good, and some are disastrous! Abraham had just buried the earthly remains of his dear wife Sarah at the God-blessed age of 127 years. Abraham also was well advanced in years—so he needed to make certain that the all-important promise of God was in good hands. As a first step, he called on his most trusted servant for this assignment, and commissioned his "chief of staff" for a special and sacred duty.

This trusted servant pretty much took care of all of Abraham's serious business. However, this particular assignment was so unusually important that Abraham required that his servant subscribe to an oath:

"I will make you swear by the LORD, the God of heaven and the God of the earth, that you will not take a wife for my son from the daughters of the Canaanites, among whom I dwell; but you shall go to my country and to my kindred, and take a wife for my son Isaac" (Genesis 24:3–4).

What do you think? Does that sound a bit pre-arranged? Indeed, it does—and of course, it was! However, such marital arrangements were common. Maybe it seems a bit crude to us: *"Go and fetch a wife for my son, Isaac, but she is not to be from this country in which we dwell. I want you to go back to where my kindred are living, and there you will be able to find a wife for Isaac from among our relatives."*

As has been said, this may sound a bit tactless to us, yet present-day unarranged marriages in our country are not going so well either, are they? It was recently reported that eight years of research reveal that about 31% of all marriages in the United States of America end in divorce! (Other studies place this figure at a whopping 50%!) However, we are told that this number drops dramatically among God's people who are dedicated to the truth of His Word and His never-failing guidance. For them, divorce is and should be an abomination! Indeed, the LORD God couldn't be clearer on the subject:

For the LORD God of Israel says that He hates divorce (Malachi 2:16).

Therefore, it is our constant prayer that each of our children and grandchildren will marry someone who is committed to a Bible-centered Christian faith. And during their marriage, our parental prayers and solid Christian advice will continue with constant concern and love. We never stop being loving parents!

But let's get back to Abraham and Sarah. Without question, they had much to pray about. They fully understood that there were also idolatrous influences "back home." Yet it also appears that the knowledge of the one true God was still at least in evidence among the relatives of Abraham. So, off Abraham's servant went, fully equipped for the four hundred miles or more journey with ten camels, fellow travelers, and needed supplies.

Finally, after weeks of travel, they arrived at the city of Haran. As far as they knew, Abraham's brother, Nahor, still lived there—but first things first. As one might expect, the travelers and the camels were in genuine need of a good, healthy drink of water. Well, what do you know—just what they needed—a well on the edge of the city.

This was good timing. It was evening. OK . . . but why was that a good time to be at the well? It so happens that evening was the usual time when many young ladies came to the well to draw water for their various evening needs. Now . . . that was interesting. Everything seemed to be falling into place, right? However, as a true believer in the LORD God and feeling totally unequipped for this special assignment . . . with whom could Abraham's servant discuss this situation? Well, as God's children generally do, he talked it over with God. This was his silent prayer:

"O LORD God of my master Abraham, please give me success this day, and show kindness to my master Abraham. Behold, I stand here by the well of water, and the daughters of the men of the city are coming out to draw water. Now let it be that the young woman to whom I say, 'Please let down your pitcher that I may drink,' and she says, 'Drink, and I will also give your camels a drink'—let her be the one whom You have appointed for Your

servant Isaac. And by this I will know that You have shown kindness to my master" (Genesis 24:12–14).

Prayer is good, agreed? However, this prayer of Abraham's servant sounds a bit too specific . . . don't you think? Maybe the servant should have left the details in God's very capable hands. On the other hand, it does sound like a prayer of faith. So the question is: How will God answer that kind of prayer? Well, sometimes our LORD surprises us with His answer. We've all experienced that, haven't we? There are times that God's answer to our prayers is totally in accord with what we had in mind. Well, that prompts us to pray with careful forethought, doesn't it? As the saying goes: "Be careful what you pray for!"

That is exactly what happened with Abraham's servant. The servant had barely finished his prayer—and there she came, a beautiful young woman with her water-pitcher on her shoulder. Accustomed to this chore, she swept by Abraham's servant and made her way down to the well. She adeptly drew water from the well, filled her pitcher, and confidently ascended the incline—a very ordinary and simple task for her. The servant's eyes never left her but were glued to her every move. Perhaps he secretly wondered, *"Could this possibly be the one?"* This all seemed too good to be true. The servant just had to go ahead with his planned request—so he blurted it out, **"Please let me drink a little water from your pitcher." So she said, "Drink, my lord"**(Genesis 24:17–18).

Abraham's servant was well-pleased by the gracious manners of this young lady, but he must have been entirely swept off his feet when he heard her say, **"I will draw water for your camels also, until they have finished drinking"** (Genesis 24:19).

Was this really happening? The servant was utterly amazed and silently pondered this entire scenario: *"What a gracious young lady. She fulfilled my request—and more! Everything is happening according to my prayer!"*

The camels had finished drinking. Now what? Astonished by it all, the servant took from his supply bags some special gifts: **a golden nose ring weighing half a shekel, and two bracelets for her wrists weighing ten shekels of gold** (Genesis 24:22) *(Note: A shekel=1/2 ounce—an approximate day's wage. Apparently, nose rings are not an invention of the 21st century, after all!)* These were elaborate gifts, yet Abraham's servant felt compelled to give them to the young lady in thankfulness for her kindness.

But what followed was undoubtedly God's continuing answer to the servant's prayer. Listen to this: She went on to explain that she **was the daughter of Bethuel, Milcah's son, whom she bore to Nahor** (Genesis 24:24). Really? These specific answers to his detailed prayer were astounding! Besides, this very gracious young lady went on to explain that they had plenty of room and provisions for the servant, his aids, and all of his camels. She invited him and his entire entourage to their home!

Now, we realize that hospitality was a common trait among the people of that day—but this was well-nigh unbelievable! Besides the generous offers, she was a member of Abraham's family—the very ones that Abraham had requested that his servant meet! Everything seemed to fit! *(Note: Abraham and Nahor were brothers. Thus, Isaac and Bethuel were cousins).*

When they arrived at Bethuel's home, Abraham's servant explained the entire incident and the reason for his visit to Bethuel and Laban *(Rebekah's brother)*. After listening attentively, they figured it out: **"The thing comes from the LORD; we cannot speak to you either bad or good. Here is Rebekah before you; take her and go, and let her**

be your master's son's wife, as the LORD has spoken" (Genesis 24:50–51).

Now, we might wonder about their readiness to release Rebekah into the hands of a stranger. Abraham had been gone for decades, but they remembered him and felt somewhat comfortable that the servant was acting on behalf of kinfolk. Besides that, their words indicated that they recognized the hand of the LORD God in all of this. Immediately, this drew them close to their traveling guest.

Not only that, but they might well have been aware of the promise of the Messiah that Isaac carried. What a special honor: Rebekah could become the mother of the children from whom the Seed of the woman would finally be born. This was a blessing beyond anything that could be named! Joyfully they had become convinced, gave her into the hands of Abraham's servant, and sent her on her way with this blessing: **"Our sister, may you become the mother of thousands of ten thousands; And may your descendants possess the gates of those who hate them"** (Genesis 24:60).

Absolutely! As the mother of the children of Isaac she would indeed become **the mother of thousands of ten thousands**, for she would be the spiritual "mother" of all the faithful believers down through the generations. Besides that, as the bride of Isaac she would be among those special few in the genealogy of Christ Jesus, the Seed of the woman, the Savior of all the world. To add to that, her offspring could go about their calling fearlessly and **possess the gates of those who hate them**. In other words, regardless of what their enemies—Satan and those who follow him—might do in opposition to the LORD God and His people, the blest of the LORD would always be victorious!

Indeed, my friends in Christ, the golden thread of God's gracious love in the promised Seed miraculously ties all believers together as His joyful and thankful family. What a special favor is ours: We see the beauteous ribbons of Christmas intricately woven into the lives of His people down through the generations. However, it is a very long way from Eden to Bethlehem—and Satan is very alert to capitalize on any and every weakness of faith found among God's people. Nevertheless, the assurances of God made in the Garden of Eden stood secure. It would happen. Christmas would come! Blessed are those of us who are privileged to make this journey and accompany the saints of old in prayer:

> *Welcome, O my Savior, now!*
> *Joyful, Lord, to you I bow.*
> *Come into my heart, I pray;*
> *Oh, prepare yourself a way.*
>
> *Crush for me the serpent's head*
> *That, set free from doubt and dread,*
> *I may cling to you in faith,*
> *Safely kept through life and death. (CW 28:4,5)*

PRAYER

I thank You, LORD, for permitting sinful beings like me to become so intricately involved in realizing the fulfillment of Your promise of salvation for the whole world. Time and again, I wonder about my next step in life as I prayerfully try to make decisions that are in keeping with Your will. I pray for Your Spirit, O LORD, that I may confidently, trustingly, put one foot in front of the other, fully realizing that my life is in Your good and gracious hands. For I fully realize, that as You have done wondrous things for Your people in the past, I may confidently place my life into Your loving hands every minute of every day. For I know that You will make all things work together for my good. To that end I pray in my Savior's name. Amen.

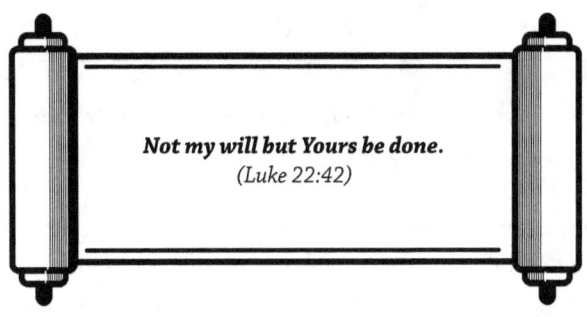

Not my will but Yours be done.
(Luke 22:42)

TWO NATIONS ARE IN YOUR WOMB

One of the primary blessings that most young married couples expect is God's gift of children. Consequently, it becomes a rather difficult shock when it doesn't happen. Suddenly they are faced with the unexpected possibility that one or the other of them is sexually sterile. Isaac and Rebekah were joined together in joyful, holy wedlock—but the happiness of their young married life was soon accompanied with sadness. Time passed . . . but Rebekah did not conceive. As it was with Sarah and Abraham, so it seemed to be with Isaac and Rebekah. It appeared that she might be barren.

Isaac and Rebekah found themselves in a quandary similar to that of Abraham and Sarah. As you recall, Isaac was the sole bearer of the Eden Covenant—that all-important God-given promise, and so their circumstance was particularly heart-rending for Isaac. As children of God, what should they do in this predicament? Of course, Isaac pleaded with the LORD God for offspring—a normal concern for all of God's believing people. Without question, only God could help. Sometimes God's answers to our prayers are different than we expect—but in this case, God's response was exactly in keeping with what Isaac wanted. Rebekah conceived. Praise the LORD!

It wasn't long before Rebekah detected movement within her womb. That, of course, was not out of the ordinary, but something rather unusual about her pregnancy made Rebekah cry out in distress: **"If all is well, why am I this way?"** (Genesis 25:22)

Something was so different from what she had expected—so again, as a believing child of God, she took it to the LORD in prayer. Our LORD answered and gave her the reason for her particularly strange feeling:

"Two nations are in your womb, two peoples shall be separated from your body; one people shall be stronger than the other, and the older shall serve the younger" (Genesis 25:23).

First of all, the LORD made something very clear to Rebekah: She was going to be the mother of twins! In the words of the Almighty Himself, she would be the mother of two nations, so to speak. But there was something else revealed to her that was even more significant: The oldest, the first-born child, would be subservient to the one born second. This seemingly small detail was unusual, for normally the older son would have some advantages over the younger. In this case, however, God Himself reversed this customary order. So, what did that finally mean? How would this all play out? It was a rather challenging wrinkle, to say the least.

Well, let's watch and observe the ramifications of this unusual twist. When Rebekah went into labor, the first baby born had reddish skin and was very hairy. They named him Esau. And what was the meaning of the name Esau? Of course, "hairy." *(Not Harry, but hairy!)* The second baby came into this world holding on to his brother's heel—so they called him Jacob, which meant quite literally, "seizing by the heel." They were very different already from birth. Unquestionably, they were certainly not identical twins! As a matter of fact, they were opposites in many ways. This was already apparent when they were struggling with each other in their mother's womb and causing their mother such distress.

Well, the boys grew up—and guess what? Their differences became even more prominent with each day of development. Esau became a skillful hunter, an outdoors man—a man of the field. Such noticeable interests were certainly acceptable in themselves. But there was something else that was of great concern to Isaac and Rebekah. It appeared that Esau lived only for the present. His interest in spiritual matters was rather minimal, to say the most. He lived his life for this world only. He seemed to carry on as though the promise of the Messiah and God's continual presence in his life were of little or no particular interest or concern to him. It was scary! It could well have reminded them of Cain, about whom they might have heard.

This worldly attitude of Esau seemed to complicate matters, for after all he was the first-born, and as such, he automatically had the special rights of a first-born son. Since God was fully aware of future happenings, maybe it was to that pronounced difference in the boys that God was referring when He specifically declared: **"The older shall serve the younger"** (Genesis 25:23).

To what specifically did this customary practice relate? For one thing, the first-born would normally receive a double share of inheritance from his father's wealth. More importantly, he would stand to be blessed with that all-important promise of God concerning the coming Savior. So the reason for God's reversal of the customary order of things with respect to Rebekah's twin boys was becoming more and more evident.

How could this be resolved? I suppose we could ask endless questions. Why this and why that? On the other hand, we can simply realize that all was in God's very capable hands, for we know that He certainly had everything well designed for the blessing of His kingdom and His people. There we go—that is definitely the wiser choice.

As time went on, Jacob and Esau became grown men. In fact, Esau had already become quite deeply involved with the neighbors and coupled with Hittite women! Yes, idolatrous women! This obviously added some urgency to this strange situation. It appeared that God would have to intervene somehow. But how and when?

As the boys matured, their differences became more prominent. Jacob couldn't help but become concerned by Esau's increasingly worldly attitude. For after all, the older son was entitled to his father's blessing. But what could Jacob do to approach this very sensitive matter? Suddenly, an incident in the lives of the two boys gave Jacob the opportunity to force the issue.

Here's what happened: Esau had been out in the field, likely hunting or carrying on some other outdoor activity. He came home exhausted and was as hungry as a bear coming out of hibernation. It just so happened that Jacob had been doing some cooking, creating a fine aroma. Esau arrived in his usual burly fashion and got a whiff of the pot of stew cooking on the fire. Man, he was hungry! So in his customarily demanding tone he ordered Jacob: **"Let me eat some of that red stew, for I am exhausted!"** (ESV Genesis 25:30)

Hmmm. Likely, Jacob began to wonder. *"Maybe this is a good time to broach the matter that has been bothering me for some time."* In Jacob's view, the birthright that Esau possessed as the older son seemed misplaced. To further galvanize his thinking, likely Rebekah had shared with him the words of God, declaring that **"The older shall serve the younger"** (Genesis 25:23).

Since Esau appeared to care nothing for his birthright, it seemed to Jacob that it was time to broach the question. So he laid it on the line: **"Sell me your birthright as of this day"** (Genesis 25:31).

Tired and hungry, Esau responded emphatically and without hesitation: **"Look, I am about to die; so what profit shall this birthright be to me?"** (Genesis 25:32)

In other words, and typical of Esau's attitude, *"Why are we talking about this birthright thing? I'm totally tuckered out and starving. What do I care about my birthright? I want something to eat!"* But Jacob wasn't satisfied; he wanted this matter clearly settled, once and for all.

So Jacob countered: **"Swear to me as of this day." So he** (Esau) **swore to him** (Jacob)**, and sold his birthright to Jacob. And Jacob gave Esau bread and stew and went his way. Thus Esau despised his birthright** (Genesis 25:34).

OK. Clear enough! But was that the end of the matter? Not really. You see, this episode concerned the matter of the birthright only—and there still remained the much more significant matter of the all-important blessing of the promise of the Messiah. That was priceless above all earthly blessings.

What added complications to this serious matter was the fact that father **Isaac loved Esau because he ate of his game** (Genesis 25:28). It appears that Isaac was not thinking straight in his elderly years, for he seemed to be more interested in the taste of Esau's "game" (venison) than in anything else . . . including the all-important preservation of the promise of God concerning the coming Savior of the world.

As time went on, and Esau's worldly ways became more and more prominent, it seemed to Rebekah and Jacob that the situation was becoming urgent. Esau's two wives of the Hittite population were a constant aggravation. In fact, they **were a grief of mind to Isaac and Rebekah** (Genesis 28:35). The Hittite immorality and idolatry were well known; this godlessness was in front of them every day right under their noses in their own family!

However, it was far more than that. Rebekah couldn't forget it, nor should she. God's promise of the Seed of the woman through whom the whole world would be blessed with God's love and forgiveness was in jeopardy. And as far as Rebekah was concerned: *"The promised Savior born from a Hittite idolater? Never!!"*

Now, to further set the scene of events, it was obvious that **Rebekah loved Jacob** (Genesis 25:28) as her favorite son. The reason for her favoritism? Well, for one thing, she was certainly well aware that it was God's will that the promise of God concerning the coming Messiah should be carried via her son Jacob. Besides, she knew that Jacob faithfully recognized the importance of having the one true God and His blessing in his life.

But how could Rebekah promote her strong feelings? Maybe she should have simply prayed about it and left it in the hands of God—for after all, whatever the LORD promises, He is fully capable of finishing, without the interference of "reasonable" people. But that kind of thinking was not appealing to Rebekah.

All of us are guilty of such appraisals now and then, aren't we? Sometimes we have the notion that as long as our motives are righteous, a bit of logical engineering is acceptable. After all, the end justifies the means . . . doesn't it? Not really. Nevertheless, sometimes we might succumb to the notion that God needs a little "help!" Apparently, that was Rebekah's thinking. Might it be far better to join the 17th century hymn writer and confess with heart and souls?

> *I leave all things to God's direction;*
> *He loves me both in weal and woe.*
> *His will is good, sure His affection;*
> *His tender love is true, I know.*
> *My fortress and my rock is He:*
> *What pleases God, that pleases me. (CW 414:1)*

PRAYER

LORD God, my life is filled with decisions that must be made every day. It is not always clear to me what I should do. I wish to function according to Your good and holy will, but sometimes my sinful nature gets in the way. Sometimes things are not moving in the direction that I think they should, and I become a bit over-zealous in trying to steer them. LORD, help me realize that the ultimate outcome of matters in my life is always totally in Your hands. Help me to make good judgments that are in accordance with Your will and then leave it all in Your wise, loving, all-knowing, and all-powerful hands. I know that in so doing, frustrations will be avoided, and outcomes will result according to Your will and always for my blessing. Help and strengthen me so to do in the name of Your Son Jesus, who so eloquently prayed to His heavenly Father from the sacrificial altar of the cross: **"Not my will but Yours be done"** (Luke 22:42). Amen.

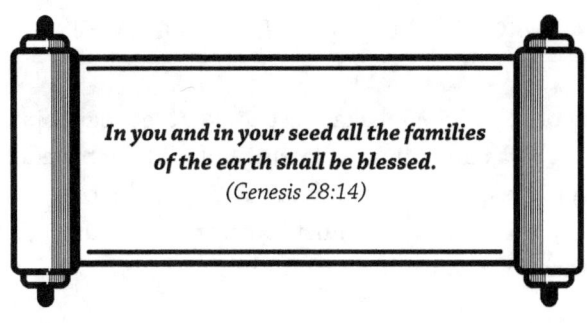

REASON OVERTAKES FAITH

Isaac had grown quite elderly and for all practical purposes was blind. He wisely surmised that it was time to make some final arrangements with his family. So one day he called Esau to his side and made this startling announcement:

"My son . . . behold now, I am old, I do not know the day of my death. Now therefore, please take your weapons, your quiver and your bow, and go out to the field and hunt game for me. And make me savory food, such as I love, and bring it to me that I may eat, that my soul may bless you before I die" (Genesis 27:1–4).

The time had come! The day for bestowing that all-important blessing had arrived! And of course, as one might expect, Rebekah had done a little eavesdropping and overheard the entire conversation between Isaac and Esau. Now what? Well, one thing was certain in her mind: She had to do <u>something</u> in order to prevent this "mistake" from happening! But what?

Well, in Rebekah's mind, whatever she did she would have to do quickly! Esau, abiding by his father's wishes, had already left to hunt. With his skill it wouldn't take very long for him to bag the desired game. Besides, Esau was anxious to return on this very special day in his life, for when he returned, Isaac would bestow on him that coveted blessing.

In her way of thinking, Rebekah just couldn't let that happen. As you remember, this was no ordinary blessing but was the benediction that carried with it the golden thread that was tied to the Messiah. So, she determined that somehow she must intervene. Once again, she was convinced that she had to "help" God a bit.

Rebekah came up with a plan. As we know, she was good at that. First, she had to find Jacob and explain to him what was about to happen. Jacob listened attentively as his mother explained her proposed course of action. Rebekah instructed Jacob to choose two choice kids from among their herd of goats. After they were butchered, she would prepare the meat as Isaac enjoyed it. Since Isaac was practically blind, Jacob would pretend to be Esau. In the guise of his brother, Jacob was to take the prepared goodies to his father. Isaac would presumably eat of the specially prepared meat . . . and bless Jacob.

It all sounded a bit underhanded to Jacob . . . but maybe workable. However, Jacob was concerned about some rather important details. For example: Esau wore different clothing and . . . remember . . . he had hairy skin. Even though Isaac was blind, he was no dummy. He would smell his son's "gamey" clothing, feel his skin, and recognize that Jacob was not Esau! Not a problem—leave it to Rebekah.

Hurriedly she gathered up some of Esau's smelly hunting clothes for Jacob to wear. Then she covered some of Jacob's exposed skin with the hair-covered skin from the goats they had butchered. Well now, that might seem a bit extreme! But remember, Esau was <u>really</u> hairy! Let's see . . . was there anything else? There didn't appear to be. They were ready but bursting with anxiety—fearful that their meticulous preparations might not work as they hoped.

So, with prepared goat meat in hand, Jacob approached his blind father—but there was one thing that they could not camouflage—his voice! Jacob knew that it was impossible for him to imitate that husky, deep voice of Esau. Would this be a dead give-away? Try as he might, Jacob could not get the voice thing right. As a result, even though Isaac was blind, he sensed that something was not quite "kosher." As he talked with Jacob, Isaac became suspicious. The voice he heard sounded like Jacob. Could this be the "straw that breaks the camel's back?" Well, it might have been. But, after all, Isaac was well aware of his hearing problems and various other deteriorations.

Then, palpable tension filled the air as Isaac invited Jacob: **"Please come near, that I may feel you, my son, whether you are really my son Esau or not"** (Genesis 27:21). Nervously, Jacob approached his father! Isaac ventured, **"The voice is Jacob's voice, but the hands are the hands of Esau"** (Genesis 27:22). And because of a lingering doubt, Isaac felt constrained to ask one probing question, **"Are you really my son Esau?"** (Genesis 24:27) How could Jacob not have had a lump in his throat as he answered, **"I am."** (Genesis 24:27).

Apparently Isaac became convinced that he was blessing Esau—and therefore he spoke those all-important, world-changing words of blessing upon his son Jacob! **"Let peoples serve you, and nations bow down to you. Be master over your brethren, and let your mother's sons bow down to you. Cursed be everyone who curses you, and blessed be those who bless you!"** (Genesis 27:29)

Much meaning is crammed into those few, short but significant sentences—words that God moved Isaac to use. Thus the LORD God placed Jacob at the very center of God's promise to everyone—nations far and wide. Jacob's kinfolk would need to realize his God-appointed status and give him due honor. As the carrier of God's promise to all people, as it was with Abraham, so it would be with Jacob: All who would oppose him would oppose God. And all who would oppose God would be cursed!

So, the matter was settled, right? Not exactly. Though Esau couldn't care less about receiving the promise of God concerning the Messiah, nevertheless he was jealous of his father's blessing. After all, he felt he deserved it simply because he was entitled to it! So what was going to happen when he found out that the blessing of his father had been stolen by his brother, Jacob? Well, we shall soon find out because . . . here came Esau down the rugged path with a haunch of venison across his shoulder.

He arrived shortly after Jacob had left. There was his father Isaac, sitting comfortably in his favorite chair. Obviously he had just eaten and was maybe preparing for a nap when Esau entered. Something didn't seem right to Esau. For one thing, he could see that his father was not waiting for him in anticipation of that planned, special meal.

Well, it didn't take long for Esau to put two and two together. *"My brother Jacob! Where is he? The blessing! This was the day for father to bestow that all-important blessing on me! Has my brother somehow taken advantage of my blind father? Is it possible that somehow or other Jacob has deceived our father? Am I being cheated out of what is rightfully mine . . . again?"*

Satanic thoughts rumbled through his mind and prodded him on. "First, I lost my birthright to my brother . . . now I have lost my father's coveted blessing." Esau was filled with rage. He was convinced, beyond a doubt, that he was his father's favorite son. Besides, he was the first-born! Yet, somehow—in some way Jacob had stolen everything that was rightfully his. As one might expect, Esau's hatred toward his brother boiled over. The Devil took control of his heart, and he was crazed with rage and hatred toward Jacob. His sinful anger became so intense that . . . he vowed to kill Jacob—really! And that was no idle threat!

Rebekah had left the premises, but she got wind of Esau's hateful tirade. She was certain that Esau was capable of doing exactly what he threatened. As a result, Rebekah had three primary concerns for Jacob.

1. Jacob must have a wife, but <u>not</u> from among the local population.

2. Jacob's safety had to be assured.

3. The blessing concerning the Seed of the woman had to be preserved.

So, first of all, Jacob must have a wife. No wife—no seed. Should he marry from among the Canaanites just to have a wife? Never! As we remember, her present daughters-in-law, the wives of Esau, were a constant grief to her. In fact, they were driving her nuts! Rebekah confessed to Isaac: **"I am weary of my life because of the daughters of Heth; if Jacob takes a wife of the daughters of Heth, like these who are the daughters of the land, what good will my life be to me?"** (Genesis 27:46)

It appears that Isaac finally shared her concerns—but what should be done about it would be a bit more complicated. Well, for one thing, Isaac still remembered well what his father, Abraham, had done to obtain a wife for him. That had worked out well. Maybe it was time to do the same for Jacob. That would resolve all of the issues of concern. Jacob would be safe. He could very possibly find a wife among his relatives.

Above all, through Jacob and his wife the blessed promises of God concerning the woman's Seed would be preserved. Problem solved!

Arrangements were quickly made, and Jacob was prepared to go back to the homeland where Abraham's servant had discovered Rebekah. Once there, Jacob was to check in with Bethuel, Rebekah's father, and with Laban, Rebekah's brother. What a relief!

When all was said and done, it appears that Isaac was totally on board. Apparently he forgave Rebekah's conniving methods and recognized that Jacob was indeed the God-appointed heir to the all-important promise of God. As a result, he sent his son on his way with this special blessing:

"May God almighty bless you and make you fruitful and multiply you, that you may be an assembly of peoples; and give you the blessing of Abraham, to you and your descendants with you, that you may inherit the land in which you are a stranger, which God gave to Abraham" (Genesis 28:3–4).

"The blessing of Abraham"—nothing could be of higher value! Yes, from Jacob's seed would come that One, the Seed of the woman, through whom all the nations of the Earth would be blessed. Jacob and his offspring would possess that God-ordained, marvelous privilege, the grandest blessing that any human would ever possess and carry. Together with that promise, his offspring would one day possess the land on which they dwelt. From there they were to become a shining beacon, brightly flooding all the world with the Gospel of God's love through the Messiah.

Fortified with the blessing of his parents, Jacob left his mother and father to journey back to the place where Rebekah, his mother, had grown up. But first we need to stop along the way to observe something rather unique and prophetic in the life of Jacob. Indeed, it was a God-ordained happening that this chosen vessel of God would never forget. Here's what happened: On the way, he stopped for the night to sleep under the stars. And what a night it became! He experienced a most graphic and magnificent dream. But it was more than a dream—it was a vision that would be indelibly fixed in his memory for the rest of his life.

Many of us have dreams—but this was totally out of the ordinary. It was so real and so wonderfully beautiful that words fail in description. But let's allow our minds to wander a bit as our LORD recreates this majestic theophany for us in His Word:

Jacob beheld a ladder—it was a huge and a gloriously inviting stairway reaching up to the very gates of heaven. And upon this heavenly structure he saw the angels of God ascending and descending. **And behold, the LORD stood above it and said, "I am the LORD God of Abraham your father and the God of Isaac; the land on which you lie I will give to you and your descendants. Also your descendants shall be as the dust of the earth; you shall spread abroad to the west and the east, to the north and the south; and in you and in your seed all the families of the earth shall be blessed. Behold, I am with you and will keep you wherever you go, and will bring you back to this land; for I will not leave you until I have done what I have spoken to you"** (Genesis 28:13–15).

It's breathtaking, isn't it? And if it's breathtaking for us, how about Jacob? It was indelibly fixed in his mind all the days of his life. As we try to visualize this magnificent vision in our mind's eye, we are swept out of this world of sin and find ourselves for an instant at Jacob's side. There we behold the very LORD God of heaven and earth standing before the gates of heaven. There we hear the LORD God of heaven and earth speak that monumental blessing to Jacob. This marvelous promise of God echoes from the heavens and reaches across thousands of years to the very manger-crib in Bethlehem.

"In you and in your seed all the families of the earth shall be blessed" (Genesis 28:14).

Praise the LORD! From the offspring of Jacob One would come, through whom you and I as well as all the nations of the Earth would be blessed with God's love, His gracious forgiving mercy and restoration, through the promised Messiah.

Talk about a dream—a vision—an appearance of the living God! This was a blessing that would carry Jacob on through all of the challenging times that lay in his future. Oh, to be sure, Satan would do his best to scuttle this beautiful, gracious, life-giving plan of God. Nevertheless, what Jacob saw would absolutely happen, for Jacob had God's word on it, and nothing could beat that!

Without question, it is a long way from Eden to Bethlehem—but God kept His promise every inch of the way! The cradle for the Messiah, the cradle which God had created with the children of Abraham, often seems to be on the brink of collapse. At times it may seem to be falling apart. The promise of the Seed of the woman may seem lost because the carriers of that blessing appear to be so weak and frail. Sometimes their faith falters, and they become deceitful and conniving. Indeed, their confidence in the LORD and His way often becomes feeble. As a result, they resort to their own devised, crafty methods.

Without a doubt, Satan is watching. He never quits but tries to take advantage of every shortcoming of God's people. Indeed, at every turn he continues in his effort to "throw a wrench in the gears" of God's promise of salvation for the world. Yet, without a doubt, Christmas would come! The advent of the Messiah, the Seed of the woman, remained absolutely certain because it rested in the merciful hands of the LORD God of heaven and earth. He made a promise that He would restore to us what we had lost in the Garden—and He would keep His promise as He always does.

And so we joyfully and confidently pray with the believers down through the generations:

Jacob's Star in all its splendor
Beams with comfort sweet and tender,
Forcing Satan to surrender,
Saved us from the wily Foe.

From the bondage that oppressed us,
From sin's fetters that possessed us,
From the grief that sore distressed us,
We, the captives, now are free. (TLH 90:5–6)

HALLELUJAH!

PRAYER

I thank you, LORD God, for Your gracious mercy. My forbearers of the faith were but dust as am I. Their lack of faith and stumbling in the way which You have outlined in Your Word are only too familiar. I find it to be so in my life also. It is so amazing that You, the Mighty God of heaven and earth, patiently work with us weak mortals to produce such marvelous results. Therefore, I pray, O LORD, that I may keep my mind and heart fixed upon the blessings of Your love for me and for all people. In a world where unbelief and idolatry rage, fill me with Your Spirit that I may serve You with heart and soul and reach out to my fellow pilgrims with Your mercy, forgiveness, and love. And I pray that Your promises in the Seed of the woman, our Messiah, may always be and remain in the center of my life. In His holy name I pray. Amen.

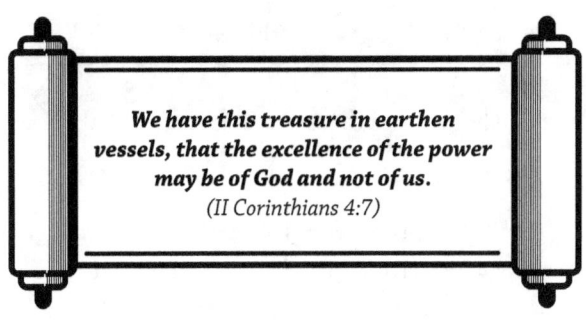

We have this treasure in earthen vessels, that the excellence of the power may be of God and not of us.
(*II Corinthians 4:7*)

THE DECEIVER IS DECEIVED

We know that Jacob was no paragon of godly virtue, but who among us is? The fact of the matter is: God has to work with what He has available—and let's face it, He doesn't have much to work with. Nevertheless, God is determined to preserve His chosen people in faith and bring them through this world of sin to be with Him in heaven forever—no matter what!!! It isn't easy—but when God makes a promise, He will keep it!

Yes, in spite of all of his deceit and underhanded trickery, we can say of Jacob what is said of Abraham: **He believed in the LORD, and He accounted it to him for righteousness** (Genesis 15:6). Sometimes God's promises were far beyond reason—at other times they might have seemed impossible—nevertheless, he believed the LORD God and everything that was promised by Him. And we might add, even though Jacob's thoughts, words, and deeds would condemn him before God, the Spirit-produced heartfelt faith in God's promises would rescue him.

We are amazed that in the same way the LORD makes use of us— frail, faltering, faulty, sinful beings—to carry His precious Word of forgiveness and life far and wide throughout this world. Why us? The Apostle Paul explains: **We have this treasure in earthen vessels** (II Corinthians 4:7). We clods of clay carry within us the most precious treasure that can be found on this side of eternity. This **treasure** of God's love for lost sinners in the Seed of the woman is ours to have, to hold, and generously give to others—corrupted, sinful beings though we be!

Astonishing, isn't it? In the strength of His Spirit, we struggle with our sinful nature, we do battle with Satan, we fight the good fight of faith in the middle of this world of sin controlled by the Evil One. As we continue to declare His Word and pronounce the blessing of God upon sinners like us—when all is said and done—the LORD God works His miracles through us!

I suppose every one of us might wonder, *"Why me? Why did God choose me—a pot of fragile clay—born a sinful being of sinful beings—to carry and deliver the most precious message that mankind will ever hear?"* Well, there is a very good reason why God uses us feeble beings for this glorious task . . . just as He used Jacob. Here's God's reason: **That the excellence of the power may be of God and not of us** (2 Corinthians 4:7).

There we have it! There's the answer! We're not much with which to work, but nevertheless God uses us to cause miraculous things to happen. Yes, it is through us that <u>He</u> builds His kingdom of grace and mercy in the midst of a world lost in sin. The result? **The people who walked in darkness have seen a great light; those who dwelt in the land of the shadow of death, upon them a light has shined** (Isaiah 9:2). And who is responsible—who brought this about? There can be no question about it—God does it all! Therefore He deserves all the glory and praise! We are merely His instrument through whom He works. All glory be to <u>Him</u> alone! OK. So we have that straight, don't we?

Now back to Jacob and the happenings as recorded in Genesis 29. When we left him, he was on his way, quite literally, to find a wife . . . remember? As he traveled northeast to the land of his relatives and drew close to his destination, he came across a well. Just in time! The livestock needed a good healthy drink, and the water containers needed refilling. Come to think of it, maybe this was the same well that Abraham's servant had found—remember, the one at the edge of town?

As was pointed out previously, this well was a natural gathering place for the men of the field and the shepherdesses. *(Note: Female shepherds were quite common. We are told that there are quite a number of them yet today in Arabia.)* So, quite naturally Jacob struck up a conversation with some of the male workers. He discovered that they knew Laban, his uncle. Well, that was a step in the right direction. Then, while they were talking, here came a shepherdess with her father's sheep.

As we all know, there are many ways to strike up a conversation and become acquainted with a young lady. Here was Jacob's approach— maybe a bit unusual but apparently effective. It normally required at least two men to remove the very heavy stone that covered the mouth of the well. Not this time! Jacob, being a strong and virile young man, approached the well and with muscular dexterity handily removed the stone from the mouth of the well singlehandedly! Very impressive, wouldn't you say? Besides that, he went on to water the sheep for this young lady. Quite courteous . . . right?

But there was something else going on that was even more interesting. While the sheep were enjoying the fresh, clean water, Jacob was relishing the company of this attractive shepherdess. Come to find out, her name was Rachel. As they conversed, surprisingly it became evident that Rachel was Laban's daughter. That would make her Jacob's niece! Coincidence? I don't think so. With tears of joy he revealed that he was her relative—Rebekah's son!

As one might expect, they were both thrilled at this revelation. Both could hardly believe it! Jacob embraced her and kissed her. *(A common practice among relatives and close friends.)* Neither of them could hardly believe it! So, off they went to tell her father, who quite naturally invited Jacob to their home to meet the family. A wonderful, joyous, and unexpected family gathering took place. Laban welcomed Jacob into his home with open arms.

It turned out that Jacob stayed with them for an entire month. During that time it became obvious that Laban had a ton of work with all of his flocks of sheep and herds of goats as well as numerous camels and other animals. Jacob plunged right in and helped with the daily chores. Laban was impressed! With all of the many tasks in Laban's operation, quite naturally he offered to hire Jacob. Well, of course, Jacob was more than willing; he certainly wanted to earn his keep.

But there was something else that influenced Jacob. He was genuinely smitten with the love bug. He was intensely attracted to Rachel, and so decided to make Laban an offer: **"I will serve you seven years for Rachel your younger daughter"** (Genesis 29:18).

Now, there's the kind of offer that one may never hear today, right? However, Laban took it seriously. Besides, it appears that Laban was somewhat of a crafty business man. This seemed to him to be an excellent way to get some cheap labor—so Laban struck the deal with Jacob. Seven years it would be. Final "payment" would be due and paid after seven years, when Rachel would become his wife. It might seem like a huge price to pay, but to Jacob it **seemed but a few days to him because of the love he had for her** (Genesis 29:20).

To make a long story short, the day finally arrived. The seven years were up! Jacob went to Laban to collect his "wages." All seemed to go as planned. Laban got his servants together and prepared an outstanding wedding feast; Jacob and Rachel would become husband and wife—or would they? What could possibly stand in the way? Well, we shall see.

The ceremony and celebration were over; evening came; time for the new husband and wife to be alone and consummate their marriage. According to custom, Laban brought the heavily veiled "bride" to the bridal chamber where the groom was waiting. In the darkness of their bridal chamber they made love. All went well—right? Not exactly!

As the morning light gradually crept into the bridal chamber, reality also dawned. Laban's trickery was revealed, for the woman with whom he made love was Rachel's sister, Leah, and not Rachel! Oh NO! Jacob had been deceived. Yes! The deceiver was deceived! Jacob was utterly beside himself. *"Where's Laban. He'll have to answer for this . . . this terrible deception!"* So Jacob confronted his father-in-law. And what was Laban's answer? Very calmly he responded, **"It must not be done so in our country, to give the younger before the firstborn"** (Genesis 29:26).

So that was Laban's excuse for this underhanded maneuver—cheating both his daughter and his son-in-law! Jacob had been betrayed! Betrayed? Well, Jacob was no stranger to such kind of fraudulent activity, was he? How could he not be reminded of how he had misled his father in order to obtain that precious blessing? But this was different . . . wasn't it? Maybe not so much. As the saying goes, "What goes around comes around." The deceiver was deceived!

Jacob had nothing to say, but Laban did. No doubt he had carefully thought this all through. And just maybe he had a slight conscience pang for his callous deception of Jacob. Anyway, being a rather shrewd (if not dishonest) business man, and fully aware of Jacob's deep love for Rachel, Laban made this second offer to Jacob: **"We will give you this one** (Rachel) **also for the service which you will serve with me still another seven years"** (Genesis 29:27).

Ah-ha! Laban had it all figured out, didn't he? Likely, this was all planned in advance. *"Your move, Jacob; what's it going to be?"* There was one thing that was certain: Jacob's love for Rachel had not cooled even a tiny bit, and he strongly desired to have her for his wife. So what could he do? Well, he didn't need to give it much thought. He agreed to serve Laban another seven years for the privilege of having Rachel for his wife—but only under one condition: The "wages" would be paid up front—in advance.

That didn't seem to be a problem for Laban. He had grown to trust Jacob and knew him to be an honorable man. So the deal was struck, and Jacob married Rachel immediately! *(Note: Bigamy (two wives) as well as polygamy (many wives) was not unusual at that time. However, though this practice was a common custom among the people of that day, it was not, of course, in accord with God's creative plan. He created one woman, not multiple women, for one man. However, God does not hide this perversion of His creative order from us in His Word, nor does it appear that He precisely condemns such actions in His written record. However, this we recognize: Living together as husband and wife outside the bond of wedlock was absolutely forbidden! Adultery was clearly condemned. Thus we see how Jacob, though deeply in love with Rachel, did not cohabit with her as husband and wife until they were officially married.)*

As we observe all the varied activities of God's children up close, we must keep one thing in mind above all: In spite of the very questionable words and actions of God's people, there was always that golden thread of faith that was preserved in their hearts by the Spirit. Sorrow over their sins and shortcomings was regularly obvious, and above all Jacob as well as Isaac and Abraham before him believed God's promises in the coming Messiah. It alone was accounted to them for righteousness.

Yes, my friends, without a doubt, it's a long way from Eden to Bethlehem. All the while God's people knew by faith that they were privileged to be part of God's magnificent and marvelous journey toward that day of salvation. So it is with us. Our activities as God's people working in His kingdom are far less than they ought to be. The distractions of this world of sin, Satan and our own selfish flesh weigh us down constantly.

We recognize our shortcomings, we see our sins. Daily we repent and pray to be guided by His Spirit. By faith we cling to the promises of God. We hold fast to the salvation that God has provided for us and all people in the Seed of the woman, Jesus Christ, our Savior and Lord. Yes, and by steadfast faith in Him and His work of redemption, we are accounted as righteous before His gracious throne! Without a doubt, it is purely Amazing Grace!

Oh, what a privilege it is to be a part of God's family that carries His blessing and willingly, freely gives God's forgiving love away in every way we can. May our gracious LORD fill us with His Spirit that we may regularly repent of our shortcomings and failures in our thoughts, words, and deeds! So also may we continually be about the business of giving away that most precious gift of God's forgiveness and life in the Seed of the woman. To that end may each of us ever sing with a repentant heart and soul:

> With broken heart and contrite sigh,
> A trembling sinner, LORD, I cry.
> Your pard'ning grace is rich and free—
> O God, be merciful to me! (CW 303:1)

PRAYER

LORD God, my Maker and Redeemer, I bless You each and every day for bringing me into Your kingdom of grace and mercy. Each day Your mercies are new. Each day I pray that I may walk in Your grace and avoid every evil in thought, word, and action. However, this is a constant struggle for me because I dwell in a world of sin and godlessness. Besides, my corrupted nature hounds me every step of the way in my life, encouraging me to adopt the life-style of the unbelieving world around me. And, yes, Satan never quits in his desire to have me in his kingdom of sin and death. Yet, just as your mercies are new every morning, I pray, forgive my shortcomings. Blot out my transgressions. Give me peace in Your forgiveness. And having experienced Your loving kindness, by the power of Your Spirit may I be a ready transmitter of Your forgiving love to others. Just as Abraham, Isaac, and Jacob believed in Your promises, and it was accounted to them for righteousness, so may it be with me. For the sake of Jesus, the promised Seed, I pray. Amen.

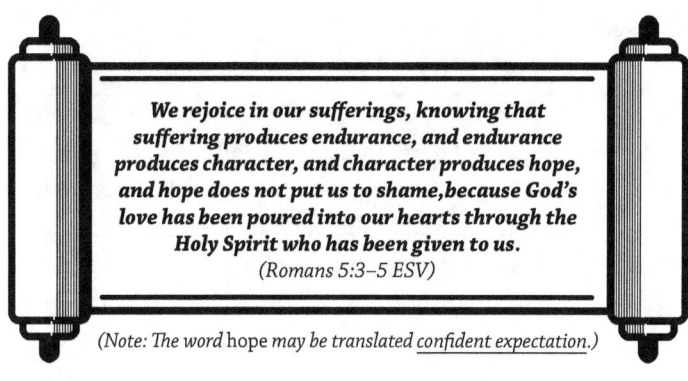

We rejoice in our sufferings, knowing that suffering produces endurance, and endurance produces character, and character produces hope, and hope does not put us to shame, because God's love has been poured into our hearts through the Holy Spirit who has been given to us.
(Romans 5:3–5 ESV)

(Note: The word hope *may be translated* <u>confident expectation</u>.)

IT WAS TIME TO GO

Time was up! After serving Laban a total of fourteen years, Jacob's obligation to Laban was complete. His diligent labors had produced tangible and rewarding results, and Jacob was ready to leave. However, Laban wouldn't hear of it, for he had seen how prosperous he had become through the diligent labors of Jacob blessed by the LORD God. What would he do without him? He pleaded with Jacob to stay longer, but his appeal seemed to fall on deaf ears.

Laban decided that he had to give Jacob some meaningful reason to stay. So in order to convince Jacob, he made him a rather attractive offer. He promised to share ownership of some offspring from his huge flocks and herds. Well, what do you know? Finally, after fourteen years of dedicated duty, Jacob would finally be compensated materially for his devoted labor. It seemed to Jacob that the offer was too good to pass up—so after considering it a bit, Jacob agreed.

Although Jacob realized that Laban's offer was generous, he wanted to be fair with his father-in-law, so Jacob proposed that he would choose only the less desirable animals for his share. For example, it seemed that the speckled and spotted among the goats as well as the black lambs among the sheep generally were considered inferior. Besides, without marking or branding, that would enable them to keep track of ownership quite easily. Done! That seemed more than fair to Laban, so he quickly agreed.

But then the unexpected happened, as all children of God have experienced. Out of the blue, so to speak, comes this blessing from God that we did not expect. Blessed is the person who recognizes it as such! Well, here was Jacob's unexpected gift of divine favor: his share of the livestock increased dramatically, multiplying so rapidly that within a few years Jacob became very wealthy!

As one might expect, as a result of this remarkable increase in Jacob's flocks and herds, a rather common trait of humanity emerged— jealousy! Yes, resentful jealousy surfaced among the sons of Laban. It arose with such an unpredictable intensity that Laban felt that he had to deal with it lest his entire operation be threatened. So what could he do?

Well, he simply decided to change the terms of his agreement with Jacob—yes, break the verbal contract! To Laban that was a minor matter of shrewd business practice, so he did it! That should take care of the problem, right? Well, momentarily, yes—but finally, no. What he didn't realize was this: He was actually dealing with God—and when God blesses, no puny little effort of man and/or Satan can stand in His way.

So the whole thing became an effort in futility for Laban. Whenever he changed the terms of the agreement with Jacob, God's blessings on Jacob followed suit. Laban tried this distressing maneuver ten times— but it didn't matter, for his strategy didn't and wouldn't work. In spite of Laban's calculated intentions, God blessed Jacob all the more. Laban became frustrated to the core! He just couldn't understand why this was happening.

Do you think that maybe with this lesson we can all learn something about ourselves with the LORD God in our own lives? I think so! Maybe it should go without saying . . . but maybe not . . . so we'll say it anyway: God's blessings are not dependent upon our neighbor's actions.

Sometimes we may find ourselves victimized by ruthless people—folks who are not guided by decent, godly principles and wish to take advantage of us. It may be that we are forced to sever our relations with them. But fear not, walk with God; let His Word be our guide! For as long as this world stands, it shall ever be true:

> *If you but trust in God to guide you*
> *And place your confidence in Him,*
> *He'll give you strength and stand beside you*
> *When days are dreary, dark, and dim.*
> *For those who trust His changeless love*
> *Build on the rock that does not move.*
>
> *Sing, pray, and keep His ways unswerving,*
> *Perform your duties faithfully.*
> *And trust His Word; though undeserving,*
> *You'll find His promise true to be.*
> *God never yet forsook in need*
> *The soul that trusted Him indeed.* (CW 444:1&4)

Finally, after Laban put up with the "bellyaching" of his sons for a number of years, and Jacob labored under their intense scrutiny, the angel of God appeared to Jacob in a dream and instructed him that it was time to go: "**I am the God of Bethel, where you anointed the pillar and where you made a vow to Me. Now arise, get out of this land, and return to the land of your kindred**" (Genesis 31:13).

OK! According to God's calendar, it was time for Jacob to return to his homeland, the land of Canaan. In His directive, God jogged Jacob's memory a bit and reminded him of that wondrous revelation at Bethel and Jacob's vow at that time. Jacob must never forget his ultimate purpose clearly etched in his soul with the finger of the living God. Every happening in Jacob's life was designed to prepare him for God's primary purpose—namely, promoting the promise of salvation in the Seed of the woman.

All of God's special people are His chosen servants with a purpose. As such we are strengthened by God to carry out His gracious design for us often through opposition and conflict. That's how it is in this ol' world. But let's not forget, tribulations are character building and faith strengthening. It's all a necessary part of our labors in His kingdom. As we well remember, Abraham and Isaac had periods in their own lives whereby God challenged them through various trying lessons in faithfulness. It was by the way of trials and suffering that they took a firmer hold on the LORD God and His ever-present, gracious activity in their lives.

In that respect we think of the words of the Apostle Paul, who by inspiration of the Spirit was caused to remind us that **we rejoice in our sufferings, knowing that suffering produces endurance, and endurance produces character, and character produces hope, and hope does not put us to shame, because God's love has been poured into our hearts through the Holy Spirit who has been given to us** (Romans 5:3–5 ESV).

So it was with Jacob. It was important for him to see the unmistakable hand of the LORD God working in his life and on his behalf every single day. So, praise the LORD, Jacob did recognize the guidance of God and responded immediately. Without hesitation and with confident action, he organized his departure. He called his wives, Rachel and Leah, and explained his plan to them.

It was no small task. His livestock numbers were huge. His children numbered eleven sons and one daughter. Rachel was pregnant with her second child. Joseph was very young and required special attention, so family and servants all had to pitch in. Besides all of the preparations, Jacob wanted to leave without notifying Laban, who was some distance away, tending to his operations. With minimum preparation, they were ready. Off they went, embarking upon the approximate 400 mile trek toward Canaan and the place where Jacob's father, Isaac, still lived.

It was bound to happen, and it did: Three days passed before Laban heard of Jacob's departure. Laban could hardly believe it! In his mind, this simply could not happen! Things had been going fantastically well. Besides, he was secretly aware that his prosperity was in large part due to the diligent labors of Jacob blessed by God. Laban quickly informed his family of his attempt to intercept Jacob. Then he and his sons were off in hot pursuit.

After a few days of dedicated travel, they caught up to Jacob and his huge, slow-moving entourage. Although Laban had been planning to verbally "let Jacob have it," it appears that his tirade was rather measured. There was a reason for that, as Laban explained in his first words to Jacob:

"It is in my power to do you harm. But the God of your father spoke to me last night, saying, 'Be careful not to say anything to Jacob, either good or bad'" (Genesis 31:29 ESV).

Thankfully, Laban heeded this warning from God. However, since Jacob had lived for years accepting Laban's decisions regarding everything, he now felt it was time (and maybe past time) to forcefully "stand up" to his father-in-law. Jacob had labored with total dedication for years while under Laban's unfair and dishonest practices. Furthermore, Jacob was well aware and readily confessed that his wealth was alone the result of God's blessing. So he demanded:

"What is my offense? What is my sin, that you have hotly pursued me?...These twenty years I have been with you. Your ewes and your female goats have not miscarried, and I have not eaten the rams of your flocks. What was torn by wild beasts I did not bring to you, I bore the loss of it myself. From my hand you required it, whether stolen by day or stolen by night. There I was: by day the heat consumed me, and the cold by night, and my sleep fled from my eyes. These twenty years I have been in

your house. I served you fourteen years for your two daughters, and six years for your flock, and you have changed my wages ten times. If the God of my father, the God of Abraham and the fear of Isaac, had not been on my side, surely now you would have sent me away empty-handed. God saw my affliction and the labor of my hands and rebuked you last night" (Genesis 31:36–42 ESV).

It was all true—every last word! And Laban knew it. Jacob's father-in-law was pretty much deflated—so after a few minor exchanges, they parted peacefully, and Laban proclaimed this benediction upon Jacob:

"The LORD watch between you and me, when we are out of one another's sight" (Genesis 31:49 ESV).

OK! One bridge was crossed, but Jacob was not "out of the woods" yet, and he knew it. As he and his unwieldy assembly came closer and closer to his former home, memories of years gone-by began to dominate his mind. Though communication systems that we take for granted today were thousands of years in the future, Jacob was certain that Esau would hear of his returning home and probably be waiting for him. Then what would happen?

Jacob's conscience gave him no rest, and we understand why—for after all, even though it was God's will that he should be the carrier of the promise of God, he had slyly and craftily taken the matter into his own hands. As we remember well, he had taken advantage of his brother and obtained Esau's birthright for a bowl of soup! Besides, he had entered into an ill-advised plot with his mother, Rebekah, in order to gain the blessing from Isaac that his father intended for Esau. Jacob vividly remembered that before he left his home and headed up north, Esau had vowed to kill him! Without a doubt, he was well aware that Esau was fully capable of making his threat a reality. Now he would have to "face the music," so to speak.

Well, Jacob finally and wisely determined that his problems were best left in God's gracious and merciful hands. He would simply confront the consequences of his actions, head-on! So he sent messengers before him to inform his brother that he was returning home.

Now, what about Esau? During those twenty years of separation from his twin brother, what had happened in his life? Well, we don't know very much. However, it appears that he had become quite wealthy in his own right during Jacob's twenty-year absence. He too was the proud owner of much livestock, and he had many servants as well. As a matter of fact, after Jacob returned to Canaan with his huge flocks and herds, grazing areas became rather crowded. It wasn't long before Esau rounded up his livestock and moved south. His offspring were the Edomites, whom we will meet later.

But as of now, when Esau was informed that his brother Jacob was returning, of course he prepared a welcoming event. But what kind of a welcome would it be? After twenty years was Esau still holding on to that fierce grudge that he deeply felt when Jacob had left? Was he still intent on taking the life of his only brother Jacob? These were thoughts that surely ran through the mind of Jacob. As a result he was filled with remorse for his underhanded trickery and feared for his life at the hands of Esau.

So when Jacob was told that Esau was coming to meet him with four hundred men, we can well understand that "he was shaking in his boots." Jacob wasn't about to take any chances, considering the possibilities. He had to prepare for the worst possible scenario, and so he devised a strategic plan. He determined that he would employ a type of military operation in order to survive. He divided his large troop of people and livestock into two bands and put some distance between them. His reasoning was, **"If Esau comes to the one company and attacks it, then the other company which is left will escape."** (Genesis 32:8).

More importantly, Jacob earnestly prayed: **"O God of my father Abraham and God of my father Isaac, the LORD who said to me, 'Return to your country and to your kindred, and I will deal well with you': I am not worthy of the least of all the mercies and of all the truth which You have shown Your servant; for I crossed over this Jordan with my staff, and now I have become two companies. Deliver me, I pray, from the hand of my brother, from the hand of Esau; for I fear him, lest he come and attack me and the mother with the children. For You said, 'I will surely treat you well, and make your descendants as the sand of the sea, which cannot be numbered for multitude'"** (Genesis 32:9–12).

Jacob hadn't forgotten that into his care and keeping God had placed a future nation which would be born of his children. Even more importantly, from his offspring the Messiah would come, who would crush the head of Satan and deliver mankind out of the bondage of sin and death. His seed—all who would cling to that promise of the coming Messiah would one day cover the earth—"as the sand of the sea, which cannot be numbered for multitude." Yes, down through the centuries the whole world would be filled with souls who would be watching and waiting, praying and singing:

> *Hark the glad sound! The Savior comes,*
> *The Savior promised long;*
> *Let every heart prepare a throne*
> *And every voice a song.*
>
> *He comes the captives to release,*
> *In Satan's prison held.*
> *The gates of brass before Him burst;*
> *The iron fetters yield.*
>
> *He comes the broken heart to bind,*
> *The bleeding soul to cure,*
> *And with the treasures of his grace*
> *To enrich the humble poor.*

Our glad hosannas, Prince of Peace,
Your welcome shall proclaim,
And heav'n's eternal arches ring
With your beloved name. (CW 12:1–4)

PRAYER

Lord, my God, as I face the future of unknowns, I generally make plans. Yet, I know that You have THE plan for my life. I need to be reminded of that often. Time and again my plans go awry. But rather than struggle to maintain my ideas and my ways, I need to learn to leave all things to Your direction—relax in Your grace and love, and wait on You and Your blessings to be revealed. Fill me with trust and confidence in You and Your ways and guidance. For then I will reap blessings far beyond anything that I could possibly devise or plan. In the name of my Savior, I pray. Amen.

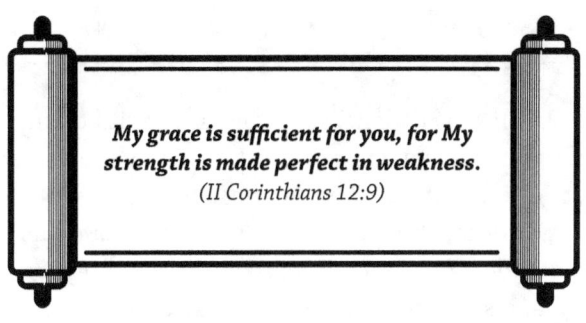

My grace is sufficient for you, for My
strength is made perfect in weakness.
(II Corinthians 12:9)

WRESTLING WITH GOD

The stage was set for that breathtaking, historic meeting of Jacob and Esau. As has been mentioned, the ravages of Satan had crippled the relationship between these two brothers. The deceptive dealings of Jacob with his father, Isaac, and his fraudulent behavior with his brother, Esau, had lain somewhat dormant in the heart and mind of Jacob for twenty years. Now they arose to haunt his conscience with guilt and gave him no rest. Esau's vow to kill him, though latent in Jacob's mind for all those years, now became a very real possibility.

Jacob surmised that extra precautions were in order. Besides dividing his company into two groups, he surmised that maybe he could appease Esau with gifts—so he sent his servants to meet Esau with a number of droves of livestock. Each drove or group was made up of goats and sheep, camels and colts, cows and bulls, donkeys and foals. One after another, each drove would be presented as gifts to Esau as an attempt to pacify his brother . . . but would it work? Was that enough?

What else might be wise preparations for this dreaded meeting? As the shadows of night blanketed the desert and the meadows, Jacob determined that it might be well to remove his most prized, God-given possessions—his two wives and his children—from immediate danger, so he led them across the brook Jabbok, where in a safe place they would wait—wait for the dreaded meeting.

That night Jacob stayed alone. And what a night it became! In the midst of night, someone mysteriously came to him. It was an angel . . . but yet . . . it was a Man. An unusual engagement took place as he and this Angel-Man wrestled. There was no time out—all night long these two contenders fought for dominance. The strong body of Jacob was stretched and strained to its limits as this exceptional wrestling match went on for hours. Was it physical wrestling? It appears so. Was it a spiritual struggle? Apparently. In either or both cases, it was certainly an intense marathon!

There was no winner in this night-long contest. As the morning light across the desert floor ushered in a new day—the shadows of night gradually began to disperse from the woods on the banks of Brook Jabbok. As if to conclude this intense struggle, the Man merely touched Jacob's hip, and immediately it slipped out of joint. Suddenly—in a moment—strong Jacob became weak. Yet Jacob held this Man in his grip with all the strength that remained in his tortured body. Finally, the Man spoke and urged, **"Let me go, for the day breaks"** (Genesis 32:26).

Breathlessly, Jacob countered, **"I will not let You go unless You bless me!"** (Genesis 32:26)

Why did Jacob request a blessing? Well, he had concluded that this was no ordinary man. He couldn't be! Some have suggested that this was the very Son of the living God Himself. Maybe! In any case, Jacob was moved to require this Man's approval— His blessing. The mysterious Man answered, **"What is your name?"** (Genesis 32:27) To which Jacob weakly replied, **"Jacob."**

The mystical Man responded, **"Your name shall no longer be called Jacob, but Israel** ("Prince with God")**; for you have struggled with God and with men, and have prevailed"** (Genesis 32:28).

Jacob was so mystified by this entire ordeal that his curiosity overwhelmed him. He just had to ask: **"Tell me your name, I pray"** (Genesis 32:29).

Calmly, the Man answered with a question of His own: **"Why is it that you ask about My name?" And He blessed him there** (Genesis 32:29). It was as if He were saying, "Why do you ask about My name? Certainly you know who I am." Then, suddenly . . . it was over . . . the Man was gone . . . Jacob was left spiritually blessed and physically crippled.

How can we describe this God-inspired meeting? It was awesome—soul inspiring—thrilling. Literally, it was out of this world! Jacob had experienced something so divine—so mysterious—so wonderfully real. He was convinced, beyond a shadow of a doubt, that he had been struggling with God Himself! This Man had to be God! Therefore, he named the place Peniel (face of God), **"For I have seen God face to face, and my life is preserved"** (Genesis 32:30).

The struggle was over. The result? Without question, Jacob was a different person both spiritually and physically. From that day until the day he died, he was severely handicapped in body. However, spiritually he was where God wanted him to be—for after that soul-stirring experience, Jacob was a totally changed man. Finally, he was moved in the spirit to turn himself over to God completely—body and soul! As it has been said, he "let go and let God be God!"

In the past Jacob had been very competent mentally and strong physically—but from that day forth his total strength was found alone in the LORD God. Lest he forget, he was quickly reminded of his complete dependence upon the LORD as he hobbled along on his lame hip . . . for the rest of his life.

Was this never-to-be-forgotten ordeal helpful for Jacob? Many might wonder, *"How could such a physical handicap be useful? In what way could this possibly contribute to his service to God? From that day on he was a physical cripple!"* Now, let's not jump to conclusions—as it has been said, "It's not a good exercise plan to spend much time jumping to conclusions!"

Do you remember how the Apostle Paul had also learned that lesson very well . . . from none other than the Lord Jesus Himself? Yes, he struggled with a God-given **thorn in the flesh** and **pleaded with the LORD three times that it might depart**. And what was the divine answer? **"My grace is sufficient for you, for My strength is made perfect in weakness"** (II Corinthians 12:7–9).

What blessing or blessings do you and I have that are constant reminders of our total dependence upon God? What, in our lives, might be a continual reminder of the necessity of God's perpetual presence and blessing every single second of our lives? Think about it. Then praise the LORD for such special reminders—whatever they might be.

What a night for Jacob! Previously he had made all of the preparations that were humanly possible—but now all of that seemed unimportant. Yes, he knew that Esau was on his way toward that fear-filled meeting, but in his halting state Jacob was ready! Yes, he was fully prepared. How could that be so . . . now? Answer: Because now he finally realized that his life, his cause, his purpose, his reason for living were all in the gracious hands of God. Yes, now he was fully prepared!

With his mind and heart saturated with **the peace of God, which surpasses all understanding** (Philippians 4:7), he went about the orderly task of gathering his children from among his servants. They should be with their mothers, Leah and Rachel, as well as with their two maidservants. And then, as Esau was approaching, Jacob stationed himself in front of his family, and in total submission bowed himself to the ground seven times as his brother approached. What would Esau do? How would he react?

As the sun arose that day, the fields and the woods were alive with God's creative beauty—but the future of God's marvelous kingdom of grace, with all of its promise of salvation for the entire world seemed once again to be hanging in jeopardy. Satan had done his best to sow the seeds of a lasting hatred between these brothers and hoped for a serious conflict. Tension hung thickly in the air as the brothers drew closer to each other.

But then, as Esau came nearer, Jacob was astonished. He caught a glimpse of Esau's countenance, and instead of anger and hatred he detected an obvious benevolence on Esau's face. Could this be true? He could hardly believe it—but it was there—it was so! Then, with a sudden impulse and arms outstretched, Esau came running toward Jacob. He grabbed his brother with his strong arms and held him close. He **fell on his neck and kissed him, and they wept** (Genesis 33:4). As tears of joy rolled down their weathered faces, there was no doubt about it—all was forgiven—all was behind them. During those intervening years God had changed Esau's heart! God had brought Esau to forgive his brother! Forgiving love prevailed. Satan's agenda was stifled. The kingdom of the living God was victorious, as it always is, when the love of God dominates words and actions!

My friends, it's a long way from Eden to Bethlehem—but gradually God's people inched along toward the fullness of time when the Seed of the woman would be born, and all the world would join in celebrating the everlasting love of God for us all in Christ Jesus! Maybe we have learned an important and godly life-lesson here. As a result, let us sing with renewed spiritual strength and vigor, the words of that beloved seventeenth century hymn:

My God has all things in His keeping,
He is my ever faithful friend.
He grants me laughter after weeping,
And all His ways in blessings end.
His love endures eternally:
What pleases God, that pleases me. (CW 414:4)

PRAYER

LORD, my God, many are the times that I approach critical matters in my life with my reasoning mind but without heartfelt prayer and recognition that You alone hold the key to success. LORD, I pray, give me a full measure of Your Spirit, that I with Jacob may continually pray for Your blessing upon my life. Fill me with Your endless love for me that it may spill over in kindness toward those close to me as well as to all people. Be with me and guide me every day that I may make good and righteous judgments as I face various tests and trials in my life. I pray, O LORD, that You will guide and lead me in the paths of righteousness in all things, that Your name may be glorified. In the holy name of the Seed of the woman I pray. Amen.

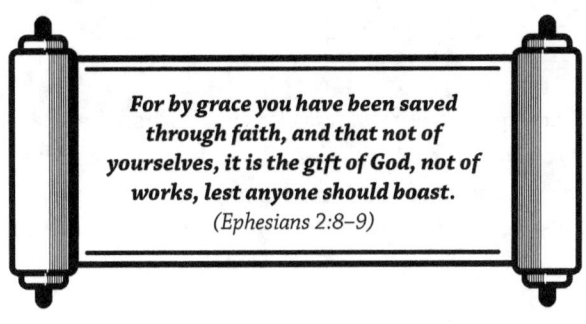

*For by grace you have been saved
through faith, and that not of
yourselves, it is the gift of God, not of
works, lest anyone should boast.*
(Ephesians 2:8–9)

FIRST THINGS FIRST

Bethel *(house of God)* was a special place in the mind and heart of
Jacob. Bethel was not a house—it was not a church—it was simply
a very special place with some very pronounced memories for Jacob.
After his wrestling with God by the Brook Jabbok and surviving his
ordeal with Esau, he could think of no better place to go than to Bethel.

It was there at Bethel, as you recall, that God had appeared to Jacob
twenty years before. At that time Jacob was about to leave his father's
house and homeland and travel to Mesopotamia in search of a bride.
During those many years away, Jacob had grown closer to his heavenly
Father than ever before. He had been humbled by God's overwhelming
love and blessing. Indeed, he had wrestled with God Himself! Those
deeply-felt spiritual experiences dominated his heart and mind. So
before Jacob and his family approached Bethel, there was something
very important that Jacob felt obliged to do . . . something that maybe
he should have dealt with long ago.

So here is the setting: In days gone by, it appears that Jacob had
been somewhat lax in guiding his family in spiritual matters. While he
was under Laban's "roof," so to speak, he had apparently overlooked a
serious spiritual problem in his household. It was past time to deal with
this long-standing issue.

What was the problem? Here it is: Jacob's father-in-law, Laban,
together with his in-laws spoke of the true God and seemed to have
a relationship with Him—but they had also adopted some of the

idolatrous practices of their friends and neighbors. They had become rather synchronistic in their religion—that is, they had attempted to melt together the religion of the true God with the man-made idolatry prevalent in the land. That NEVER works—not then—not now—not ever!

Of course, this sad circumstance has always existed and is very prevalent in our day also. New religions are invented all the time! Why? As has been mentioned previously, mankind was created to have a very close association with God, the one Creator of all. When humans lose sight of the true God in their lives, by an inner need they are prone to invent a god. This is an obvious attempt to fill that God-vacant-void in their lives. Well now, that poses a question: How does one invent a god? How does one produce a religion to fill the vacuum in one's soul?

Well, apparently, that's not difficult to do. Mohammad did it—Joseph Smith did it—Mary Baker Eddie did it—Herbert W. Armstrong did it. People do it all the time! Here's the recipe:

First, take a little bit of imagination and create a supreme being. Add a heavy dose of what one considers to be charitable, noble, and loving deeds toward others. Next, stir in a full measure of what makes one feel good. Blend this together with a generous amount of biases and religious concoctions that others have produced. Season it all heavily with a generous amount of rules, directions, and requirements. When such recipes are followed, the designated supreme-being will be happy with you—and there you have it. Voila! A new religion is born! Oh yes, finally be sure to generously share this "recipe" with others at every opportunity!

These Satanic brews have different names, different practices, and different fillers, but in the end they are all the same. "How so?" you might ask. It's very simple. The following quotation probably answers that question better than I can:

"When we examine the "religious phenomena" in the non-Christian religions and compare them with those of the Christian religion, we find again that the non-Christian religions—the other forms of religion— seek to establish good relations with the deity by way of works, while the essence of the Christian religion consists in the exact opposite, by faith, not of works" (*Christian Dogmatics*, F. Pieper, Volume I, page 17).

Once again, it is good for us to remember what Moses wrote by inspiration of the Spirit of God, and to spell out very clearly God's religion (as given to Abraham): **He believed in the LORD, and He accounted it to him** [Abraham] **for righteousness** (Genesis 15:6). Basically and simply, what did Abraham believe and to what did he look forward? Basically, our Lord Jesus answers that for us: **"Abraham rejoiced to see My day, and he saw it and was glad"** (John 8:56).

There it is: Abraham believed God's promise of deliverance from sin and death through the Seed of the woman. Abraham looked forward by faith to the fulfillment of God's promise of the coming Messiah, while we look back to the fulfillment of that same promise and behold the Seed of the woman born in Bethlehem. Therefore, we **are all sons of God through faith in Christ Jesus. . . . There is neither male nor female; for you are all one in Christ Jesus. And if you are Christ's then you are Abraham's seed, and heirs according to the promise** (Galatians 3:26, 28–29).

The Apostle Paul sums it all up rather concisely when by inspiration of the Spirit he declares to all the world: **By grace you have been saved through faith, and that not of yourselves; it is the gift of God, not of works, lest anyone should boast** (Ephesians 2:8–9). God's freely-given grace and love are received by us purely by faith—that is, by trust in His gracious, forgiving love freely granted to us in our Savior, Jesus Christ, the promised Seed of the woman.

There's the God-given reason why the religions and the worship created by man compared to the religion and worship of the one true God are absolutely, diametrically opposed to each other. The religions created by man are <u>always</u>, without exception, produced on the premise of winning their imagined supreme being's favor by what one says and/or does. However, the true God says, **"Because of your sinful nature, that is impossible, for there is not a just man on earth who does good and does not sin"** (Ecclesiastes 7:20).

That is the very reason why God established His plan of salvation for us. We are saved to live with Him now and forever, for we (like Abraham) simply believe His gracious, forgiving love for us bestowed on us through the love-labors of the Messiah, the Seed of the woman. This blessed truth was demonstrated once and for all time and for all people when God fulfilled His promise made in the Garden of Eden. His Son became the Seed of the woman, who came into this world for one purpose and one purpose only—namely, to fulfill all righteousness for us and then to sacrifice His perfect life as a ransom for the souls of every man, woman, and child who has ever been born and who ever would be born on the face of this Earth. Briefly, He came to be our Messiah.

The Apostle John is inspired to say it very simply and to the point: **God so loved the world that He gave His only begotten Son, that whoever believes in Him should not perish but have everlasting life** (John 3:16).

That, my friends in Christ, is the most precious blessing we will ever possess. In our Savior we have **everlasting life**. Everything that was stolen from us in the Garden of Eden is restored in the Messiah.

Just think of it, we have the privilege of celebrating God's love for us every single day of our lives. Yes, we celebrate Christmas every day that we live. The birth of the promised Seed of the woman, God's loving gift to us, is always at the center of our lives—our reason for living—our purpose in life. For through the gift of the Seed of the woman, God's own Son and our Savior, we are restored to be what we were created to be in the beginning: God's own people for time and for eternity.

There is no greater blessing—there is no higher calling—there is nothing more special in our lives than to know that we are all the children of God by faith in Christ Jesus! The Apostle John is inspired to spell it out in all of its glorious beauty: **Behold what manner of love the Father has bestowed on us, that we should be called children of God! Therefore the world does not know us, because it did not know Him. Beloved, now we are children of God; and it has not yet been revealed what we shall be, but we know that when He is revealed, we shall be like Him, for we shall see Him as He is** (I John 3:1–2).

OK . . . getting back to our joyful journey as we travel with God toward that wondrous day of fulfillment. We re-connect with Jacob who is trying to deal with a rather serious spiritual problem among those who were near and dear to him. Before they approached that special place of worship, Bethel, Jacob called together all of his household, those in his immediate family as well as his servants and herdsmen. He was direct and concise as he spoke to them in no uncertain terms: **"Put away the foreign gods that are among you, purify yourselves, and change your garments. Then let us arise and go up to Bethel; and I will make an altar there to God, who answered me in the day of my distress and has been with me in the way which I have gone"** (Genesis 35:2–3).

How did they all respond? Praise the LORD! They complied without a whimper. What was the first thing that Jacob required to end all of this syncretistic religious practice? All of the jewelry, images etc. connected with idolatry were to be buried in the ground! Was that it? Did that take care of the problem? Of course not—but it was a good beginning.

Obediently, members of Jacob's household got rid of everything connected to idol worship. That was the easy part, but to change the hearts and minds of those near and dear to him was quite another matter. That was something that Jacob was not capable of doing. That was God's business. Only the Spirit of God could plant that essential gift of faith and love for the one true God of heaven and earth into their hearts. It was Jacob's job to bring the truth of God to them in every way he could. This was a necessary and constant labor to be carried out in an-ongoing basis—and Bethel was a good place to begin.

What memories flooded through Jacob's mind as he approached this special place—Bethel. The dream . . . the ladder reaching into the heavens . . . the angels ascending and descending upon it . . . the LORD God appearing at the very gate of heaven . . . and that magnificent blessing poured forth from the very God of heaven and earth:

"I am the LORD God of Abraham your father and the God of Isaac; the land on which you lie I will give to you and your descendants. Also your descendants shall be as the dust of the earth; you shall spread abroad to the west and to the east, to the north and the south; and in you and in your seed all the families of the earth shall be blessed. Behold, I am with you and will keep you wherever you go, and will bring you back to this land; for I will not leave you until I have done what I have spoken to you" (Genesis 28:13–15).

Remembering and embracing these tremendously powerful happenings, Jacob thankfully went about the task of building an altar of stone for sacrifice, worship, and praise. And then once again God favored him with special words of assurance. First, God reiterated the blessing bestowed upon him when he and God had wrestled by the brook Jabbok: **"Your name is Jacob; your name shall not be called Jacob anymore, but Israel** (contender with God) **shall be your name"** (Genesis 35:10).

Then the LORD God went on to remind him once again of that steadfast promise that was made to him—that unconditional pledge that was first announced to Abraham: **"I am God Almighty. Be fruitful and multiply; a nation and a company of nations shall proceed from you, and kings shall come from your body. The land which I gave Abraham and Isaac I give to you; and to your descendants after you I give this land"** (Genesis 35:11–12).

It's so amazing, isn't it? Centuries had passed since God first promised Abraham that the land on which he and his offspring dwelt would one day belong to them and their descendants. Yet, after all of that time, they didn't own a single acre of land—with the exception of a small burial plot for Sarah that Abraham had purchased from one of the Canaanite tribes. But that was it. Yet the promise stood. When God makes a promise, He will always, without exception, keep His Word. One day that land would be theirs. And from that land they would become, as Simeon so graphically proclaimed centuries later, **a light to bring revelation to the Gentiles, and the glory of Your people Israel** (Luke 2:32).

They were destined by God to become a beacon of salvation in the midst of a world of sin. The glory of the LORD God would emanate forth from this tiny nation to every people on the face of the globe. And with God's blessing, the peace of God in the promised Messiah would cover the Earth. "Kings" in God's eyes would carry God's message far and wide throughout the world. That is exactly what our Savior, the LORD Jesus Christ—the promised Seed of the woman, was talking about when He commissioned His disciples shortly before ascending into the glories that were His before the world began:

"Go therefore and <u>make disciples of all the nations</u>, baptizing them in the name of the Father and of the Son and of the Holy Spirit, teaching them to observe all things that I have

commanded you; and lo, I am with you always, even to the end of the age" (Matthew 28:19–20).

Indeed, Christmas will finally come, as God had promised in the Garden of Eden—but we must be reminded, it is a long way from Eden to Bethlehem. However, it is good for us—it is faith strengthening to take this journey with our LORD—for by taking this trip we clearly see how God's plan of salvation for the whole world gradually emerged, inch by inch, step by step, year by year, according to His will. Without a doubt, what God promised would happen according to His good and gracious will, in spite of the faltering faith of His people and the evil inventions of Satan. So may we ever pray:

PRAYER

LORD God, Your grace is sufficient for me. My life in this sin-corrupted world has many twists and turns that often come upon me unexpectedly, but that's life in this world dominated by Satan. Through it all, I have one anchor that I use regularly to keep my life on an even keel. That sure and stable rudder in this unstable sea of life is You and Your Word. The world around me is generally on a course that is not in keeping with Your Word. Sometimes my sinful flesh and Satan urge me to give the world with all of its godlessness a try—but when I remember Your love for me, I am reminded of Your everlasting Truth, guiding and leading me in Your ways. And I am buoyed up by Your strength and gracious guidance. Please, LORD, keep on speaking to me and continue to guide me—for without You I would be swept away in the vicious currents of Satan's lies, sin, and spiritual slavery. But with You and Your words as my rudder, I can withstand the most vicious storms of life. In other words, my prayer shall ever be:

Gracious LORD, take my hand,
Lift me up, help me stand.

I must have You in my life every day, LORD.
Help me trust in every word that You say.
Turn all doubts and any fears far away, LORD.
Gracious LORD, take my hand.

Gracious LORD, take my hand,
Lift me up, help me stand.
Guide the choices that I make for each day, LORD.
If I miss the mark and then go astray,
Call me back and help me walk in Your way, LORD.
Gracious LORD, take my hand.

Gracious LORD, take my hand,
Lift me up, help me stand.
Then when comes the final time of earth's stay, LORD,
Fin'ly lead me from this world of decay,
To Your mansions in the sky far away, LORD.
Gracious LORD, take my hand.
(Poems of Prayer & Praise, p. 7)

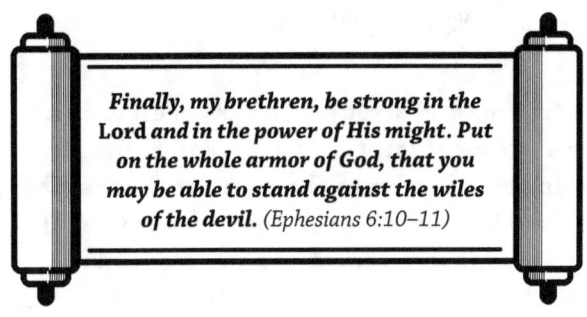

JOSEPH—GOD'S SPECIAL AGENT

It was a sad day in Jacob's life. His dear wife, Rachel, would no longer be at his side as a constant companion—the one who was right for him—the one God gave to be with him until death. She was received in the spirit into her heavenly home while giving birth to Benjamin. Jacob lovingly laid the earthly remains of his dear bride—that precious gift from God—to rest near Bethlehem.

Jacob's father, Isaac, also breathed his last breath at the God-blessed age of 180 years. Isaac was a man of God, and though he had faults and weaknesses as we all have, he lived in faith—he was a servant of the living God who believed His promises and was carried by God's angels to his eternal home in heaven. In their new-found friendship, Jacob and Esau came together and buried their father.

Now it was Jacob's turn to captain the ship of salvation. There would be many tumultuous storms in the days ahead. Threatening hurricanes of evil and Satan's tsunamis would pound at the hull of God's saving ship of life. Yet, much like the ark at the time of the world-wide flood, the vessel of life, the earthly kingdom of the living God, would survive. Why? Because, like with the ark, the LORD God was steering her course. And so His people aboard the vessel of His earthly kingdom continued to confidently pray:

God is our refuge and strength, a very present help in trouble. Therefore we will not fear, though the earth gives way, though the mountains be moved into the heart of the sea; though its waters roar and foam, though the mountains tremble at its swelling. There is a river whose streams make glad the city of God, the holy habitation of the Most High. God is in the midst of her, she shall not be moved; God will help her when morning dawns. The nations rage, the kingdoms totter; He utters His voice, the earth melts. The LORD of hosts is with us; the God of Jacob is our fortress (Psalm 46:1–7 ESV).

In accordance with God's perfect will, Jacob and his entire family with his servants, flocks, and herds, patiently settled in the land of Canaan—that country which would one day be theirs. Yes, one day . . . but for the present they lived as strangers in a foreign land . . . as did their forbearers before them. General intermingling and close friendships in the community were not possible, for coarse idolatry dominated the hearts and lives of their neighbors. This created a significant barrier against genuine friendships.

In many ways, we can relate to that, can't we? As the society around us day by day grows more worldly—as the saving Word of the LORD God of heaven and earth is cast aside by many like a dirty shirt—as the morals of the world are determined by the desires of the sinful nature of humanity rather than by God, we may feel more and more like foreigners in a strange land. The 19th century hymn writer puts his finger on it rather well when he describes our life in this world like this:

> *I'm but a stranger here;*
> *Heav'n is my home.*
> *Earth is a desert drear;*
> *Heav'n is my home.*
> *Danger and sorrow stand*
> *Round me on ev'ry hand.*

Heav'n is my fatherland;
Heav'n is my home.

Therefore I murmur not;
Heav'n is my home.
Whate'er my earthly lot,
Heav'n is my home.
And I shall surely stand
There at my Lord's right hand.
Heav'n is my fatherland;
Heav'n is my home.
(CW 417:1,4)

Yet, while he was here on this side of eternity, God had a job for Jacob, as He does for us. Jacob's God-given ministry—his divine mission was to faithfully carry the promise of God regarding the Seed of the woman one step closer to its fulfillment. That was the one God-given mission that Jacob was commissioned to faithfully perform in the midst of a sin-dominated world.

Actually, when we stop to think about it—and we should—we too, who have joyfully experienced the fulfillment of God's promise, have one particular God-given mission to carry out. What is it? You guessed it! Our Savior tells us what it is: **"Go into all the world and proclaim the gospel to the whole creation"** (Mark 16:15 ESV).

The Apostle Paul, through the power of the Spirit of God, knew that very well. He was fully aware that the entire city of Rome, as well as the lands round about, was saturated with false gods. The streets of the city were lined with statues built to honor the bogus, imagined gods of the people. But the apostle was not in that idolatry-ridden land in order to make friends and spend his time chumming around in godless ventures. He was there, above all, to tell them the truth about life with the LORD God in this world—a life that would continue on forever in eternity.

And so, standing amidst their idolatry and in full recognition of their godless living, the Apostle Paul shouted out for all to hear: **I am not ashamed of the gospel of Christ, for it is the power of God to salvation for everyone who believes . . . for in it the righteousness of God is revealed from faith to faith; as it is written, "The just shall live by faith"** (Romans 1:16–18).

And so it is with us, for—

> *Can we whose souls are lighted*
> *With wisdom from on high,*
> *Can we to those benighted*
> *The lamp of life deny?*
> *Salvation! Oh, Salvation!*
> *The joyful sound proclaim*
> *Till each remotest nation*
> *Has learned Messiah's name.*
> (CW 571:3)

So, as we continue in our spirit-strengthening, God-ordained journey toward the fulfillment of His promise, let's see how Jacob's son Joseph fits into it all. We are told that Joseph had grown to be a seventeen-year-old, handsome young man. But there was a serious problem in Jacob's household that involved Joseph. A problem? Yes, there was; in fact, it became a very grave matter. Surprisingly, Jacob allowed his sinful nature to get in the way, and he himself contributed to the difficulty.

Clearly and simply, here it is. There was no doubt that Jacob loved Joseph <u>more than any of his other sons</u>. What? Immediately, a red flag goes up, doesn't it? As we are no doubt aware, favoritism shown by a parent toward one child in a family is a recipe for serious animosity and disruption. Nevertheless, it happened in Jacob's household.

For some reason Jacob considered Joseph to be special. We may wonder why—so what's your guess? Here's mine: Maybe it was because Joseph was the first-born son of his favorite wife, Rachel. We also know that Jacob's special love for Joseph was only too obvious—it was out there for all to see. As one might expect, Joseph's brothers were fully aware of it and clearly resented their father's partiality. As a result, what happened? You guessed it: They began to thoroughly despise Joseph himself! Given the sinful nature of humanity, it was understandable—but sad, nevertheless.

Is there anything that could make matters worse? Yes, there was . . . and it did! Jacob was guilty in the first place, and he was genuinely guilty in the second instance. First, he threw another log on what was already a burning fire of resentment. Here's what he did: Jacob made the mistake of procuring a special tunic for Joseph. So was that some kind of an unpardonable gesture? The boy had to have clothes, didn't he? Well, yes. The trouble was this: It was not just any garment normally worn by the working individual of the day; a simple piece of clothing for Joseph would not have posed a problem for the brothers.

Here's the problem: A shepherd's garment was usually short-sleeved, maybe thigh length and colorless. This normal type of clothing enabled free movement for the various chores of the shepherd's activity. The garment made especially for Joseph, Jacob's favorite son, was clearly "over the top," extravagantly different from anything worn by the common shepherd. As a matter of fact, this was a rather dignified garment, long-sleeved and ankle length, made beautiful with colorful pieces throughout. Such a tunic was worn by the elite, those of high financial standing with dignified positions of authority.

So now the "fat was in the fire," so to speak. The coals of resentment that had simmered among the brothers of Jacob's family were suddenly doused with the fuel of this open and obvious partiality. The brothers' jealousy burst into scorching fires of bitter passion. **When his**

brothers saw that their father loved him [Joseph] **more than all his brothers, they hated him and could not speak peaceably to him** (Genesis 37:4). What was Joseph's attitude? Amazingly, he seemed to be completely oblivious to the seriousness of the situation. In fact, he gave the impression that he enjoyed the special treatment of his father and didn't mind parading it before his brothers. Was there anything that could make this matter worse? Once again: Yes, there was—and did!

Matters came to a head when Joseph had some rather pointed dreams. They were simple and clear—easily understood—graphic in content and obvious in their meaning—and Joseph decided (for whatever reason) to share them with his brothers: **"There we were, binding sheaves in the field. Then behold, my sheaf arose and also stood upright; and indeed your sheaves stood all around and bowed down to my sheaf"** (Genesis 37:7).

"Joseph! Do you realize that you just threw more fuel on the already flaming inferno?" There was no doubt at all in the minds of his jealous brothers; they got the point of the dream immediately! **"Shall you indeed reign over us? Or shall you indeed have dominion over us?" So they hated him even more for his dreams and for his words** (Genesis 37:8).

Then, to make matters worse, Joseph had another dream. *"Oh, no!"* we might be saying to ourselves. *"Keep it to yourself, Joseph."* Not a chance! Joseph just had to share it not only with his brothers but with his father also: **"Look, I have dreamed another dream. And this time, the sun, the moon, and the eleven stars bowed down to me"** (Genesis 37:9).

Let's count. How many brothers did Joseph have? Eleven, right? And then there were his mother and his father—the sun and the moon. It all added up—clear as crystal! By this time, even Jacob was getting uneasy and sternly rebuked him: **"Shall your mother and I and your brothers indeed come to bow down to the earth before you?"** (Genesis 37:10)

Well, the brothers couldn't take it any longer. Their anger was at the boiling point. They grabbed their work tools and were out the door! They had enough of such prideful talk and self-promotion. They simply left to take care of their flocks in the field lest their indignation toward their brother boil over into serious action.

We might wonder: *"What has this to do with the promise of God, the promise of salvation for all of humanity through the Seed of the woman?"* And I suppose that the happenings in the life of Joseph are often presented as just interesting stories without any connection with God's ultimate plan of salvation. However, nothing could be further from the truth! In fact, unknown to Joseph and Jacob and certainly far from the thinking of the brothers, God had chosen Joseph for a very special assignment in this joyful—though often times difficult journey to Bethlehem.

Indeed, the life of Joseph has much to do with God's blessing for the world. As we read on, we shall see! To fuel our curiosity a bit—where do you think Joseph's graphic dreams came from? His imagination? Not at all! God planted them in Joseph's mind. The reality of those dreams would play out in their total graphic clarity in future days. As a matter of fact, none of the God-guided happenings in the Bible are just coincidences or merely nice stories about occurrences in the lives of God's people. God tells them to us so that we can see and learn how He works in our lives also to accomplish His purposes. In fact, that very matter is addressed by the Apostle Paul in these Spirit-inspired words: **Now all these things happened to them as examples, and they were written for our admonition, on whom the ends of the ages have come** (I Corinthians 10:11).

It is truly astonishing, isn't it? God takes what He has to work with, sinful and corrupt human beings. Through these unlikely candidates God develops His plan of love for humanity magnificently well, and always in accordance with His will. He prepares things in such a way that His ultimate goal of salvation for all mankind will finally be realized in all of its wonder and glory. In other words, God is always in the driver's seat. He was there then, and He is there now in our lives. Make no mistake about it! He takes our actions, prayers, failures, weaknesses, and shortcomings—and causes them all to fall into place in such a surprisingly wonderful way that His will is always done in us and for us. If we but pay attention, we will be utterly amazed!

Why does God keep on doing this? Answer: Simply because He loves us. He has drawn us into His kingdom by the power of His Spirit and planted the gift of faith in our hearts—faith in His promises—faith in His forgiving love poured out upon us through His Son, the Seed of the woman, Jesus Christ. Through the Spirit-given faith in His goodness, we become united with our gracious LORD God—and having become one with Him, we confidently walk with Him through life, knowing that our lives begun here with Him will finally melt into the eternal bliss of heaven. Yes, our loving God causes this to happen in spite of our fallacies, shortcomings, and mistakes.

In the following chapters we will discover tremendous testimonies to the everlasting truth of God's love, guidance, and blessing for us all. May the LORD ever be and remain in our lives and cause us to pray with all believers in the words of that well-known hymn writer, Isaac Watts:

> *Oh, that the Lord would guide my ways*
> *To keep his statutes still!*
> *Oh, that my God would grant me grace*
> *To know and do his will!*
>
> *Order my footsteps by your Word,*
> *And make my heart sincere;*

Let sin have no dominion, Lord,
But keep my conscience clear.

Assist my soul, too apt to stray,
A stricter watch to keep;
And should I e'er forget your way,
Restore your wand'ring sheep.

Make me to walk in your commands—
Tis a delightful road—
Nor let my head or heart or hands
Offend against my God. (CW 462:1–4)

PRAYER

Lord God, help me always to realize that my life and the lives of all Your people are in Your hands. Sometimes things happen in my life that I don't fully understand. Sometimes I briefly wonder, *"Why?"* Yet by faith I know that You make all things work together for good for Your children who are Yours through faith in Your Son, our Savior and Lord. I pray, O, Lord, that You will give me a humble spirit with which I may bow to Your will in all matters of faith and life. Inspire me always to bow to Your will that I may, by faith, make Your way my way. In all things, bless me with Your merciful love and Your gracious forgiveness of my weaknesses. Pour out Your Spirit in full measure upon me. And so may I live in peace, correcting what can be corrected and readily accepting Your will in all things that are beyond my abilities and wisdom. So may I live and so may I die, resting in Your hands of grace. In the name of the Seed of the woman, Your promised Redeemer, I pray. Amen.

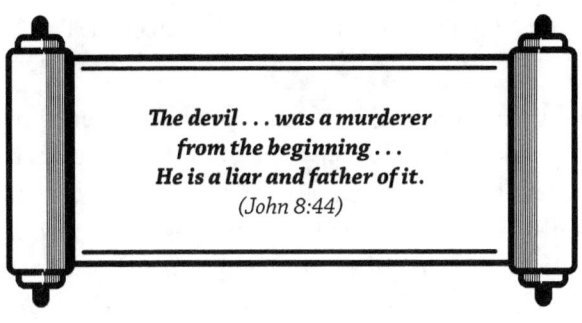

GOD PREPARES JOSEPH FOR HIS MINISTRY

Jacob was generally concerned about the well-being of his family. So, out of fatherly interest in his sons' welfare and not fully aware of the brothers' jealous anger against Joseph, he sent his favorite son to check-up on his brothers. Supposedly, they had gone to Shechem, about fifty miles from where they dwelt in Hebron. There they were seeking good grazing grounds. So off Joseph went in search of his brothers.

The princely coat, especially crafted for Jacob's special son, swept the morning dew from the face of the grasses and flowers of the fields as Joseph strolled through the countryside. Anyone seeing this young man with his tunic of many colors would likely not forget it. Joseph's regal attire definitely caused him to stand out among the *plain folk*, and that may be why a local countryman inquired as to his purpose. He was bound to wonder: *"What would such a princely dressed person be doing out here in the wilderness?"*

When Joseph asked about his brothers, without hesitation the man quickly directed him to Dothan, a change in his brothers' destination. No matter. That merely meant that another twenty-five mile trek lay ahead. Joseph didn't mind. He was enjoying his pleasant hike across the sandy plains and over the gentle hills. However, what awaited Joseph was not so pleasant.

When he was yet a great way off, his brothers spotted him coming. Who could mistake that audacious garment of many colors flapping in the gentle breeze? As the brothers caught sight of Joseph's princely swagger, evidently some of them were thinking: *"Here we are, out in the middle of nowhere. Our father is far away. Who will know what we do out here in no-man's land? So, now is our chance to put this father-favored-fraternal nuisance in his place."* What an opportunity for the Evil One! And be assured, Satan was doing his very best to cultivate such hateful thoughts among the brothers. As they glanced at each other, they were certain that they shared a common mood: **"Look, this dreamer is coming!"** (Genesis 37:19)

Then one of the brothers shockingly but vigorously suggested: **"Come therefore, let us now kill him and cast him into some pit"** (Genesis 37:20a).

Whoa! This was getting out of hand, don't you think? Their deep and loathsome resentment towards their brother was worse than anyone thought—but there it was, clearly on display! And doubtless the Devil was egging them on. Their extreme envy of their brother had reached its limit, and they were acting like madmen with no conscience. However, they knew they would have to give an account to their father. *"What will we tell him? How will we cover up such a loathsome deed? On the other hand, having committed murder, lying will be easy."*

Finally, with Satan's prompting, this plausible fabrication was suggested: **"We shall say, 'Some wild beast has devoured him.' We shall see what will become of his dreams!"** (Genesis 37:20b)

Satan was having his way with the brothers. Anger, envy, murder, and then lying about it to their father—that is Satanic work at its best! Our Savior had him pegged correctly, **a murderer from the beginning . . . a liar and the father of it** (John 8:44).

Again, I suppose you might wonder, *"What has all of this to do with God's promise of the Seed of the woman who would bring salvation to the entire world?"* Well, for one thing, we clearly see an obvious attempt on the part of the Devil to block God's plan of salvation for all people. And we are well aware that breaking a link in the golden chain of God's promised redemption for all humanity was his constant goal. But there is more to it than that—so we'll be patient, and eventually we will see God's love for His people and the world's salvation miraculously unfold before our very eyes as we observe Joseph in his service to the LORD God.

So let's reset our thinking a bit. Reuben, as all the other brothers, was very likely deeply disturbed by the favoritism shown to Joseph by his father. It is also safe to say that Reuben too detested the princely attitude of Joseph, accentuated by the garment of grandeur paraded before them. Besides, Joseph's seemingly self-serving dreams were difficult for Reuben to swallow. That goes without saying. But murder? That kind of dreadful action was shocking and totally unacceptable to this brother.

Somehow, Rueben had to come up with a plan to placate the fierce anger of his siblings. He knew that he had to devise a scheme to punish Joseph in such a way that his brothers' wrath would be appeased. It had to be something drastic but yet short of taking the young man's life! As Joseph came ever closer, Reuben knew that he had to act quickly. So he blurted out a hastily devised mode of operation:

"Shed no blood, but cast him into this pit which is in the wilderness, and do not lay a hand on him" (Genesis 37:22a).

This hasty suggestion was made to buy time. He felt that he had to come up with a delaying tactic so **that he might deliver him out of their hands, and bring him back to his father** (Genesis 37:22b).

So here came Joseph. He was likely looking forward to a joyful, brotherly greeting from his siblings. Besides that, he was no doubt weary from the seventy-five-mile trip on foot, and one might presume he was hungry—so the "welcome" he got was doubtless a huge surprise. As Joseph sauntered into camp, there was no word of greeting or welcoming gesture of any kind. Without a single word, the brothers grabbed him, roughly stripped him of his coat of many colors, and into the pit he went. Thud!

(Note: There were various pits or cisterns in the area for collecting water. They were relatively deep. At that particular season they were mostly dry, as was the one into which Joseph was cast.) Now what? Well, at least the brothers followed Reuben's advice to that point. They seemed to be comfortable with this arrangement . . . at least for the time being.

Amazingly, they sat down to eat their lunch as though nothing had happened. One cannot imagine how the brothers could be so cruel and inhumane as not to be bothered by what they had just done! One wonders what must have been going through their minds as they ate in silence while they could hear Joseph pleading for mercy.

Obviously, their quickly contrived plan was somewhat shortsighted. The question that remained and must have been on each of their minds was, *"What do we do now? Can we actually leave him in the pit to starve to death? What will we tell our father?"* While Reuben was off on an errand, these were deeply anxious moments for the brothers. But then suddenly and to their surprise an answer to their dilemma seemed to be staring them in the face. A company of nomadic Ishmaelites was traveling through with their camels, bearing the usual trading fare of spices, balm, myrrh etc., on their way to Egypt.

A solution to their problem plus a bit of financial gain clicked in Judah's mind: **"What will we gain if we kill our brother and cover up his blood? Come, and let's sell him to the Ishmaelites and not lay our hands on him; after all, he is our brother, our own flesh and blood"** (Genesis 37:26–27 ESV).

This seemed to be a way out of their quandary, so they jumped at the chance to finish this terrible ordeal!

Roughly they extracted Joseph from the pit and maybe wondered. *"Hmm. What might we get for him? After all, he is a healthy, strong, and handsome young man. He should fetch a good price."* We don't know if they bartered a bit or not. Primarily, they just wanted it done! So they sold him to the traders for twenty shekels of silver (twenty days' wages), not a bad price for a slave! But most of all, they were finally rid of their father's pet son and the source of constant aggravation. Joseph was off to Egypt—to be marketed as a servant . . . for some foreigner.

So, is that it? Well, not exactly. The brothers still had to deal with Reuben and their father. They didn't have long to wait. When Reuben returned, immediately he checked on Joseph. Surprise, surprise! He was not in the pit! Reuben was filled with fear and despair at the same time. He felt responsible: **"The boy isn't there! Where can I turn now?"** (Genesis 37:30 ESV) Reuben felt a fierce responsibility. *"What ever happened to Joseph? What can I do? How shall we face our father?"*

The brothers held their secret well and didn't reveal a thing. One might suppose that they urged Reuben to calm down and invited him to join them as they got their heads together to decide on a plan by which they would bring this matter to their father. *"Let's see . . . his coat . . . that despicable, beautiful coat. It was lying on the ground where they had angrily stripped it from Joseph's body before throwing him into the cistern. Wouldn't that be an appropriate item to use to break the calculated and dreadful news to their father? Cruel . . . but satisfying!"*

But how could they influence their father to draw conclusions even without their saying a word? They needed blood . . . yes, some blood. So, they **killed a kid of the goats and dipped the tunic in the blood** (Genesis 37:31). What satanic brazenness!

It must have been a long seventy-five mile trip as they made their way back to their father, Jacob. Can you imagine the fake sadness they displayed when they actually went before their father with that bloody garment in their hands and asked their bogus question? **"We have found this. Do you know whether it is your son's tunic or not?"** (Genesis 37:33)

What a bunch of hypocrites! Of course it was Joseph's colorful garment that his father had tailored especially for his son! Poor Jacob—a victim of his sons' devilish scheme. Immediately Jacob recognized the tunic, for it was one of a kind. It was Joseph's . . . no doubt about it! The only conclusion that Jacob could draw from this blood soaked garment was that a **wild beast has devoured him. Without doubt Joseph is torn to pieces** (Genesis 37:33).

Jacob mourned uncontrollably for his dear son Joseph. All the comforting of his children was useless. **"For I shall go down into the grave to my son in mourning." Thus his father wept for him.** (Genesis 37:35). Sad . . . sad . . . sad. And Satan laughs. Murder and misery are his stock in trade; he doesn't ever quit, and he never will quit until this world is swallowed up in the fire of God's final judgment.

The Lord God must contend with such devilish wickedness as He in merciful love moves things along toward His goal of salvation for the world. But make no mistake about it, God's will will always be done! Yes, at times happenings may seem completely out of sync with God's intentions—but as we watch and wait, we will see how God takes even the evil intentions of Satan as well as the scheming and lying of those who walk in his footsteps and uses them for His own good purposes.

We must never forget that God's calculated purpose and His will, from the instant of man's fall into sin in the Garden of Eden, was to give redemption and salvation to all mankind through the Seed of the woman. Amazingly, God's plan called for the use of imperfect people like you and me to produce the perfect solution to the world's dilemma of sin and death. The workings of our gracious God through seemingly impossible odds make each episode in this wondrous journey exciting and fill us with deeper appreciation of God's good-hearted love for us all.

Before us is a very vivid example of that very thing. Although Joseph didn't look much like anything useful in God's plan as he was being hustled away as a slave, yet we must be patient and observe the workings of God. The LORD God will demonstrate for us how He will use this young man in a most unusual way to further His plan of salvation for the world. Yes! Joseph will be used by God in a most exceptional way to produce a nation from which the Messiah—the Christ, the Savior of all the world, will be born.

Maybe we wonder: *"Did God's people always remember—did they always function as those who were especially called to bring God's redeeming love to mankind?"* That's not difficult to answer, is it? Of course, they did not! To put it another way: *"Was God's gracious plan always before them and in their heart?"* Again, obviously not! Nevertheless, God wove each of these episodes into His salvation-mosaic, resulting in an awesome, God-inspired design. Even the horrendous actions of Joseph's brothers, evil as they were, became a piece in that God-ordained puzzle that took centuries to complete.

So, let's follow Joseph a bit more as we watch the LORD our God splice the details together for His ultimate masterpiece of deliverance for humanity. And as we do that, may each of us be strengthened by the Spirit of God to recognize God's wondrous workings every day in each of our lives. As we do this, may we pray each day:

What God ordains is always good;
His will is just and holy.
As He directs my life for me,
I follow meek and lowly,
My God indeed
In ev'ry need
Knows well how He will shield me;
To Him then, I will yield me.

What God ordains is always good;
This truth remains unshaken.
Though sorrow, need, or death be mine,
I shall not be forsaken.
I fear no harm,
For with His arm

He will embrace and shield me;
So to my God I yield me. (CW 429:1 & 5)

PRAYER

LORD, my God, the wickedness of man is always there, close to the surface, ready to boil over in deplorable acts. We witness it every day in this world of sin—killing, maiming, raping, murder, wars, and threats of evil actions are only too prevalent every single day. We recognize thoughts and actions in our own hearts, minds, and lives that are evil and unbecoming to Your children whom You love and came into this evil world to save. LORD, I pray, fill me with Your Spirit that I may heartily repent of my offenses and strive by the power of Your Spirit to put all evil far from me. Indeed, O LORD, I pray each day, deliver me from evil. To the glory of Your holy and forgiving name, I pray. Amen.

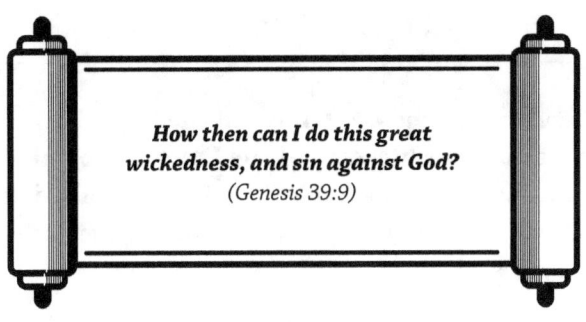

How then can I do this great
wickedness, and sin against God?
(Genesis 39:9)

JOSEPH'S ONE-LINE SERMON

So, here we are in Egypt, some two hundred miles southwest from where Joseph had been sold by his brothers to the Ishmaelites as a slave. There we might observe businessmen as they busily hawk their goods on the streets of Egypt—and of course they were making a special effort to market their prized offering—a Hebrew slave boy by the name of Joseph!

And would you believe it? It just so happened that one of Pharaoh's officers, Potiphar by name, was looking for a slave. Not any slave would do, for he wanted someone who was young, strong, and intelligent—someone who could manage some of the officer's affairs. The word came to Potiphar that some Ishmaelite traders had a slave for sale who might be exactly what he needed. Was this a stroke of luck? God says, *"No. It's all according to My plan. Watch and see."*

Joseph could have been sold to anybody. There were many in Egypt who bought slaves on a regular basis for construction work, road repair, field work, home maintenance, and the like. At this particular time, among them was Potiphar—an officer in the service of the most powerful man in Egypt. Well, Potiphar liked what he saw in Joseph and purchased him.

As we might expect, Potiphar recognized the abilities and honesty of Joseph and soon placed him in charge of his entire household and all of his possessions. And **the LORD blessed the Egyptian's house for Joseph's sake; and the blessing of the LORD was on all that he had in the house and in the field** (Genesis 39:5). Indeed, it shall ever be true that godliness always results in blessing for the doer as well as for those he serves.

Joseph was simply doing what he was responsible to do—dutifully making his rounds in Potiphar's palace—continually caring for his several required chores as well as making decisions and managing the affairs of the estate. Now, Potiphar had an attractive wife who had not a single thing to do but primp and parade around the palace. Besides, she probably felt somewhat unappreciated by her busy husband.

Suddenly, there was Joseph, **handsome in form and appearance** (Genesis 39:6b). Of course, she took special notice of this new slave, a handsome young man. And as time passed, not only did she notice Joseph, she also became lustfully intrigued by him! She had time on her hands—too much time. Day after day she silently observed this gifted young slave laboring zealously and humbly as he carried out his assigned duties.

In the course of time, Potiphar's wife began to **cast longing eyes** on Joseph. Then one day she blurted out her craving and lustful desires: **"Lie with me!"** (Genesis 39:7)

Joseph was astonished, and of course immediately refused! His responsibilities were to manage the affairs of Potiphar—which did not include an affair with his wife! She was off limits, as any godly person would know.

Since Joseph was a normal, virile, red-blooded young man, far away from his family and anyone that he knew—would he finally fall for her sexual enticement? Beyond his dedication to his boss, Potiphar, there was something else that guided Joseph's words and actions. There was an overriding clear voice in his mind and heart that moved him to cry out: **"How then can I do this great wickedness, and sin against God?"** (Genesis 39:9)

There's the answer—the voice of conscience, responding to the will of God. This overrode every other possible thought or desire in Joseph's mind. Even before the sacred commandments were written on tables of stone at Mount Sinai, Joseph knew sin when he saw it. In one sentence he preached one of the grandest sermons ever to cross human lips. Its application to sinful situations that come before God's people constantly in life is simple and God-ordained. It is a compass that guides every Christian's conscience, heart and action. **"How then can I do this great wickedness, and sin against God?"**

But that didn't stop the temptress. She wanted Joseph, and she was accustomed to getting what she wanted! It's interesting to note how her godless attitude was graphically portrayed by a playwright in this way: When Joseph preached his glorious one-line sermon, the seductress responded by flinging her flowing skirt over the bust of her idol-god that stood in the corner of her room. Then she vigorously stated in typical irreverent fashion: "Now, god will not see!" To which the actor, playing the part of Joseph, unwaveringly responded with the godly answer: "My God sees!" In fact, that is what Joseph effectually was saying.

Nevertheless, she did not give up, and Satan was urging her on. Without a doubt, the evil one was well aware that he had an ally in the sinful nature of mankind. So, being a master at temptation and an expert at promoting seduction, Potiphar's wife became his perfect host. When the LORD God does not rule in one's life, the human becomes easy game for Satan. So, day after day after day the temptress flung herself before Joseph, urging him to lie with her. By God's grace, Joseph wavered not a smidgen. His answer was always the same.

Finally, one fateful day as Joseph entered Potiphar's house to tend to his several duties, he noticed something rather strange. None of the men servants or workers were visibly at their daily labors. Apparently they all had the day off. Joseph became suspicious. Was this a trap? Maybe. At the very least, this was a dangerous time to be in the house alone with this sex-crazed woman.

Then suddenly, it was too late to think about it! The lustful woman approached Joseph, grabbed him by his outer garment, and once again seductively whispered, **"Lie with me"** (Genesis 39:12).

Joseph knew that she wasn't about to take "no" for an answer. Not this time! His only conceivable recourse: He tore loose from her, left his garment in her hand, and fled from the house. *"But, Joseph, this is a woman who usually gets what she wants. Remember? People do her every bidding day after day. Besides, as William Congreve concisely put it in* The Mourning Bride"*:

> Heaven has no rage like love to hatred turned,
> Nor hell a fury like a woman scorned.

This woman was not about to permit what she considered to be insolence and humiliation to go unpunished! Immediately, with Joseph's outer garment in hand, she called in servants and vigorously charged: **"See, he** (Potiphar) **has brought in to us a Hebrew to mock us. He came in to me to lie with me, and I cried out with a loud voice. And it happened, when he heard that I lifted my voice and cried out, that he left his garment with me, and fled and went outside"** (Genesis 39:14–15).

The father of lies was having a "hay day"! First, unashamed sexual lust—then accusatorial lying: *"This Hebrew man tried to rape me!"* She repeated the same false witness to her husband. Of course, Potiphar was furious. And without bothering to check the facts, he ordered that Joseph be thrown into prison!

What a turn of events! First, being sold as a slave . . . and then suddenly finding oneself in prison with common criminals. Well, now, how did Joseph react? Did he resentfully complain to God, *"Why? Why? I was simply trying to do Your will, LORD! How—why did You let this happen to me?"* Or did he offer the usual current complaint, "No good deed ever goes unpunished?" Others might have had second thoughts about his actions and wonder if it might have been better to simply enjoy the "hospitality" of his temptress rather than sit in that stinking prison— but there is no sign that Joseph had any such thoughts. As a matter of fact, even in prison **the LORD was with Joseph and showed him mercy, and He gave him favor in the sight of the keeper of the prison** (Genesis 39:21).

Yes, the keeper of the prison soon recognized that Joseph was no ordinary prisoner. He saw that Joseph was kind and considerate and readily went about doing what was expected of him without complaining. Soon he was promoted to become a deputy to the warden. The reason is clearly stated. **The LORD was with him; and whatever he did, the LORD made it prosper** (Genesis 39:23).

Let us not forget that The LORD's plan of salvation is continually being worked out amidst the slime and muck of the sinfully corrupted ways of man. As we read each episode, we are moving just a tiny bit closer to observing how God's promise is kept—how Christmas finally comes with the birth of the Messiah, the world's Savior. But it's a long way, and Satan never stops in his attempts to side-track the LORD's will. Evil is his expertise—the sinful nature of mankind is his ally—the unbelieving world is his playground. But let us be patient and observe as the LORD our God causes everything to mesh together to fulfill His will.

We might wonder: *"What good could possibly happen in this place— this despicable prison? How can the LORD's will ever be accomplished in a dreadful place like this?"* The odds seem to be entirely in Satan's court. This calls for faithful patience—waiting on the LORD for the answer.

More than 350 years ago Georg Newmark did an excellent job of poetically teaching us that very point:

> *Be patient and await His leisure*
> *In cheerful hope, with heart content*
> *Then take whate'er your Father's pleasure*
> *And His discerning love have sent,*
> *Doubt not; your inmost wants are known*
> *To Him who chose you for His own. (CW 444:3)*

PRAYER

LORD, my God, I live in a world that is filled with sin of every kind. Temptations are on every hand. Satan invades the lives of people, constantly urging them to pay no attention to Your Word but rather engage in actions contrary to Your will. When I look at my own life, I must say: "Were it not for Your guidance that leads me on my safari through this wilderness, I would easily become lost and entangled in this dense, murky forest of temptation. I know that Satan lurks behind every one of Your blessings, trying to cause me to misuse Your gracious gifts to me. That is why I pray constantly, O LORD, please fill me with Your Spirit and guide me with Your words that I may be alert to the many temptations that are all around me. Give me the spiritual strength to say with Joseph, **'How then can I do this great wickedness and sin against God?'** And when my sinful flesh has its way, O LORD, please forgive me for the sake of Your Son, my Savior, the Seed of the woman, who came to pay the price of sin for us all. In His holy name I pray. Amen."

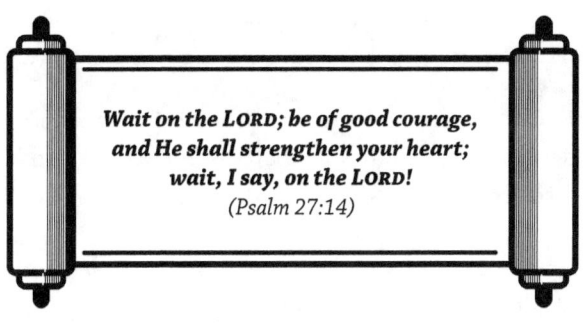

THE BLESSING OF PATIENT ENDURANCE

What exciting things can happen in a prison? Normally, not much of anything—same ol' same ol', day after day. That's pretty much the likely description of Joseph's prison life. But then . . . the boredom of this dull confinement was suddenly interrupted as the prison gates creaked open, and two sullen and glum captives were thrust through the doors. Come to find out, they were part of the staff of the Pharaoh, the king of Egypt. One was the chief butler and the other the chief baker.

For some reason they had displeased the Pharaoh, and off to prison they were sent. Well, the captain of the guard felt he was just too busy to be bothered with yet two more political inmates. So, whom should he put in charge of these hapless individuals? Joseph, of course! He was given the instructions to somewhat help them adjust to their incarceration. This seemed normal, for since Joseph had become the captain's right-hand man, he was the designated one to "show these new prisoners the ropes" of prison life and generally take care of their needs while in confinement.

Being the sensitive man that Joseph was, he immediately noticed that these two prisoners were unusually glum. Joseph showed interest in their dejection and wondered what he could do to help them. Certainly, being in prison was not exactly living in the Taj Mahal . . . no argument there. But why so unusually depressed? The reason for their sadness was revealed when they finally spoke up: **"We each have dreamed a dream, and there is no interpreter of it"** (Genesis 40:8).

Of course, many of us dream. However, our fanciful visions are usually about life's happenings, family, etc. Many a time when morning comes we can hardly remember what we dreamed, not to mention what it all might mean . . . if anything. However, the dreams of these two prisoners were special dreams and not easily dismissed. They were very graphic, shockingly real, and simply had to have a special and significant meaning. But what was it?

Now, Joseph was no stranger to the element of dreams of great significance, as we know. He had had a few of his own. One wonders if his former dreams ever crossed his mind at a time like this. If they did, he might have wondered how they could ever become reality here in Egypt—in this seemingly "God-forsaken" jail—far from his homeland and his brothers and father. There was certainly no one bowing down to him here!

Besides having the responsibility to care for these two prisoners, God had also given him the ability to interpret dreams—so first of all he taught his dejected fellow prisoners an all-important lesson in one short sentence: **"Do not interpretations belong to God?"**

It was purely a confession of faith together with a gentle reminder that he was merely an instrument of God. Then he invited: **"Tell them to me, please"** (Genesis 40:8).

It is good for us to be reminded that before God caused His Word to be written, He communicated His will to people in various ways. Sometimes He used angels to speak with mankind. Then again He used dreams. At various times we are simply told that God spoke to individuals, as He did to Adam and Eve, Noah, Abraham, Isaac, Jacob as well as Moses—with whom **the LORD spoke . . . face to face, as a man speaks to his friend** (Exodus 33:11).

Apparently God often chose to communicate with Joseph in dreams, so this form of communication from God was not at all foreign to him. And not only had God informed Joseph of His will in this way, but He had given His servant the gift to interpret his own dreams and the dreams of others as well. However, Joseph wished to make it crystal clear and he wanted others to understand that it was God who gave him the ability to understand dreams and reveal their meaning.

The chief butler, who was totally mystified by his dream, was very willing to relay it to Joseph. **"Behold, in my dream a vine was before me, and in the vine were three branches; it was as though it budded, its blossoms shot forth, and its clusters brought forth ripe grapes. Then Pharaoh's cup was in my hand; and I took the grapes and pressed them into Pharaoh's cup, and placed the cup in Pharaoh's hand"** (Genesis 40:9–11).

So, how would you interpret that dream? After giving it some thought, I suppose any of us could come up with a variety of scenarios, each of which would likely miss the mark completely! But with his special gift from God and as a mouth-piece of the LORD God, Joseph was given the correct interpretation immediately and clearly, **"This is the interpretation of it:"** (Genesis 40:12)

No doubts! Not, "I'll have to give it some thought," or "I'll get back to you on that" kind of answer. Rather, straight forward and to the point Joseph laid it out: **The three branches are three days. Now within three days Pharaoh will lift up your head and restore you to your place, and you will put Pharaoh's cup in his hand according to the former manner, when you were his butler** (Genesis 40:12–13).

Was this just a "shot in the dark" or a kind of "feel good" interpretation? Not in the least. Joseph knew and revealed the meaning of the dream without a doubt. In three days the butler was going to be restored to his former position, and that was that! So, knowing what would happen, Joseph made a simple request of the butler: **"Remember me when it is well with you, and please show kindness to me; make mention of me to Pharaoh, and get me out of this** (jail) **house"** (Genesis 40:14).

Well, it all happened as Joseph had predicted. In three days the butler was restored to his butlership and carried on with his duties as before. BUT, did the butler remember Joseph's request? Did he put in a good word for him with the ruler of Egypt? Of course not! The butler likely reasoned, *"Why should I risk my position by mentioning the kindness and the special gift of a fellow prisoner? After all, the king has no time for such petty nuisance matters."* He forgot all about Joseph's request. And Satan said, *"Good! Now Joseph will rot in prison, and God's plan of salvation-love for the whole-wide-world will be at a standstill."*

As for the baker—his dream was totally different and forecast a much different outcome. Nevertheless, Joseph "laid it on the line" and told him the truth. Once again, without a single doubt, Joseph saw it all clearly and rendered the gripping meaning of his dream. The baker's duties as baker-chef were over. He would die—hanged by the orders of Pharaoh. And so it came to pass.

But was that the end of this matter? Not yet! God was not finished. Time dragged by—two hapless years passed while Joseph continued to faithfully carry out his duties as they were given to him. How often Joseph must have prayed while in that grim, gloomy, and seemingly hopeless confinement: **"My times are in Your hand"** (Psalm 31:15). God's people both then and now need to be continually reminded that our times and God's time table are often far different. It is good for us to remember that. In fact, that is one of the reasons that the LORD is so insistent upon faith—faith—faith—trust in His gracious promises and magnanimous love.

For example, we know by faith that the LORD God loves us. He has unquestionably proved that to us. How? Through the sacrifice of His Son, our Lord and Savior, Jesus Christ—the promised Seed of the woman. As His purchased people, we certainly know by faith that His gracious care rests upon us every day—and we leave in His hands the when and how He will bless us. We simply go about our duties, praying that His will be done in His own good time and according to His own good pleasure. After all, His will has become our will; right?

Joseph had to relearn that lesson day after day after day as he patiently waited for the next happening in God's kingdom of grace. We too need to learn that lesson time and again as we struggle with decisions, conclusions, the unexpected, illnesses, and possible results. Each day of our lives should begin with a prayer like this: "LORD God, strengthen my faith. Give me patience, as I wait on Your resolution to troubling issues in my life. For I know that in Your own good time and in Your own right way, You will make all things work together for my good. Without question LORD, Your will is my will."

Added assurance is given to each of us through the inspired words of the Prophet Isaiah: **Have you not known? Have you not heard? The everlasting God, the LORD, the Creator of the ends of the earth, neither faints nor is weary. There is no searching of His understanding. He gives power to the weak, and to those who have no might He increases strength. Even the youths shall faint and be weary, and the young men shall utterly fall, but those who wait on the LORD shall renew their strength; they shall mount up with wings like eagles, they shall run and not be weary, they shall walk and not faint** (Isaiah 40:28–31).

Oh! What beautiful and soul inspiring words those are coming directly from God through His holy Prophet Isaiah! What a gift to God's people was this prophet! He has been named by many to be THE messianic prophet of the Old Testament—and rightly so. The Messianic nature of Isaiah's words will be further visited in Volume II, where we trace how our LORD God uses Isaiah to graphically point directly to the promised Messiah soon to come.

Indeed, the words from the pen of His prophet Isaiah were spoken and written for every generation of mankind and most certainly for God's people. As a result, Isaiah's God-inspired words are read, sung, and taken into our hearts with complete confidence that **those who wait on the LORD shall renew their strength they shall mount up with wings like eagles, they shall run and not be weary, they shall walk and not faint.**

Praise to the Lord
Who o'er all things so wondrously reigns.
Who as on wings of an eagle uplifts and sustains.
Have you not seen
How your desires all have been
Granted in what He ordains?
(TLH 39:2 adapted)

PRAYER

Dear Father in heaven, patience is something that many of us lack. I for one know how desperately I need to learn and relearn to show loving patience toward my fellow humans as You have so patiently shown Your constant care for me. You have loved me so much that though I was born in sin—separated from You from the moment that I was conceived in my mother's womb—yet You patiently came to me and by the power of Your Spirit redeemed me already in my infancy by the washing of regeneration and renewing me by Your infinite power. I pray that by

Your Spirit You will help me to recognize each day of my life that **my times are in Your hands**. Indeed, all things are in Your hands. Cause me diligently and patiently to keep my eyes fixed upon the work of Your kingdom and the blessings that You have promised for all Your dear children. Help me to see that in Your good time You will make all things work for good to those who love You, those who have been called into Your blessed kingdom by the power of Your Holy Spirit. Inspire me by Your Spirit to patiently wait for Your blessings every day—for by faith in You I will be empowered to mount up with wings like eagles. By Your grace I will run and not be weary. With Your strength I will walk and not faint. In the name of our loving Savior and Lord, I pray. Amen.

We know that all things work together for good to those who love God, to those who are the called according to His purpose. (Romans 8:28)

FROM PRISON TO PALACE

The future for Joseph looked anything but bright. There he was, undeservedly stuck in a dungeon with worldly-minded criminals of every sort. We may wonder: *"Why?"* And if we are caused to wonder about this, how could Joseph himself not be perplexed by the bizarre happenings that had led to his incarceration? As this rumbled through his mind, he must have prayed about it often: *"OK, LORD, how are You going to resolve this matter? I thought I had a chance for freedom through an intervention by the butler—but apparently You did not choose to use him to help me . . . at least not yet! Very likely he has completely forgotten about me. How am I ever going to get the chance to prove my innocence, LORD, and get beyond the gates of this wretched place?"*

And beyond Joseph's immediate concerns, we might wonder: *"How is God's plan of salvation ever going to progress with His 'agent' stuck in that dreadful, dreary dungeon of death?"* Everything looked very bleak at that moment. However, Satan was overjoyed, for it seemed that the plan of God for the salvation of the world was again at a standstill. Nothing could be better . . . for Satan and his evil purposes!

And so it is that many people, then and now, loudly proclaim: *"God is dead! His promises have all come to naught. Sinful man empowered by Satan rules the day."* Yet, when all seems lost, and the trials of life seem insurmountable, Joseph and all of God's people courageously cry out with hearts of faith, **"Our soul waits for the LORD; He is our help**

and our shield. For our heart shall rejoice in Him, because we have trusted in His holy name. Let Your mercy, O LORD, be upon us, just as we hope in You" (Psalm 33:20–22).

And the LORD God hears and goes about His work of wonders, as we shall see in the case of Joseph. So let's continue by observing how God gently stole into the mind of Pharaoh. Pharaoh? Of all people . . . the ruler of Egypt? Yes, indeed! There, in this ruler's mind, God created a picture for him to visualize—a dream of sorts. Was this the way that God was going to change Joseph's predicament?

Well now, that's rather interesting; right? We remember that Joseph had the special gift of interpreting dreams. Maybe, by some unexpected turn of events, God was preparing the way for Joseph to get out of that hell-hole. So let's watch and see—let's enjoy the adventure as we absorb the actions of God on behalf of His servant Joseph and in keeping with His ultimate work of salvation for everyone.

There was always something very unique about dreams sent by God, and that was the case in Pharaoh's dream also. The images were so real, so clear, but yet so puzzling. The scene of the dream took place . . . by a river—likely the Nile River. **Suddenly there came up out of the river seven cows, fine looking and fat; and they fed in the meadow. Then behold, seven other cows came up after them out of the river, ugly and gaunt, and stood by the other cows on the bank of the river. And the ugly and gaunt cows ate up the seven fine looking and fat cows. So Pharaoh awoke** (Genesis 41:2–4).

Did God make His point? Yes, He did. Did Pharaoh get it? No, he didn't! Pharaoh awakened but then simply passed the dream off as nothing important. Without question, it was a strange experience and sharply defined. But Pharaoh was doubtlessly puzzled and his thoughts likely went like this: *"Maybe it is of no significance. Maybe it's just a crazy dream. I'm going back to sleep."* Pharaoh did exactly that—back to sleep he went.

But God wasn't done with him. Not yet! He **dreamed a second time; and suddenly seven heads of grain came up on one stalk, plump and good. Then behold, seven thin heads, blighted by the east wind, sprang up after them. And the seven thin heads devoured the seven plumb and full heads** (Genesis 41:5–7).

Again his Majesty awoke. This was a bit much for the Pharaoh. Two rather strange dreams, yet so precise—so graphic and utterly real. And somehow . . . they seemed to be similar. Now Pharaoh was deeply troubled. He couldn't get them out of his mind. The dreams both seemed to point in the same direction and seemed to arrive at the same conclusion—whatever that was! They had to be describing something important—but what was it? What should he do? Whom could he call on to help solve the puzzle of his strange dreams?

Well, Egypt was awash with those who claimed to be versed in deciphering hieroglyphics, sacred writings, and what not. Maybe they could help. After all, they were the geniuses of the day who also cultivated the art of astrology. Sometimes they were referred to as "magicians." Well, if ever this Head of State needed "magicians," he needed them now!

Together with these wise men of the realm, there were other men whom Pharaoh considered to be the wisest in all of Egypt—the scientists of the day. They too were requested to come to Pharaoh's palace. Surely, someone among these highly regarded personnel could tell him what his dreams meant. So he verbally laid out his puzzling conundrum before them in all of their stark details. His band of intelligent seers and men of wisdom listened intently.

We might assume that there was much discussion and conjecture among this group of elite "wise" men. But when all was said and done, much was said and nothing was done! Nobody—not one could come up with the meaning of these strange visions. Remember, these were the intelligentsia of Egypt. If they couldn't do it—maybe it was hopeless. It was frustrating for them, to say the least!

In the midst of all of this commotion and mental anguish . . . there stood the butler. You remember the butler who had been in prison with Joseph? Well, there he was standing by to serve refreshments and offer assistance with anything. He observed as these very brightest of the kingdom struggled and strained but miserably failed in their attempt to solve the king's problem. FINALLY the butler remembered—he recalled his prison experience and how a fellow inmate had clearly interpreted a dream for him. Of course he remembered NOW! If ever there was an opportune time to mention his prison experience with Joseph, this was the time. If this wouldn't make a favorable impression on his master, nothing would!

So the butler stepped forward with his information. He revealed his experience with Joseph when they were fellow prisoners. It must have gone something like this: *"This fellow interpreted a dream for me perfectly. And things happened just as he said."* Pharaoh was at his wits' end, so he "jumped at the chance" for a resolution. He wasted no time. *"Who is this guy? Get him in here!"* Immediately members of his cabinet jumped into action. They might have had serious reservations about this proposal, but whatever . . . anything to relieve the tension of this complicated situation was welcome!

Talk about surprised! There was Joseph, carrying on his duties in prison, when "out of the blue" he was summoned to meet with the Pharaoh! What? This seemed utterly unbelievable! But that's what the man said: "You have been summoned to meet with the Pharaoh." Joseph couldn't help but wonder, *"What is this all about?"* Often Joseph had been charged with something that was entirely false. In fact, as we remember, a false accusation is what landed him in this dungy dungeon years ago. *"So what is the meaning of this? Another false accusation?"*

Well, no matter. It was worth a chance. He had to hurry and shave, get cleaned up, and change his clothes. Out of the prison Joseph went, presumably with guards close at hand. What might have been going through Joseph's mind? *"What could the ruler of Egypt want with me? What did I do this time that would require this kind of hasty appearance before this very powerful man?"*

Joseph soon found out. He had no sooner arrived in the presence of the Pharaoh when "his Majesty" began anxiously relating his puzzling dilemma. **"I have dreamed a dream, and there is no one who can interpret it. But I have heard it said of you that you can understand a dream, to interpret it"** (Genesis 41:15).

Then he proceeded to convey all the details of his dreams. They were firmly etched in his memory, for they were so utterly real, but yet so mysterious. Joseph was ready to answer immediately—but first of all: **"It is not in me; God will give Pharaoh an answer of peace"** (Genesis 41:16).

What a beautiful godly introduction. According to one's prideful nature, we might expect Joseph to make a case for himself. Now would be his opportunity to take full credit for his special gift and thus curry the favor of this powerful man. Right? After all, how many chances does a prisoner get to stand before the ruler of the land—the only one who could actually set him free? This dictatorial head of the entire nation was really asking for his help! Maybe this was the time for Joseph to make a name for himself or at least use his gift as a bargaining chip for release from jail.

It's wonderfully amazing, isn't it? After years of unfair suffering in prison, still Joseph was moved by his steadfast faith in the one true God of heaven and earth to proclaim this godly answer and confession: "It's not me, it's God who will give you the answer." Maybe we should pay attention to Joseph's simple one-line explanation, and pray that the LORD will give us such a humble and God-centered heart as Joseph had.

Indeed, may we ever sincerely recognize and confess simply: "Whatever gifts and blessings have been given to me by God, my Savior and my LORD, are not of my doing. God has given them to me, purely out of His goodness, to be used to His glory. He deserves all the credit. I just pray that I may always bear this in mind and use His blessings to me in a way that will glorify His name and cause His kingdom to come to many."

Joseph went on to confidently lay out God's message: **"The dreams of Pharaoh are one; God has shown Pharaoh what He is about to do"** (Genesis 41:25).

First, Joseph pointed out that both dreams pictured dramatically what God was about to do. Then Joseph went on to reveal the meaning of his God-sent dreams:

"Seven years of great plenty will come throughout all the land of Egypt; but after them, seven years of famine will arise, and all the plenty will be forgotten in the land of Egypt; and the famine will deplete the land. So the plenty will not be known in the land because of the famine following, for it will be very severe" (Genesis 41:30–31).

Was that it? Well, that's all that was asked of Joseph. I suppose Joseph could have walked away, leaving this mighty man to come to grips with what to do with this "bomb shell" that was dropped in his lap. But just as God gave Joseph the ability to interpret dreams, He also gave him the gift of a marvelous insight into resolving such a serious national crisis, so he followed up immediately with the solution:

"Now therefore, let Pharaoh select a discerning and wise man, and set him over the land of Egypt. Let Pharaoh do this, and let him appoint officers over the land, to collect one-fifth of the produce of the land of Egypt in the seven plentiful years. And let them gather all the food of those good years that are coming, and store up grain under the authority of Pharaoh, and let them keep food in the cities. Then that food shall be as a reserve for the land for the seven years of famine which shall be in the land of Egypt, that the land may not perish during the famine" (Genesis 41:33–36).

Genius! The solution was simple and yet so profound. Of course, it was simple and profound because it was God-given! All the intelligent counselors to the Pharaoh were speechless. It was surprising that no one questioned Joseph's interpretation nor the solution. Joseph was so absolutely certain that he did not equivocate for a second, for he knew that these dreams were directly from God. Therefore, the proposed necessary action was also guided by his unwavering faith in the blessing of the LORD God.

Pharaoh and all his intelligent advisors were no doubt taken aback by this rather straightforward proposal. Indeed, it sounded so thorough—so workable. Miraculously they were on board immediately without a contrary word!

BUT there was another problem. The administration of such a program was somewhat more than challenging, even overwhelming to Pharaoh—yet he believed Joseph. Therefore he knew that he had to act. But that was easier said than done. How was he going to find such an individual who would be capable of carrying out such a huge nation-wide program in this vast country? Apparently there was no-one among his advisors who could "fill the bill." He sincerely asked, **"Can we find such a one as this, a man in whom is the Spirit of God?"** (Genesis 41:38)

Now, those words are somewhat interesting, aren't they? "The Spirit of God?" As far as Pharaoh was concerned, that was an all-important point. Belief in a god of some sort was common and considered to be a virtue. After all, the individual to be put in charge had to be caring, compassionate, honest, and an individual who had the ability and readiness to work hard! To many, then and now, these credentials constitute the spirit of God. On the other hand, could it be that this Egyptian Pharaoh, who was surrounded by idols, saw the hand of the true God in all of this? Could it be possible, or is it wishful thinking that a measure of the knowledge of the one true God was still lingering in existence among the Egyptians at that point in history?

Whatever the reason, the one who had the necessary credentials was . . . without question . . . standing right in front of them! It was Joseph! Above all, Joseph showed all the signs of having the godly wisdom necessary to carry out this huge program for the entire nation of Egypt, so Pharaoh made the decision right then and there—on the spot! Joseph was appointed! Efficient, wouldn't you say? As one of my history professors pointed out, "The most efficient government in the world is a benevolent dictatorship. The trouble is, it's practically impossible to find a dictator who is benevolent!"

Pharaoh spelled out the details of Joseph's appointment and position clearly: **"You shall be over my house, and all my people shall be ruled according to your word; only in regard to the throne will I be greater than you"** (Genesis 41:40).

Then besides this regal position in government, all the lavish perks of royalty were showered upon Joseph. To demonstrate full confidence in Joseph, Pharaoh removed his signet ring—the one used to stamp official documents. (The stamp of this ring authorized federal works projects and any other official statements or documents requiring the approval of the ruler of the nation). Pharaoh placed this ring on Joseph's hand, giving him unusual authority. Besides that, Joseph was provided with garments of fine linen, a gold chain was draped around his neck, and he rode in the number-two chariot. (This was equivalent to Air Force II in the U.S.A.)

Everything in Joseph's life changed. Within minutes he went from the prison to the palace—from reprobate to ruler. All of this happened by the will of God and to the dismay of Satan. The Evil One cheered when Joseph was sold into slavery, but now he had to sulk in defeat as the will of God carried the day, as it always does. **Happy is he who has the God of Jacob for his help, whose hope is in the LORD his God, Who made heaven and earth, the sea, and all that is in them; Who keeps truth forever, Who executes justice for the oppressed, Who gives food to the hungry. The LORD gives freedom to the prisoners** (Psalm146:5–7).

But there is more! Since Joseph was going to be in the public eye constantly, of course his name had to be changed to one of Egyptian origin. Zaphnath-Paaneah became his official moniker. None other than the daughter of the priest of On became his spouse. Two sons were born to this marriage. His firstborn was named Manasseh, meaning *one who forgets*: **"For God has made me forget all my toil and all my father's house"** (Genesis 41:51).

Yes, he was still well aware all of the terrible treatment he had endured at the hands of his brothers, but the blessings of God overshadowed them all, as they always do.

The name of the second son was Ephraim, meaning *double fruit*: **"For God has caused me to be fruitful in the land of my affliction"** (Genesis 41:52).

So, thirty-year old Joseph began his new occupation as "Secretary of State" of the country of Egypt.

This agent of God lost no time. Immediately he established the annual procedures for gathering up one-fifth of all of the grain produced in Egypt and safely stored it in granaries dispersed throughout the country. During the seven years of plenty, the LORD blessed their harvests with vast quantities of various types of grain. The store houses became so full that even with meticulous records, they lost count of the amount of grain that was put in storage.

Finally, the seven years of bumper crops came to an end, as Joseph had predicted under God's direction, and the period of extreme drought was upon them. This was the case not only in Egypt, for this devastating condition was felt throughout the entire then-known world. And there sat Egypt in the middle of it all with its granaries bursting at the seams.

Soon word spread far and wide that Egypt was the only place around where there was abundance. Many from nations round about must have wondered: *"What luck! It's amazing that Egypt had the foresight to prepare in such a marvelous fashion. How did they know that this drought was coming?"* But there was really no mystery, was there? We know, don't we? And God's special agent, Joseph, knew.

So what does this have to do with God's promise in the Garden? Well, my friends, it has everything to do with it! Don't you see? Everything that we have been reviewing is by no means accidental. As a matter of fact, every last detail from God's promise of salvation in the Garden of Eden to the last day of the world is under God's supervision and direction.

Let's think for a bit about the happenings before us. Why was Joseph sold into slavery? Why was he subjected to temptations by Potiphar's wife? Why was he cast into prison? All of these events came from evil motives, right? And we know that God is not the author of evil. Yes, God took what was evil and caused it to work for His eventual planned blessing for the whole world! Astounding—isn't it?

Similarly, why did the butler have a dream there in prison? Why was Joseph given the gift to interpret dreams? Why was he given the ability to properly interpret the dreams of the Pharaoh? Why was he elevated to such a princely position, administering a federal program that was astonishing, to say the least? Accidental? Not at all. Coincidence? Not a chance. Joseph knew. The Apostle Paul knew, and he was moved by the Spirit to say so: **We know that all things work together for good to those who love God, to those who are the called according to His purpose** (Romans 8:28). Not <u>some</u> things, not a <u>few</u> things but **all things work together for good to those who love God**. God sees to it!

At this point we begin to recognize more and more that events were being set in place by God, step by step, to establish that nation—that kingdom promised to Abraham. Remember? **"Your descendants shall be as the dust of the earth; you shall spread abroad to the west and the east, to the north and the south; <u>and in you and in your seed all the families of the earth shall be blessed</u>"** (Genesis 28:13).

That nation would be made up of the descendants of Jacob. As you remember, Jacob was Abraham's grandchild. From that nation the Christ would be born. So, inch by inch and little by little we are moving ever closer to the fulfilled promise that had been made in the Garden.

It's a long way from Eden to Bethlehem, yet what a joyful trip it is as we observe the hand of God moving things along according to His will and in His own good time.

So it is yet today. Our lives in this world of sin may become filled with trials. Physical, mental, or spiritual conflicts may weigh heavily upon us—but, my friends, know that it shall ever be as true as God's truth itself: God uses them all to accomplish His purpose in our lives. The Apostle Paul was inspired to say it, and we pray that as we make our way through this world, we too will be moved by the Spirit of God to join with him and confess with steadfast faith: **We also glory in tribulations, knowing that tribulation produces perseverance; and perseverance, character, and character hope** (confident expectation). **Now hope does not disappoint, because the love of God has been poured out in our hearts by the Holy Spirit who was given to us** (Romans 5:3–5).

Our lives are made up of many unforeseeable twists and turns which we do not expect. We are constantly making prayerful adjustments, and as we adjust to the workings of the LORD, we will recognize Him blessing us far beyond our fondest expectations. For which reason we earnestly pray:

> *My God, my Father, make me strong,*
> *When tasks of life seem hard and long,*
> *To greet them with this triumph song: Your will be done.*
>
> *Draw from my timid eyes the veil,*
> *To show where earthly forces fail,*
> *Your pow'r and love must still prevail: Your will be done.*
>
> *With confident and humble mind*
> *Freedom in service I will find,*
> *Praying thro' ev'ry toil assigned: Your will be done.*
>
> *Things deemed impossible I dare,*
> *Yours is the call and Yours the care;*
> *Your wisdom shall the way prepare: Your will be done.*
> *(CW 468, 1–4)*

PRAYER

LORD God, many are the severe ups and downs of life. They would be terrifying if I did not realize that my times are in Your hands. I will make mistakes, but they will not ruin my future. In fact, in spite of any shortcomings in my life, I am able by Your grace to see beyond them to my tomorrows. In confidence and peace, I realize that You are there to bless every minute of every day. So also I pray that You will give me an extra measure of Your Spirit that I may joyfully reach out to others with Your blessings of love and freely share with them what You have given to me. Thus, may my "granaries" filled with Your gracious goodness, in the promised Seed of the woman, be generously shared with all at every opportunity. In the name of the promised One—our Lord and Savior, Jesus Christ. Amen.

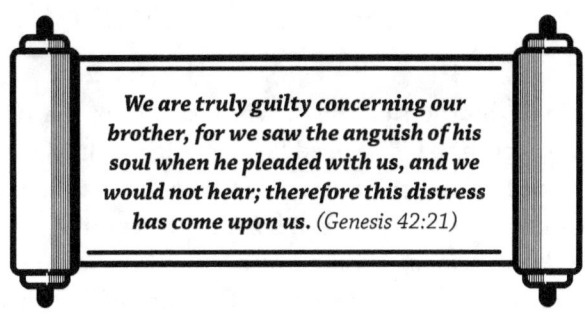

We are truly guilty concerning our brother, for we saw the anguish of his soul when he pleaded with us, and we would not hear; therefore this distress has come upon us. (Genesis 42:21)

A (KIND OF) FAMILY REUNION

And so it happened—exactly as Joseph had been moved by the Spirit of God to predict: In the land of Canaan as well as throughout much of the inhabited world, God sent a devastating drought. At first people managed to get by—but soon the reserves were gone—livestock died—people suffered—famine and hunger were everywhere. How long . . . how long? Month after month and year after year went by with no respite from this life-threatening condition. When would it finally end? We know, don't we? Seven long and suffering-years—that's how long! But the general public was not privy to that bit of wisdom. As a result they were at their wits' end.

In Canaan Jacob felt the helplessness and stress endured by his family. They were simply clueless as to a solution. Finally, decisions had to be made for their survival, so Jacob instructed his sons, **"I have heard that there is grain in Egypt; go down to that place and buy for us there, that we may live and not die"** (Genesis 42:2).

Egypt! How could Jacob's sons not remember? *"That's where the Ishmaelites were going when we sold our brother into slavery. But no matter; that's over. Who knows what finally happened to him?"* Maybe that briefly crossed their minds—but likely they didn't give it another thought.

So the sons of Jacob together with many others from Canaan prepared for a trip to Egypt. However, at the request of Jacob, Benjamin would not join his brothers on this survival expedition. Jacob already had lost one son born to his beloved Rachel. With such trips as this, there were risks involved, so he refused to take the chance of some calamity befalling the remaining son born to his favorite spouse. Just as well. His other ten sons, traveling with a number of burden-bearing donkeys, could handily take care of this life-saving effort without the extra responsibility of caring for their "little" brother.

But of course they would have to meet with the "Secretary of State" of Egypt. (And we know who that was, don't we?) Unknown to them, their brother Joseph was directly in charge of the voluminous stock-pile of grain held in their neighboring nation. Egypt's benevolent offer to share its precious produce with other nations became well known. People came from far and wide to take advantage of this oasis of grain in the midst of a starving world. The bountiful produce was carefully distributed, and records were scrupulously kept.

But in the midst of the frenzy of people from everywhere congregating in Egypt for their last chance for survival, another event was playing out with much more serious implications. This was the activity of the LORD God. It was occurring quietly—without notice of the general public. Yes, my friends, God was moving events gently and slowly toward His pre-ordained purpose of establishing the nation from which the Savior of all the world would be born. It was under construction in Egypt, and Joseph was in the center of it all!

Did Jacob know? Did the brothers realize how and for what purpose God was using them? No, they did not. Furthermore, would the brothers recognize Joseph when they were required to meet with him? Certainly not! We must remember that a number of years had passed since those despicable acts had taken place on the plains of Dothan. Besides that, Joseph had matured and changed in appearance. But especially, this man was next in authority to the very Pharaoh of Egypt!

Under such circumstances, who among the brothers would be able to identify Joseph? Not one!

To further add to his disguise, as we remember, Joseph was fully decked out in all of his princely finery. And beyond that, his position in the Egyptian government automatically demanded complete respect from those around him. Servants were everywhere on hand catering to his every need. Indeed, Joseph was the farthermost thought in the brothers' minds as they approached this "Egyptian" of high authority. As was the custom, they bowed down before this magistrate with their faces to the ground. *(Ah-ha! Remember Joseph's dreams?)*

And what about Joseph? Did he recognize this company of ten men bowing in obeisance before him? Absolutely! He recognized them immediately. His past moved through his mind like a 3-D movie. His tunic of many colors—his dreams—their hateful resentment and mistreatment—selling him as a slave! Now there they were before him—prostrating themselves with their faces to the ground. The very scene that was vividly portrayed in his dreams years ago was now being played out dramatically in real life!

Joseph carefully counted them. There were only ten! Where was the eleventh? Had something happened to one of his brothers? He had to know! But yet . . . he couldn't ask them—at least not at that point. So to stall for time he quickly devised a plan. He vigorously charged: **"You are spies!"** (Genesis 42:9)

Surprised by this accusation, they strongly denied it! They knew that such a crime was punishable with the death penalty. Trembling in fear, they responded: **"No, my lord, but your servants have come to buy food. We are all one man's sons; we are honest men; your servants are not spies"** (Genesis 42:10–11.)

Joseph would not relent, so they tried to bargain with him. They explained that they were sons of their father who dwelt in Canaan. They divulged that one of their brothers had died and their youngest was home with their father. *"Ah-ha!* (Joseph quickly surmised) *One had died—that would be me. And one was home—that would be Benjamin!"*

That's just what Joseph wanted to hear. He had not seen his genetically full-brother, Benjamin, for many years. Oh, how he longed to see him and embrace him. Somehow, someway Joseph had to come up with a plan to bring Benjamin into his presence without revealing his own identity to his brothers. He needed time to think—so he quickly instructed, *"You're going to prison."*

Before they could even protest, the guards on duty shuffled them off as Joseph had commanded. There they sat in captivity for three long days while Joseph thought through his next move. When he had concluded a plan, he instructed that they be brought before him. Here was Joseph's decision: *"One of you will remain in my custody. The remainder of you will go back to your father. Then you will make a return trip. When you come back you must bring your younger brother with you. Thereby* **'your words will be verified, and you shall not die'"** (Genesis 42:20).

In Joseph's eyes, the real reason for their coming was secondary. He would take care of that "food thing" in his own way, but that was not nearly as important to him as seeing his brother Benjamin.

The brothers really had no choice. Nevertheless, as they stood before this officer of the Egyptian government, they felt somewhat humiliated. The primary question in their minds was obvious: *"Why are we being treated in this way? Out of all of the people who came to Egypt to buy food, we were singled-out and given a difficult time. Besides that, we have even been jailed for three long days! Why?"*

Well, they didn't have far to look for their answer. In their minds and hearts the reason lay smoldering deep down in their consciences. Their action against Joseph had so seared their minds and hearts that they had never forgotten that fateful day many years ago. They remembered with grief–stricken hearts, when out there on the highlands of Dothan, their intense hatred for their brother Joseph had driven them to actually consider killing him!

His desperate pleas still lingered in their minds as they with callused hearts had watched him being dragged off to Egypt to become a slave. They couldn't help but seriously consider that somehow they were presently being punished for this crime against their brother. With guilt-ridden hearts they were convinced that their terrible action in years gone by had to be the reason for the dire situation in which they found themselves. Finally, their talk among themselves concluded with this admission, **"We are truly guilty concerning our brother, for we saw the anguish of his soul when he pleaded with us, and we would not hear; therefore this distress has come upon us"** (Genesis 42:21).

As they stood before this magistrate of Egypt, Reuben verbally exploded. In no uncertain terms he vigorously reminded his brothers how he had urged them on that fateful day years before: **"Did I not speak to you, saying, 'do not sin against the boy;' and you would not listen. Therefore, behold, his blood is now required of us"** (Genesis 42:22).

They all recognized Reuben's words to be absolutely on target. None of his brothers challenged him, for in their minds, he was right. *"This has to be retribution for our dreadful sins of years ago. Without a doubt, we are being punished particularly because of our horrendous treatment of our brother."* And, of course, Joseph witnessed it all. Finally, he heard from the very lips of his brothers' a recognition of their despicable action on that life-changing day. At long last he was witnessing his brothers' acceptance of responsibility for their vicious actions against him.

Now, we might wonder about the language factor. The Jews spoke in the Hebrew tongue, and the Egyptian language was totally foreign to them. In fact, a Psalmist speaks of the verbal communication of the Egyptians as a **strange language** (Psalm 114:1). However, as we well remember, Joseph had a number of years to assimilate that **strange language** of the Egyptians, and he readily communicated with the Egyptian people as an officer of the state.

Yet, by no means had he forgotten his native tongue. He fully understood every word spoken by his brothers. However, to serve his ultimate purpose, when he talked with his brothers, he spoke to them through an interpreter. As he listened to his brothers rehearse those agonizing happenings from years ago, and above all witnessed their admission to their sins against him, he was simply emotionally overcome. His love for his family welled up within him. He had to turn away from them for a bit to hide his tearful reaction.

How true it is: Owning up to one's sins in genuine repentance is good reason for fellow believers to rejoice—even shed tears of joy. And when this happens with close relatives, such an emotional response is good. So what happened with Joseph? Was he ready to finally disclose his true identity? Not yet! As far as Joseph was concerned, the final conclusion of the matter had to be left for another day. Remember, his immediate concern was to see his dear brother Benjamin.

So after he composed himself, he returned to the job at hand. He directly ordered that Simeon be bound. Yes, before the fearful eyes of his brothers he was led away, destined for prison as a pawn. In no uncertain terms the remaining brothers were instructed to return home—with one stern stipulation: When they would return to Egypt for more supplies, they were under strict orders to bring Benjamin with them.

So what about their original purpose for coming to Egypt? Well, Joseph had not forgotten. In his benevolent goodness Joseph instructed his servants to fill the brothers' bags with grain—and secretly to place their payment back into the mouths of their bags. Together with all of that, Joseph instructed members of his staff to provide his brothers with extra provisions for their trip back home.

So with their pack donkeys weighed down with grain—their conscience burdened with their past sins—their brother Simeon left behind as a hostage prisoner—they began their homeward journey. It was all so unreal to them—so mind boggling. There were so many questions in their minds—their heads were spinning with uncertainties—but no answers!

Maybe the most bothersome of all was that strange but absolute demand of the Egyptian "Secretary of State" to bring their youngest brother with them on their return trip. Why would this magistrate of the Egyptian government care about their youngest brother? Why would he want to see him? That was not only strange but maybe impossible! How were they ever going to convince their father to permit Benjamin to accompany them on their next trip back to Egypt? With heavy hearts they trudged along on that two-hundred mile journey back home.

A day's journey was behind them and it was time to rest, feed and water their beasts of burden, and set up camp for the night. When one of them opened his bag of grain to retrieve some grain—OH, NO! There, in the mouth of the sack was the money that they had paid for the produce! What's next? One problem after another! Now what's going to happen? How could they ever return to Egypt? For surely, then and there, they would be accused of theft and lawfully executed! How could this be happening to them? And . . . why? Question after question raced through their minds. But again . . . no answers!

Well, all they could do was to continue homeward and lay it all out to their highly respected father, Jacob. Maybe he would have a solution. Their trip was arduous, to say the least. As they carried their burdens in their minds and hearts, there was little talking . . . much thinking . . . no answers. Finally, they arrived home. Before their father they systematically laid out all of their strange experiences as well as the requests of **the man, the lord of the country** (Genesis 42:33).

Jacob's response came quickly and firmly: *"My youngest son, Benjamin? The only son I have left from my beloved wife Rachel? No! No! Never! Why did you even mention that you had a younger brother? Joseph is gone, Simeon is gone. And now, Benjamin is supposed to go back with you? Not a chance!"* **"If any calamity should befall him along the way in which you go, then you would bring down my gray hair with sorrow to the grave"** (Genesis 42:38).

Often times, as we view the horrendous agony of God's people, our heart goes out to them. Yet we also remember that our loving God sees it all and makes **all things work together for good to those who love God, to those who are the called according to His purpose** (Romans 8:28). His marvelous plan for saving the world from sin and everlasting death through the Seed of the woman was always first and foremost in the mind and actions of God. The operation of salvation and restoration for us all was in the making. Let's never lose sight of that central truth and the focus of God in these challenging events.

Jacob thought about and likely prayed about the entire matter for many days. *"Was there another way? There had to be. For how can I as a loving father watch my youngest son, my only remaining son from my precious wife Rachel, leave for Egypt?"* Yet a decision had to be made. The purchased grain was almost gone, and the famine persisted. Lives were at stake. But try as he might, Jacob could not come up with an acceptable solution. Finally he agreed . . . somewhat: "Go back and buy us some food. But <u>Benjamin will not go with you!</u>"

Now what? Well, as far as Jacob was concerned, Benjamin would not join his brothers on their trip for survival—that was not an option! But Judah was just as absolute in his position. He simply refused to go back to Egypt without Benjamin. For "the man" had unequivocally stated, **"You shall not see my face unless your brother is with you"** (Genesis 43:3).

Judah was totally convinced that the Egyptian prince meant exactly what he said. As a result, an argument ensued between Judah and his father. Finally Judah clearly pointed to the obvious: **"If we had not lingered, surely by now we would have returned this second time"** (Genesis 43:10).

Well, "when push came to shove," Jacob had no choice but to accept the terms of the "man." But one last effort, on Jacob's part, was made to curry the favor of the Egyptian "Secretary of State." Jacob insisted that they gather some of the few items that they had left—their best fruits of their land—and present them to this Egyptian LORD: **"A little balm and a little honey, spices and myrrh, pistachio nuts and almonds. Take double money . . . and take back . . . the money that was returned in the mouth of your sacks; perhaps it was an oversight. Take your brother also, and arise, go back to the man. And may God Almighty give you mercy before the man, that he may release your other brother and Benjamin. If I am bereaved, I am bereaved!"** (Genesis 43:11b–14).

PRAYER

O LORD, there are conflicts galore as I continue to make my way, one step at a time, through my own everyday life. Yet none seem to be quite so difficult as the ones experienced by my forefathers and mothers in the faith. However, I also realize that many of the difficulties in my life are brought about by myself. Yes, sometimes I am my own worst enemy. How is that so? It is because I fear . . . when I should trust—imagine the worst . . . when I should believe—faint . . . when I should be confident. Yes, I should face the future with all the difficult decisions and opposition that await me, knowing that You are there. You know what I need, and You have promised to provide everything that is necessary to cope with whatever comes my way. Yes, I should realize that You alone, by Your Spirit, can work miracles in my life—if that's what it takes. In the end, You will undoubtedly make all things work together for my good. Please, LORD, give me the spiritual courage to simply place my life into Your loving hands—for I am assured by Your Word to me that You will always make all things work for my good, for now and forever. In the name of my Savior and Lord, Jesus Christ I pray. Amen

To that end may we join fellow believers down through centuries and sing with heart and soul those age—old Bible-based words:

How firm a foundation O saints of the LORD,
Is laid for your faith in His excellent Word!
What more can He say than to you He has said
Who unto the Savior for refuge have fled?

"Fear not, I am with you, Oh, be not dismayed,
For I am your God and will still give you aid;
I'll strengthen you, help you, and cause you to stand,
Upheld by my righteous, omnipotent hand.

"When through the deep waters I call you to go,
The rivers of sorrow shall not overflow,
For I will be with you your troubles to bless
And sanctify to you your deepest distress."
(CW 416:1,3–4)

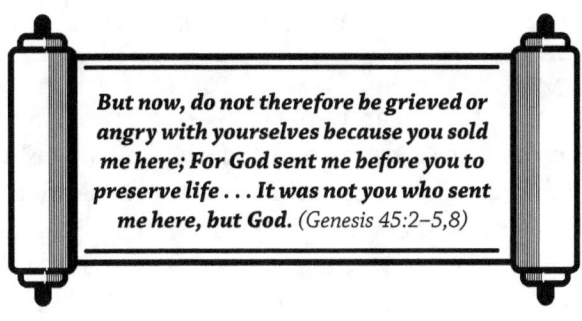

But now, do not therefore be grieved or angry with yourselves because you sold me here; For God sent me before you to preserve life . . . It was not you who sent me here, but God. (Genesis 45:2–5,8)

IDENTITY OF THE "MAN" REVEALED

With a trembling heart and no doubt a fervent prayer to the LORD God, Jacob had come to terms with the necessity of his sons' trip to Egypt, so he sent them on their way. Their travel bags were filled with a plethora of gifts for the "man." Besides that, double money for the grain was in their satchel, for they were returning the money found in their sacks during the previous expedition. But the most important treasure of all was young Benjamin. Father Jacob gave his blessing to this necessary trip, though he retained many reservations.

The obvious question that had to be uppermost in the minds of Jacob's sons was this: *"What kind of a reception will we get? Will we all be subjected to slavery under the "man" who seems to be able to see right through us? Or maybe we will become subservient to the mighty Pharaoh himself."* In spite of all their concerns and reservations, they had to take the chance.

The trip went smoothly, and finally they arrived at their destination. There they waited, with trembling hearts, for an answer to their bewilderment. They were met by an official of the government, who ushered them before the second-in-command in Egypt, Zaphnath Paaneah (Joseph). Immediately, the "big man" gave the brusque and concise order: **"Take these men to my home, and slaughter an animal and make ready; for these men will dine with me at noon"** (Genesis 43:16).

What? They were totally surprised by this kind of treatment. What was the meaning of this generous and cordial hospitality! Nevertheless, what should they do? There was nothing else they could do than simply follow the directions of the steward toward the "man's" house. This was absurd, they thought. *"Why would this powerful man invite us to his house—say nothing of the order for dinner besides?"* They couldn't help but wonder: *"Maybe it's because of the money that we discovered in our bags. Maybe he is finding a reason to take all of us into unending slavery here in Egypt!"*

Suddenly they were at the door of Joseph's home! They made one last attempt to mitigate the situation that they were certain was moving toward total disaster! Very politely, but in desperation, they approached the "man's" steward [and interpreter],: **"O sir, we indeed came down the first time to buy food; but it happened, when we came to the encampment, that we opened our sacks, and there, each man's money was in the mouth of his sack, our money in full weight; so we have brought it back in our hand. And we have brought down other money in our hands to buy food. We do not know who put our money in our sacks"** (Genesis 43:20–22).

The steward kindly assured them: **"Peace be with you, do not be afraid. Your God and the God of your father has given you treasure in your sacks; I had your money"** (Genesis 43:23).

What! They were totally stunned! Then, to add to their shock, the steward brought their brother Simeon out to them. He was safe and sound! It was all so surreal. Were they dreaming? To add to their astonishment, the steward guided them <u>into</u> Joseph's rather luxurious home. As was customary, water was brought for them to wash their feet. *(This was a normal practice of hospitality for guests. It was a very welcome practice especially after plodding through a couple hundred miles of sandy and dusty trails.) And,* of course, their donkeys had been taken away and were cared for with a generous helping of fodder.

Finally, the announcement was made: "The 'man' was coming." They didn't know what to expect from him, but because the steward was so very cordial and helpful, their fears were somewhat allayed. Buoyed by this unexpected, kind treatment, they prepared to present their gifts to the "man." When he entered, they properly bowed down before him. Joseph's emotions were so close to the surface that he dared not become too involved with a response. In fact, he sort of by-passed their carefully prepared gifts and proceeded to ask, **"Is your father well, the old man of whom you spoke? Is he still alive?"** (Genesis 43:27)

And there before him stood his younger brother, Benjamin. Joseph wanted to grab him and hug him—his one and only full brother . . . but he refrained and only asked: **"Is this your younger brother of whom you spoke to me? God be gracious to you, my son."** (*Benjamin was about 23 years of age.* Genesis 43:29)

The brothers assured the "Egyptian" official that their father was still alive and in good health. No sooner had they answered him, when suddenly the "man" left. He simply had to leave. He was so overcome with feelings of emotion and extreme joy that he retired into his private chambers, where he sobbed and wept in thankfulness. When he had somewhat composed himself, he returned. With face washed and hair combed, he gave the order: **"Serve the bread."** (*In other words, "Let's eat."* Genesis 43:31)

Generous helpings were served by the "man" himself to each of them from the lavishly filled table. They couldn't help but notice the special attention given to Benjamin, whose serving was five times as much as anyone else's! Somewhat bewildered, but thankful for this tremendously lavish reception, they relaxed, conversed (in the best way they could), laughed, ate, and of course drank freely! So, was that it? Maybe now was the time for Joseph to reveal his true identity to his family? Well . . . not yet.

Joseph was thoroughly enjoying the company of his brothers, especially Benjamin. He really wanted his full-blood brother to remain with him in Egypt. But how could he bring that about? After some hurried consideration, he came up with an interesting scenario. First, he instructed his steward to fill the bags of his brothers with grain. Once again, the steward was instructed to return their money to them by putting it in their sacks. Now, here comes the most ingenious part of his plan: Into Benjamin's bag, together with the returned money, the steward was instructed to hide Joseph's personal silver cup. So how was Joseph going to use this slyly executed maneuver to gain extended company with his brother Benjamin? Watch and see.

With happy hearts, good memories of the night before, and maybe less trepidation, early in the morning the brothers were on their way. When they were barely out of the city limits . . . what a surprise! Here came the steward. According to Joseph's detailed instructions, he overtook them and immediately laid down his charge against them, *"We have treated you so well, and what thanks do we get? One of you has stolen my master's silver cup—his very special cup from which he drinks. Besides, this is the cup he uses in his practice of divination. How could you do this to him?"* (Note: Divination was practiced by many ancient cultures such as the Babylonians, Egyptians, Greeks, Romans, and sometimes even the Hebrews. It was an attempt to interpret omens, dreams, foretell the future, etc. Divination was thoroughly condemned by God, through Moses in Deuteronomy 18:10ff. But in order to play Joseph's role as an Egyptian to the very end, the servant was likely instructed to add this detail about divination. Besides, Joseph's God-given ability to interpret dreams may well have been misunderstood and simply categorized as divination.)

Of course, the brothers couldn't believe it. They were beside themselves. Confidently they responded: *"We didn't do it. Check our bags, and you will see."* They were so certain of their innocence that they readily permitted a search of all of their belongings. Furthermore, they even promised that if the silver cup were found in any one of the brother's bag, that one would be turned over to the steward for severe punishment, even death! In fact, they were so positive that they were not guilty that they promised to become slaves of the Egyptian government if the silver cup would be found in their possession. The steward assured them that all of that was not necessary. Only the one in whose sack the cup was found would be held accountable. He would become the steward's slave!

So with the brothers' permission, the servant began the search. One by one, sack by sack, from the eldest to the youngest. The steward's acting was superb; he could have won an award for his performance! Finally, the servant arrived at the sack of Benjamin—and again he played his role well. *"Oh, what is this? The silver cup!"* There it was in Benjamin's sack, of course, exactly where the servant had placed it!

The brothers were in complete disbelief. How could this be? They were overcome with astonishment and terror. They tore their clothes in fear of what lay before them—but they had no choice; they had made a promise. Meekly they loaded their cargo on to their donkeys and followed the steward back to the city. Filled with confusion and fear, they returned to face the judgment of the Egyptian prince.

Strangely, the man was still at his house. It was as though he were waiting for them. (In fact, he was!) They came before the Egyptian prince and in total surrender threw themselves at his feet. The man, appearing totally indignant, firmly inquired, *"What have you done? How could you think that I would not discover this?"* The undeniable evidence was there. What could the brothers say in defense? Judah spoke for them all: **"God has found out the iniquity of your servants; here we are, my lord's slaves, both we and he also with whom the cup was found"** (Genesis 44:16).

Notice how Judah saw this as God's retribution. One wonders: *"Was Judah here speaking of the current charges or maybe about the sin of previously selling their brother into slavery?"* Very likely that dreadful crime committed years ago hung over them like a shroud. It may well be that Judah was seeing this as the punishment that they deserved for that vicious and loveless deed carried out so many years ago. From the day that they had stood before their father and lied to him about the apparent demise of their brother, their consciences would give them no rest. Maybe slavery under this "man" would do something to salve their aching hearts.

Surprise, surprise! Joseph declined their offer with these words: **"Far be it from me that I should do so; but the man in whose hand the cup was found, he shall be my slave. And as for you, go up in peace to your father"** (Genesis 44:17).

Think about it. Could this be one final test by which Joseph would attempt to uncover the present attitude of his brothers' hearts? Maybe Joseph wanted to know if they could be so hard-hearted as to leave their youngest brother behind to become a servant.

Humbly and sincerely, once again Judah stepped forward to speak for the brothers. His words were remarkably eloquent as he pleaded his case before the man: *"I realize that I have no right to ask this of you. After all, you are like Pharaoh, the ruler of this mighty kingdom of Egypt. However, do you remember asking about our father and brother? We responded by telling you that our father is elderly, and we truthfully admitted that we have one younger brother. He is the only child left of his mother, and his father loves him dearly."*

"You no doubt remember that you wanted to see our younger brother as proof that we were telling the truth. You made it perfectly clear that you would refuse to see us again unless we would bring our younger brother with us. We were ready to abide by your wishes , but our father was very reluctant to allow this. He was blessed with just two sons born of his dear wife, Rachel. One disappeared and was likely torn to pieces by some wild animal. If our

father were also to lose his youngest son, he will surely die in his grief. And we feel that we would be responsible for such a tragedy."

So, finally, Judah pleaded: *"Please, take me as your servant and let the lad go free. I simply cannot bear to do this to my father."* (Paraphrased from Genesis 44:18–34)

Joseph got the picture very well. His brothers had changed. Although Judah did not fully admit to the crime that they had committed against their brother Joseph twenty-five years previously. Nevertheless, they seemed to be truly sorry also for that sin. Judah's words demonstrated a love for Benjamin and their father that had not been apparent before. Joseph was overtaken with this display of love and compassion shown by Judah for his family.

Once again Joseph's emotions overflowed; quickly he turned to his Egyptian servants and ordered them to leave the room, for he wished to be alone with his family. After his servants had all left the room, Joseph released his pent-up emotions and **wept aloud** (Genesis 45:2). All of his anxiety and inner tension poured forth in tearful release. The "man" turned to his brothers and revealed in all simplicity, as well as clearly speaking in the Hebrew tongue, directly to his brothers:

"I am Joseph"
(Genesis 45:3).

His brothers were stunned. They couldn't speak a word but only stared in disbelief. Joseph continued in a tone of happy and godly forgiveness: **"Please come near to me. I am**

Joseph your brother, whom you sold into Egypt. But now, do not therefore be grieved or angry with yourselves because you sold me here; for God sent me before you to preserve life. . . . It was not you who sent me here, but God" (Genesis 45:2–5,8).

What a beautiful, powerful, forgiving, and faith-filled assurance he expressed to his brothers!

It is amazing, isn't it? Joseph could clearly see that the things which occurred in his life—all of them—were the result of God working for a beneficial and blessed purpose. Their selling him into slavery—his being purchased by Potiphar—the episode with Potiphar's wife—his time in prison—the butcher and baker, their dreams and his ability to interpret them—the request that he come before Pharaoh and interpret those mysterious dreams—his resulting status as "Secretary of State" for the entire nation of Egypt—his ability to establish a system to counter the extreme drought and famine in Egypt and thereby be an aid to the people of Egypt and many lands round about.

Because of all these events, Joseph knew that he had been put in his position by God to provide for the family of Israel in which the promise of salvation for the whole world rested. Without reservation Joseph fully understood that God managed it all! The Satan induced evil promoted by the brothers—the lust filled actions of the wife of Potiphar—even the idolatry practicing nation of Egypt became instruments in God's hands to fulfill His will. God made a promise in the Garden that mankind would be rescued from the evil hands of Satan—and the cursed Devil would not be able to stop it, try as he might. Every evil word or action put in God's path became His instruments for good! Hallelujah! Praise the LORD!

What wonderful lessons God teaches us as we watch and observe Him at work accomplishing His purposes for the blessing of His kingdom— His people—and for all mankind. Yes, Christmas will come—the

Messiah will be born—but it will also be a long and trying journey from Eden to Bethlehem. God's chosen people through whom He would fulfill His promise will falter and sometimes fall in their weak faith. But the fulfillment of God's promise through the Seed of the woman was never in question, for it was in God's hands.

Yes, Joseph was a key player in God's marvelous plan of salvation for the world. This will become ever more obvious as we move on toward that wondrous day of blessing. To that end God's people continue to pray:

> *Our Hope and Expectation,*
> *O promised Seed appear;*
> *Come soon, Desire of nations,*
> *To this benighted sphere.*
> *With hearts and hands uplifted,*
> *We plead, O Lord, to see*
> *The day of earth's redemption,*
> *That sets Your people free! Amen.*
> *(TLH 72:4 adapted)*

PRAYER

LORD, our God, I thank You for helping me realize that though it is a long way from Eden to Bethlehem—and though the way is obstructed with obstacles and the frailty of Your servants as well as Satan's evil intentions, Your acts of forgiving love to rescue all souls from the clutches of the Evil One continue to move continually toward that day of triumph and salvation. Your desire to restore everything that was lost in the Garden is progressing well. Thank You for the opportunity to take this journey with You. For along the way I have the privilege of observing You in action on my behalf and for the salvation of the entire world. And I further pray that You will graciously open my eyes to recognize how You are working ceaselessly in my life every day. Yes

LORD, I pray that You will move me by Your Spirit to love others as You have loved me, to forgive as you have forgiven me. And so may Your kingdom come to many, that Your name may be glorified. In Your holy name I pray. Amen.

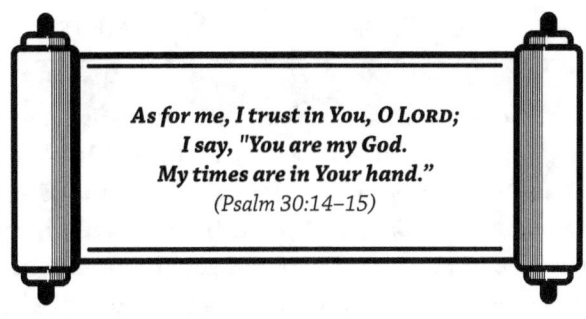

As for me, I trust in You, O Lord;
I say, "You are my God.
My times are in Your hand."
(Psalm 30:14–15)

A LIFE-CHANGING INVITATION ACCEPTED

The brothers of Joseph were in a daze. They were still trying to wrap their minds around the happenings of the last months. But . . . there was more to come! Suddenly, Joseph dropped another unexpected "verbal bomb." *"Let my father know that I am in a position to invite all of you to Egypt, with your children, flocks, and herds. I will see to it that you have some of the finest land upon which to dwell—namely, the land of Goshen. So, let's not waste time. Hurry home and bring my father down here to dwell."* (Genesis 45:13 paraphrased)

And Benjamin—his dear brother Benjamin who was so special to him . . . finally Joseph grasped him and with rivers of joy rolling down their faces, they embraced. Joseph then smothered each of his brothers in a loving embrace—so that they finally realized: *"This is really true! Yes, this indeed is Joseph. This is the one who had endured our heartless and loveless treachery. This is our little brother, the wearer of that despised princely, colorful cloak. This is that dreamer whose "ridiculous" dreams became totally true. Yes, we are bowing before him in abject submission. Everything that we had so utterly detested . . . became reality!"* What could they say? They were utterly speechless!

The good news traveled quickly; Pharaoh heard about it; he talked with his cabinet of officials. Their respect for Joseph was clearly apparent as everyone was in agreement. *Let's make this happen.* The king spoke to Joseph privately: **"Say to your brothers, 'Do this: Load your beasts and depart; go to the land of Canaan. Bring your father and your households and come to me; I will give you the best of the land of Egypt, and you will eat the fat of the land. Now you are commanded—do this: Take carts out of the land of Egypt for your little ones and your wives; bring your father and come. Also do not be concerned about your goods, for the best of all the land of Egypt is yours'"** (Genesis 45:17–20).

Isn't it thrilling to observe? Isn't it marvelous to witness the loving hand of God working out the details of His blessing for the whole world? Yes, what miraculous outcomes result as God gently, patiently but precisely moves people and circumstances to accomplish His purposes for us and for His kingdom. And He is still at work among us today and every day to accomplish His soul-saving purposes. That is why, in the midst of our everyday walk in this sin-ridden temporary dwelling place, we are moved to confidently pray to our heavenly Father:

Well You know what best to grant me;
Though my longing hopes may haunt me,
Joy and sorrow have their day.
I shall doubt your wisdom never—
As You will, so be it ever—
I to You commit my way.

If on earth my days You lengthen,
You my weary soul will strengthen;
All my trust in You I place.
Earthly things are not abiding,
Like a stream away they're gliding;
Safe I anchor in Your grace.
(TLH 426: 5,6 adapted)

So Joseph was moved to send his brothers on their way with all the necessary provisions and several changes of clothing. Of course, there was Benjamin, that special brother whom he dearly loved. He was awarded special treatment. He was endowed with three hundred pieces of silver and five changes of garments—yet no jealousy was detected among the brothers. They were all so thankful and filled with joy that they practically floated on air all the way back to Canaan. They could hardly wait to pour out their wonderful news to their father.

But could Jacob withstand such a turn of events? Could he, in his fragile, elderly condition endure the shock of hearing that his long-lost son was alive and well? Would he be able to understand the wonder of God's magnificent activity in bringing Joseph to his position of authority in the Egyptian government? And, above all, would he be able to process that totally unexpected invitation of his son, Joseph, to leave Canaan and move to Egypt?

Likely no one remembered that this too was God-ordained years before, for many centuries had passed since the LORD God had revealed to Abraham: **"Know certainly that your descendants will be strangers in a land that is not theirs"** (Genesis 15:13).

Granted, that particular revelation of God was likely not known by Jacob and certainly did not enter into consideration at that time. What was of concern was this: Jacob was up in years. News like this was almost more than this elderly, faithful servant of God could endure. In fact, his heart nearly failed when his sons revealed all of the life-changing details of Joseph's plan. Understandably, it was difficult for him to mentally grasp it all.

Could this really be true? Could his beloved Joseph still be alive? While they told him of Joseph's invitation and all the things that Joseph had said, an unspoken testimony to the truth of it all stood waiting in their yard. All of the carts with the beasts of burden sent by the Pharaoh of Egypt to carry them back to Egypt were assembled there and ready for Jacob to accept this wondrous offer. Overwhelmed and almost speechless, Jacob could not deny the evidence of these unbelievable blessings; it was all overpowering, to say the least.

Jacob was finally convinced and thankfully responded: **"It is enough. Joseph my son is still alive. I will go and see him before I die"** (Genesis 45:28).

What a job lay before them! All of their household belongings and equipment for the journey had to be gathered up. All of their workers and servants, their flocks and herds—everything had to be readied for this God-designed and long-predicted journey. After a great deal of preparatory work—at long last they were ready to hit the trail bound for Egypt.

Jacob could clearly see the unmistakable hand of God in all of this. His heart was overflowing with thankfulness and praise to the LORD God of heaven and earth. As they approached the southern-most city of Canaan, Beersheba, which marked the border between Canaan and Egypt, Jacob insisted that they stop. As they were about to leave Canaan, he had one heartfelt request. *"We must pause for a bit. For I wish to offer sacrifices of thanksgiving to the Lord God of heaven and earth, the God of my father Isaac and my grandfather Abraham."*

It was there in the darkness of night that the LORD God appeared to him in a special vision and reassured him: **"I am God, the God of your father; do not fear to go down to Egypt, for I will make of you a great nation there. I will go down with you to Egypt, and I will also surely bring you up again"** (Genesis 46:3–4).

That was all that Jacob needed. Above all, he wanted to be assured that this was all according to God's will. With that assurance he was at peace.

It was a huge undertaking, but with God's blessing Jacob was ready. Many questions likely traveled through the mind of this man of God—yet he was assured that God had ordained it and as a result He would bless them. Therefore this was the right thing to do. A seventeenth century hymn writer sums it all up well when he teaches us to sing faithfully with Jacob:

> *What God ordains is always good;*
> *He never will deceive me.*
> *He leads me in His righteous way*
> *And never will He leave me.*
> *I take content*
> *What He has sent;*
> *His hand that sends me sadness*
> *Will turn my tears to gladness.*
> *(CW 429:2)*

That's the point of that entire lengthy story of Joseph, isn't it? Israel was designated as the God-ordained nation with one purpose, to produce the Messiah, the Seed of the woman. Though the people often lost sight of their godly mission—their reason for existing as His people—God never even for an instant lost sight of His Promise nor wavered in His faithfulness to His final goal. It must have been frustrating to Satan, for whenever he laid a stumbling-block in the way, God took all of his evil devices and caused them to turn out for God's good purposes.

Do you recognize similar happenings in your life? As believing children of God, we can absolutely depend upon our LORD's faithful and loving concern for each of us. Often we do not understand when and why our lives take turns that we don't expect—but rather than wasting our time asking "why?" (as is so often done) maybe we need to spend our time in a prayer of thankfulness. It is a marvelous blessing when our LORD strengthens us to unconditionally give ourselves over to Him who loves us with an everlasting love and will always make all things work for our good.

So, another huge step was being taken toward the fulfillment of God's promise made in the Garden of Eden. There in Egypt God's chosen family would have an opportunity to grow and develop into a nation. Eventually they would return and reestablish themselves in the land which God had given to Abraham centuries earlier. As we well remember, Canaan was chosen by God to become the home of Israel, and there Christmas would finally come—the Christ would be born. Satan's head would be crushed. The whole world would be given the blessing of freedom from sin, Satan, and eternal death. In other words, everything that was taken from us on that infamous day in the Garden would be restored through the Messiah.

But we still have a long way to go, don't we? Nevertheless, we will get there as God has promised. Enjoy the travels that God has so graciously mapped out for us in His Word. As we follow that golden chain of events one link at a time, we continue to move toward that glorious day prepared by God for all of us.

PRAYER

As for me, I trust in You, O LORD; I say, "You are my God." My times are in Your hand (Psalm 30:14–15). So may it be with me, O LORD, as I confidently take one step at a time into the future with You guiding and leading me. Complications in my life are made very simple when I realize that my tomorrows are in Your hands of constant love for me. This is a life-lesson that I must learn and relearn again and again as I face obstacles and difficulties in this world. There will always be challenges and problems in my life because that is the nature of living in this sin-laden world. However, I have nothing to fear because my days, hours, and minutes are in Your good and gracious hands. LORD God,

I pray, remind me of this often as I step into each new day and close my eyes in sleep each night. I thank You, LORD, for your loving care. Without question, **my times are in Your hand**. In my Savior's name I pray. Amen.

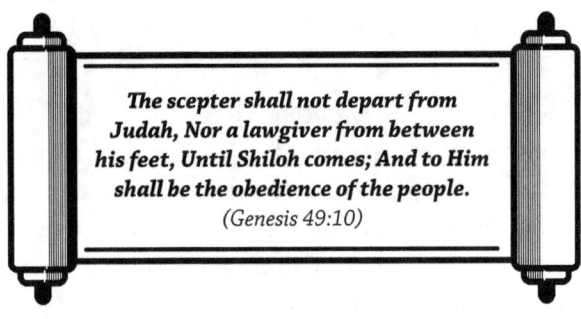

The scepter shall not depart from Judah, Nor a lawgiver from between his feet, Until Shiloh comes; And to Him shall be the obedience of the people.
(Genesis 49:10)

A SPECIAL BLESSING FOR JUDAH

Jacob dwelt in the land of Egypt for seventeen years. He and his family had a good life in the land of Goshen—and for very good reason. This area of Egypt was one of the most productive areas in the country, and the Israelites knew how to work! Immediately they went about establishing themselves as farmers, ranchers, and builders. In that pleasant section of Egypt they lived, grew, were educated, worshiped the LORD God, and enjoyed family life. And grow they did; they multiplied by leaps and bounds!

Jacob enjoyed every minute of it. Watching his family increase and develop was sheer delight—but above all, the "cradle" for the Messiah was being formed before his very eyes. The nation that was promised to Abraham was on its way in development. Jacob also realized that as Israel grew, so did his age. The LORD God had blessed him with 147 years of blessings in His kingdom. He was well aware that his work as God's servant was coming to an end in this world—and therefore some final details were in order.

With that in mind, he called Joseph before him and requested that he swear that he would carry his father's earthly remains back to the land of Canaan to be buried with Abraham and Sara, Isaac and Rebekah, as well as Leah. *(Note: As you recall, Rachel had died when giving birth to Benjamin on their way back from Mesopotamia. Her earthly remains were buried near Bethlehem.)*

Secondly, and more importantly, before he left this life, Jacob had to attend to one last very important task. What might that be? He needed to lay a special blessing upon each of his sons. His threefold blessing upon Judah calls for our special attention. The reason for giving special consideration to Jacob's God-given proclamation upon Judah was this: Judah was the God-ordained carrier of that sacred Messianic promise. For that reason Jacob's blessing upon his son Judah was and is particularly significant. Here it is:

FACET ONE

"Judah, you are he whom your brothers shall praise;
Your hand shall be on the neck of your enemies;
Your father's children shall bow down before you.
Judah is a lion's whelp; (young lion)
From the prey, my son, you have gone up.
He bows down, he lies down as a lion;
And as a lion, who shall rouse him?" (Genesis 49:8–9)

Since Judah was the tribe in which the promise of salvation would be preserved, all of the other tribes of Israel were obligated to hold the nation of Judah in particularly high esteem. The strength and ruling force of the tribe of Judah is here poeticized by Jacob: As such, Judah is described as the most powerful of all the tribes of Israel. Many would be its enemies, both spiritual and physical. But by God's grace Judah would stand strong against its most powerful and hostile opponents. This part of Jacob's blessing carries us back to that all-important promise of God given to his grandfather, Abraham:

"I will bless those who bless you, and I will curse him who curses you. And in you all the families of the earth shall be blessed" (Genesis 12:3). This is applied directly to the tribe of Judah— the tribe from which the Messiah would come. Therefore, all who would oppose the tribe of Judah would in effect be opposing God. And those hostile to God would never prevail—not then, not now, not ever! Jacob carried this thought on beautifully in the second facet of his blessing:

FACET TWO

"The scepter shall not depart from Judah,
Nor a lawgiver from between his feet,
Until Shiloh comes;
And to Him shall be the obedience of the people" (Genesis 49:10).

What has the scepter to do with the promise of the Messiah? Well, a staff or scepter was often held by rulers. As they sat on their throne or place of honor, the scepter was placed between their feet. This was symbolic of their imperial authority or sovereignty. So in Jacob's blessing he was proclaiming that the rule of Israel would remain in the hands of Judah **until Shiloh comes** (Genesis 49:10).

Shiloh! Now, who was that? It is a Hebrew word which means "rest." This ultimate "rest" is descriptive of an Individual—a Person who is to come. This God-sent Individual, the Author and Source of true rest is none other than the Prince of Peace—the Messiah—the Giver of true spiritual rest—the Savior of all the world. Through Him all mankind would find true peace, total spiritual "rest" in the midst of a world filled with hate, crime, godlessness, and violence of every kind. In Him would be found the **peace of God, which surpasses all understanding** (Philippians 4:7).

Indeed, it has been said, and we concur: This is one of the most remarkable and inspiring Messianic promises in the entire Old Testament. Jacob was moved by the Spirit of God to narrow the focus of His people down to this one individual—namely, Shiloh, the coming Messiah, the Seed of the woman, the Savior of all mankind. By faith in Him people all over the world would be gathered together into God's blessed kingdom for time and forever.

Yes, Judah would be and remain the dominant tribe among the tribes of Israel until Shiloh would come. When the Messiah, true God from eternity, would enter the picture upon this Earth, then He alone was to be the central focus for Israel and for all people the world over. Jacob was inspired to make it crystal clear: **"To Him shall be the obedience of the people"** (Genesis 49:10).

This passage from our LORD's Word is all-important—for when Shiloh would finally arrive, Judah and national Israel would then lose their special significance. Their God-given purpose will have been accomplished. Remember? Their God-given purpose was to produce the Christ, the Savior of all the world. When that divine and world-changing task would stand accomplished, then people everywhere were to look to Shiloh, the world's Savior, for their spiritual rest and peace for time and for eternity.

As has been mentioned previously, no nation in the history of mankind has ever had or ever will have such an esteemed calling, distinction, and purpose as did Israel. Yet, sad to say, when Christmas finally came, when Shiloh, the Savior of all the world was born, the very nation that was given that monumental privilege of producing the Christ would by-and-large reject Him. Likewise, they generally rejected the prophets that God sent before Him to guide them to the most precious Gift that mankind would ever receive.

Another of the saddest verses in Holy Scripture records Israel's infamous rejection of the Messiah: **He came to His own, and His own did not receive Him** (John 1:11). And in the midst of that rejection, Shiloh—the Christ—the Son of the living God—that One who left the bliss of heaven to become the Savior of all, fervently and passionately called out to his fellow Israelites:

"O Jerusalem, Jerusalem, the one who kills the prophets and stones those who are sent to her! How often I wanted to gather

**your children together, as a hen gathers her brood under her
wings, but you were not willing! See! Your house is left to you
desolate; and assuredly, I say to you, you shall not see Me until
the time comes when you say, 'Blessed is He who comes in the
name of the LORD!'"** (Luke 13:34–35)

Indeed, it shall ever be true as long as this world stands, that no one
will be able to see and confess the Christ as their Savior and LORD until
their eyes have been opened by the power of the Spirit and they have
been moved to confess by that same Spirit: **"Blessed is He who comes
in the name if the LORD!"** (Luke 13:35)

By rejecting the Christ of God, the Seed of the woman, one becomes
a stranger from the covenants of promise, having no hope and without
God in the world (Ephesians 2:12).

Now we come to:

FACET THREE

Binding his donkey to the vine,
And his donkey's colt to the choice vine,
He washed his garments in wine,
And his clothes in the blood of grapes.
His eyes are darker than wine,
And his teeth whiter than milk *(Genesis 49:11–12).*

Jacob became rather poetic in his description of Shiloh and the
kingdom of the coming Messiah. In Judah everything would be
abundant, lush, and filled with the glory of Shiloh. The tribe of Judah
in the land of promise would be blessed beyond words because of
the special purpose assigned to it. Its grape vines as well as other
produce from the field and its flocks and herds would grow and yield
superabundantly.

All of this was symbolic—a dramatic picture of the magnificent fullness of grace that would be displayed in the spiritual kingdom of Shiloh—the Seed of the woman—the Messiah—the Savior of the world, for in His kingdom nothing would be lacking. Rather, there would be abundant beauty, glory, mercy, and blessing. In Him would be found every good and perfect gift which brings true happiness and peace here as well as eternal joy forever. An unknown author does his best to capture and put into words the adoration and joy that every believer wishes to proclaim when beholding Shiloh, the Messiah, our Savior and Lord:

> *Beautiful Savior, King of Creation,*
> *Son of God and Son of Man!*
> *Truly I'd love Thee,*
> *Truly I'd serve Thee,*
> *Light of my soul, my Joy, my Crown.*

> *Fair are the meadows, Fair are the woodlands,*
> *Robed in flow'rs of blooming spring;*
> *Jesus is fairer,*
> *Jesus is purer;*
> *He makes our sorr'wing spirit sing.*

> *Fair is the sunshine, Fair is the moonlight,*
> *Bright the sparkling stars on high;*
> *Jesus shines brighter,*
> *Jesus shines purer,*
> *Than all the angels in the sky.*

> *Beautiful Savior, Lord of the nations,*
> *Son of God and Son of Man!*
> *Glory and honor,*
> *Praise, adoration,*
> *Now and forevermore be Thine!*
> *(TLH 657)*

When Jacob had finished his words of blessing upon his sons, he **drew his feet up into the bed and breathed his last** (Genesis 49:33). Joseph was very thankful to have had his father with him for the last seventeen years of his father's life. Their mutual love was obvious and openly on display. When Jacob gave up his spirit, Joseph **fell on his father's face, and wept over him, and kissed him** (Genesis 50:1). The brothers witnessed it all. That intense love between Jacob and Joseph was moving, to say the least.

However, once again the brothers' hearts were crushed. They could not help but remember. This was the very love that drove them to commit those jealousy-motivated crimes against their brother and father. Once more they were overtaken with guilt and grief for what they had done. Anxious thoughts dominated their minds. As extensive funeral arrangements were made to honor this man of God, the brothers were sick with guilt.

Their father was dead. Now what? They could not help but wonder: **"Perhaps Joseph will hate us, and may actually repay us for all the evil which we did to him"** (Genesis 50:15).

Again, their atrocious words and actions of bygone days tortured their hearts and souls. As it has been said, "Nothing is as torturous as a guilt-ridden soul." So even though their brother, Joseph, had fully assured them of his heart-felt forgiveness while their father was living . . . suddenly their father was no more.

The brothers felt compelled to clearly and openly make their confession. It was time to reveal to Joseph something that he needed to know—so in haste they sent Joseph this message: "Before your father died he commanded, saying, **'Thus you shall say to Joseph: "I beg you, please forgive the trespass of your brothers and their sin, for they did evil to you."' Now please, forgive the trespass of the servants of the God of your father"** (Genesis 50:16–17).

Finally, FINALLY, in no uncertain terms the brothers had fully confessed their terrible, godless words and actions to their father before he left this world. In turn, some of Jacob's final words were a plea for Joseph to forgive his brothers for their wicked crimes against him.

How did Joseph receive this rather unexpected request? **Joseph wept** (Genesis 50:17). In addition, when the brothers had gained an audience with Joseph, they **fell down before his face, and they said: "Behold, we are your servants"** (Genesis 50:18).

All he could do was to offer reassuring and kind words to them: **"Do not be afraid, for am I in the place of God? But as for you, you meant evil against me; but God meant it for good, in order to bring it about as it is this day, to save many people alive. Now therefore, do not be afraid; I will provide for you and your little ones"** (Genesis 50:19–21).

What a good-hearted, forgiving spirit is evident in the mind, heart, and words of Joseph! This man of God fully realized that God can easily turn evil into good. This was fully obvious to him. To be sure, his unforgettable past was sharply emblazoned on his memory. One satanic action after another—jealousy, hatred, slavery, false accusations, incarceration—God turned it all into good for Joseph and his family. And most of all, God used it all to advance His design to crush the head of Satan and restore to all humanity everything that had been lost in the Garden.

It is our heartfelt prayer that all of us will be moved to more clearly recognize the LORD God working in each of our lives every day. Of course, we will run into obstacles and trying circumstances continually as we walk through this world dominated by Satan and sin. Yet we need to be assured that God is on our side; He knows how to turn evil into good and wrong into right.

Yes, we need to be assured that God's wondrous supervision is going on in our lives constantly. Why is God so good to us? Very simply, because He loves us—because we are His very own children by faith in His redemptive love for us through Shiloh—the Messiah—our Lord Jesus Christ—God's Christmas Gift to us all. Through Him and His vicarious atonement on Calvary's tree we have the ultimate blessing of God's freely-given love. The very first words uttered by our Savior from the pinnacle of the cross will help us grasp the nature of God's truly forgiving mercy toward us all: **"Father, forgive them for they do not know what they do"** (Luke 23:34).

The first words that our Savior spoke,
While hanging on the tree,
They to His Father are addressed.
This is His final plea.
What might He say before He dies?
What should He pray for here?
What is the most important thing
To ask His Father dear?
Should He call down the wrath of God
On those who nailed Him there?
Or should He pray for respite from
The pain beyond compare?
No prayers like these would cross His lips,
Nor flow forth on His part;
But rather, mercy for the ones
Who crushed His sacred heart.
"Forgive them" was His only plea.
And to this very day,
These words of grace and love for all
Continually say,
"Forgiveness is for everyone,"
They cry out night and day.
They intercede before God's throne,
Provide for us the way
Into the presence of our God.

By faith we're now at one
With God our blessed Father, and
The Spirit and the Son.
And so these words of love and grace
Help us to boldly pray,
"Forgive us LORD, for Jesus' sake,
Our sins and faults each day."
(Poems of Prayer & Praise, page 9)

PRAYER

LORD God, Your glory, Your peace, Your forgiving love for me and for all mankind echoes forth down through the generations. Please, LORD, permit me to contribute some tiny effort to the labors of Your glorious kingdom of peace, joy, and confident hope in the midst of a world of hopelessness, sadness, and corruption. Your message of peace and joy in Shiloh, the Messiah, gives true rest, peace, joy, and life in an otherwise hopeless world. Indeed, our loving Savior clearly reminds us why He came into this world of sin when He assures us: **"I have come that they may have life, and that they may have it more abundantly."** (John 10:10). So also, **He who has the Son has life; he who does not have the Son of God does not have life** (I John 5:12). LORD God, embolden me to do my small part in giving this blessed gift of life to others. In Your holy, forgiving name I pray. Amen.

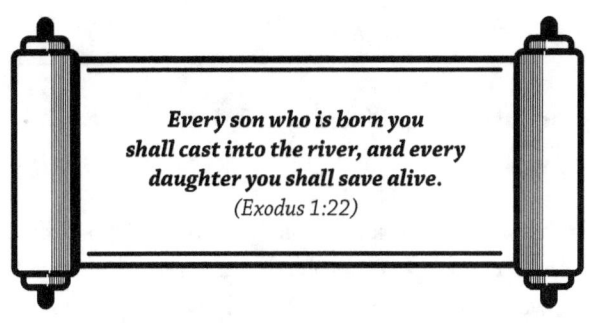

*Every son who is born you
shall cast into the river, and every
daughter you shall save alive.*
(Exodus 1:22)

GOD CHOOSES MOSES TO LEAD HIS PEOPLE

Apparently Joseph was the first of the brothers to leave this life and be ushered in spirit into the joys of eternity. At one hundred and ten years of age and having finished his earthly pilgrimage, Joseph's earthly remains were buried in Egypt. His descendants as well as the rest of the chosen children of God continued to enjoy life in Egypt.

God's chosen people became prosperous and multiplied rapidly. In the words of Holy Scripture, **the children of Israel were fruitful and increased abundantly, multiplied and grew exceedingly mighty; and the land was filled with them** (Exodus 1:7). Life was good, as the saying goes; they had plenty of everything they needed, and the blessing of the LORD God rested upon them. It is estimated that the population of Israel grew to several million during their 400 years in Egypt.

We can assume that over that period of time many different Pharaohs headed the Egyptian government. In His Word to us the LORD God calls our attention to one particular ruler of Egypt. This Pharaoh thought that he recognized a possible threat to the national security of Egypt. He summarized it like this: **"Look, the people of the children of Israel are more and mightier than we; come, let us deal wisely with them, lest they multiply, and it happen, in the event of war,**

that they also join our enemies and fight against us" (Exodus 1:9–10).

It's nothing new, is it? History books are filled with it. In this writer's lifetime our country has been involved in numerous wars, and still there are rumors of war, fears of war, threatening war, and actual war! As it was . . . so it is . . . and ever shall be. As history demonstrates, sinful humanity simply cannot and/or will not learn to live together in peace. Endless are the so-called reasons for wars among people, rulers, and nations.

The question has been rightly asked: *"When will they ever learn that wars are generally savage exercises in futility?"* History clearly documents the fruitlessness of this ungodly behavior between rulers, people, and nations—yet it goes on. From swords and bows to sophisticated guided missiles, hydrogen—atomic bombs, and now the threat of cyber warfare! Sinful humanity will not learn! It's the way of life . . . and of death!

In other words, the kingdoms of this world are just that—"of this world." As a result, wars have been fought and will continue until this world is swallowed up in the fires of God's judgment. Besides, we should never forget that Satan works overtime to stir up animosity, greed, ill will, ruthlessness, and killing! Thus it will be until this world has run its course.

Our Savior told us about the days in which we now live and describes them perfectly: **"You will hear of wars and rumors of wars. See that you are not alarmed, for this must take place, but the end is not yet. For nation will rise against nation, and kingdom against kingdom, and there will be famines and earthquakes in various places. All these are but the beginning of the birth pains. Then they will deliver you up to tribulation and put you to death, and you will be hated by all nations for my name's**

**sake. And then many will fall away and betray one another and
hate one another. Then many false prophets will arise and lead
many astray. And because lawlessness will be increased, the
love of many will grow cold. But he who endures to the end will
be saved. And this gospel of the kingdom will be proclaimed
throughout the whole world as a testimony to all nations, and
then the end will come"** (Matthew 24:6–14 ESV). So it was, is, and
ever shall be until the end!

Before us is an example of the atrocities visited upon innocent
victims by Satan's henchman. On what did Pharaoh base his horrendous
actions? He used one premise: **"In the event of war"** (Exodus 1:10).
The king of Egypt tried to solve what he considered to be a serious
national security risk for his nation of Egypt through the use (of all
things!) slavery and murder. This was his approach—atrocious as it was
even for a dictator.

To help us understand Pharaoh's thought process a bit, we should
be aware that centuries of time had passed since Jacob and his entire
family had moved to Egypt, yet in many ways the Hebrews still were
considered mere foreigners—they simply were not recognized as
belonging to the Egyptian population or culture.

The Hebrew "aliens" had their own style of life, entertainment,
schooling, religion, worship, etc. Although Joseph had been prominent
in the Egyptian government of his time, as far as the current Pharaoh
was concerned, Joseph was nothing more than a figure from the distant
past. It appears that the present king was oblivious to the situation
under which the children of Abraham had come to dwell among them
in the first place. I suppose he might have wondered: *"How and for what
reason did these people come here, anyway?"*

However, there they were, and one thing Pharaoh knew for certain:
The population of those foreigner was growing by leaps and bounds.

This was not only "getting under his skin," but he was concerned about their true allegiance to Egypt. So the king got to thinking: *"Just wait a minute, here. Maybe we can solve this huge national problem in one "fell swoop!" We can use these people for a beneficial cause and maybe at the same time curtail their population. We have plenty of work to do here in Egypt. We've got building projects, gardens to tend, farming operations to carry out, etc., etc. Why not use these foreigners . . . make slaves out of them, and we can 'kill two birds with one stone.' We'll work them so hard that they'll be totally worn out and won't have the energy to produce offspring. We can in this way limit population growth and accomplish great things for Egypt at the same time. What a brilliant scheme"*...he thought!

Well, as worldly governments do, his plan was put into motion. Pharaoh went about organizing a corps of taskmasters, who were placed in charge of huge numbers of slaves from the Hebrew population. The people of God were forced to do everything and anything that the foremen decided needed doing. They made mortar and bricks, erected buildings and built roads, worked in gardens and on farms. And of course, the work in those days was done primarily by man-power and beasts of burden. All of it was carried out under the harsh dictates and treatment of Pharaoh's cruel slave drivers. In the language of Holy Scripture: **They made their lives bitter with hard bondage—in mortar, in brick, and in all manner of service in the field** (Exodus 1:14).

But what Pharaoh didn't know was this—he was not merely dealing with Hebrew slaves, for actually he was pitting himself against God! The people of Israel were God's people, chosen not because they themselves were special in any way, but they were selected for God's special purpose. As we remember—God would use them as His cradle for the Messiah!

As a result, with God's blessing upon them, **the more they** (the Egyptians) **afflicted them, the more they** (the people of God)

multiplied and grew (Exodus 1:12). Even the king had to admit that his plan wasn't working. Slavery was not accomplishing his intended goals . . . at all. Oh, without a doubt, much work was getting done—but his chief concern was that the population growth of the children of Israel continued unabated! The harder they worked, the more children were born in Israel! That wasn't the way it was all supposed to work! That was not in accord with the king's plan!

This became an obsession with the Pharaoh—for after all, he was the "big man"—the absolute ruler of this very prosperous nation. He could solve this problem . . . couldn't he? There had to be a way to interrupt this population growth among the Hebrew people. Drastic measures were called for. So once again . . . he thought he had the solution.

So in his godless and evil mind, Pharaoh decided that the most effective way to accomplish his goal was to adopt another extremely cruel and heartless measure. In plain and simple terms, he organized a program to . . . kill the male babies AFTER they were born! Really? Yes, indeed. That was his heartless plan . . . kill all male babies at birth!

So, how could he accomplish this murderous scheme? Well, he started by finding out who the chief midwives were that served the Hebrew population. Then he gave them an order and expected them to carry it out. The order was unambiguous: "Kill the male babies! When a child is born to a Hebrew woman, if it is a male, kill him! If it is female, she may live." Doesn't that make one shudder? Of course it does! It's ugly! It's inhuman! It was gross, unmitigated murder!

But, I suppose someone might think and/or say, "*Well, those were people who didn't know any better. A slave's life didn't mean much to Pharaoh or Egyptian society at that time. They were . . . like . . . uncivilized in their murderous ambitions.*" Oh, really! So in our "enlightened" day and age, we would never permit such a slaughter of infants . . . would we? Oh, but we do! Americans do it every day! In just one year (2012), here in our "very civilized" United States of America, it has been concluded that 1.2 million lives of unborn children were legally snuffed out. In fact, since 1973, more than 57,000,000 babies were put to death right here in our own country! Yes, they were literally murdered!

Will anyone be held accountable? Absolutely! They will all be held accountable before the throne of the Almighty God, who has said clearly and unmistakably, "YOU SHALL NOT MURDER." Yet according to the laws of our land, murdering unborn babies is perfectly legal. Our government has declared the verdict: "Not guilty." My friends in Christ, this is all done in our highly civilized nation, within the confines of the law of the land.

How could such a thing be justified? As you know it is carried on in the name of "women's rights"(of all things!). Women are given the right to give a "doctor" the order: "Kill my baby!" Why? Simply because they want to! It should also be noted that in our very "progressive" society, if someone other than the mother causes the death of an unborn infant, such a person is regularly charged with murder. Of course! That's proper. On the other hand, the mother has the right to purposely commit the same crime, and it is perfectly legal! Oh LORD, have mercy and move our people to open their eyes to this gross and godless savagery committed every day in our nation . . . protected by our godless laws!

So, how did this premeditated, murderous scheme turn out in Egypt? Well, the Hebrew mid-wives secretly refused to carry out the order. Why? Because **the midwives feared God** (Exodus 1:21). PRAISE THE LORD! But Satan's henchmen were not done yet; with nowhere else to turn, the king appealed to the Egyptians at large. He ordered them all, "Kill the Hebrew male babies!" How? Here's his answer:

"Every son who is born you shall cast into the river, and every daughter you shall save alive" (Exodus 1:22). This murderous program was carried out with vigor. Of course, a huge amount of organizing had to be done in order to put this ill-conceived, satanically-engineered notion into motion. We assume that law-officers had to be assigned to observe pregnant women non-stop. After all, they had to make certain that they would catch the would-be-mother in the "nick of time" to commit this evil act.

So, when those tiny male infants came into the world, they were mercilessly torn from the arms of their weeping and screaming mothers and fathers. Savagely they were ripped from the homes of the Hebrew families amidst unbearable anguish, and into the Nile River these helpless little children were cast by the hundreds . . . yea, by the thousands! Satan, the father of lies and the promoter of murder, was having his heartless way as countless infants were flung to their watery graves!

(Note: Living in our present world, with the epidemic of abortion everywhere we may wonder: "Why didn't Pharaoh institute such a practice? Why didn't he order that all of the babies of pregnant mothers in the Hebrew population be killed before they were born?" Well, here is one possible answer: According to various sources it appears that abortion (as well as genocide) was practiced among all ancient nations of the Mediterranean world. So might it be that Pharaoh, in his evilly twisted mind wanted to preserve the female babies to become sex slaves and produce bi-racial boys, whose Egyptian genetics spared them from the genocide? In order to accomplish this, he had to wait until the sex of babies could be determined— before he selected the boys for slaughter.)

However, in the midst of all of this terror and slaughter of little infants, we need to stop for a bit, take a deep breath, and hear the wonderful story of a family of God who defied the king's order. Here's the God—inspired episode in all of its wondrous beauty: There was a Hebrew man and wife from the house of Levi, one of Jacob's sons. They had already been blessed with a daughter; then by God's grace they were also granted the gift of a son. We know how much that meant to them, don't we? Of course, they loved their son with all their heart. They took every possible precaution to hide their child from the watchful eyes of the government vigilantes for three long and watchful months.

Finally the parents had to own up to reality. As their precious son grew, this secret of theirs was bound to leak out. They were certain that the king's murdering militia would soon discover their secret, arrive at their door, snatch their only son from them—that precious gift of God . . . and put him to death. So what could they do?

The mother concocted a plan. It was a long shot and risky—but something had to be done. She made a basket out of bulrushes. *(Similar to the long, firm stalks of cat-tails)* She waterproofed the basket with asphalt and pitch, wrapped her dear treasure in a warm blanket, placed him in the basket . . . and closed the lid. With basket in hand, she cautiously made her way down to the banks of the river. Carefully she hid the basket with her beloved son in the reeds close to the river's edge. There he would be safe and perhaps be discovered by some compassionate person.

Yes, it was risky—but the LORD God oversaw it all. Trust in the gracious compassion of God filled every moment as the parents waited for the outcome of their tension-filled scheme. Maybe . . . just maybe, someone from the families of Egypt might see the basket, investigate the contents, and be moved by natural human compassion to adopt this tiny infant.

Now, there was another rather brilliant facet to the mother's plan. As you remember, they also had a daughter. Miriam by name. To her was given the very important task of nonchalantly watching from a distance. Careful surveillance was all-important, and it paid off, for soon the daughter of Pharaoh came strolling down to the river to bathe. Of course, she was accompanied by her entourage of maidens who walked along the river's edge, making certain that the princess would be safe.

The king's daughter was splashing around in the shallows—enjoying herself. Then, suddenly she stopped. *"What is that?"* she wondered as she spotted what appeared to be a basket among the reeds. *"What could that be?"*

It seemed strange that a basket of that nature was just . . . sitting there bobbing in the shallow water. She called to her personal maid and asked her to investigate. The servant brought the basket to the princess, who immediately opened it. *"Oh, it is a child. It is weeping. Why is this little infant here? I wonder, how long it has been here."* The princess was deeply moved. Upon closer examination she made the obvious deduction, **"This is one of the Hebrews' children"** (Exodus 2:6).

How could she help but be very well aware of her father's decree against all the sons of the Hebrews? Nevertheless, her womanly instinct prevailed. She just couldn't leave this little baby there. But if she turned him in to the authorities . . . well, she had no doubt as to what that would mean. This little child simply melted her heart.

Then, as though on cue . . . it was time for Miriam to enter the scene. And she most certainly did so in an extremely cool and effective way. Calmly she approached the princess and suggested: **"Shall I go and call a nurse for you from the Hebrew women, that she may nurse the child for you?"** (Exodus 2:7)

"What a nice young lady, and what a great idea!" No doubt under the circumstances, there were many young women among the Hebrew population who were bereft of a son and would be more than happy to accept such a responsibility. So this young lady's suggestion made perfect sense. Immediately the princess accepted the offer, and Miriam quickly fetched . . . (who else?) . . . her mother—the mother of infant Moses!

"What a coincidence," one might say. Except that we know better, don't we? The LORD God had His eyes set on this little child already in his mother's womb. In fact, the God-designed purpose for this son of Levi was preordained by the LORD. Is this too overpowering for our little minds to grasp? Maybe—but we must let God be God. Yes, out of all the millions of souls in the Hebrew nation, the LORD God set His eyes on this little child for one purpose and one purpose only. And that purpose was this: The predetermined time spent in Egypt by God's people was up! And this child was chosen by God to become the one who would lead His people out of Egypt to the land that was promised to Abraham, Isaac, and Jacob centuries earlier. Moreover, everything would take place according to God's timetable and in His own predetermined way.

Think of it for a moment. The promise of the Messiah made by God back in the Garden of Eden—the pledge of the Seed of the woman—the One who would come for one God-designated purpose—namely, to crush Satan's wicked head, deliver mankind from the Devil's steely grip, and restore humanity to His original, created purpose. What a pleasure it is to watch the LORD God in the center of it all. Wonderfully amazing to observe, isn't it?

Indeed, it's truly inspiring to follow along as God carefully, slowly, inch by inch, year by year, decade by decade, and century by century moved things in accordance with His divine promise. Yes, we have the opportunity to "go along for the ride"—growing in faith as we take each step with God, fully aware of where we are going and how God manages each detail perfectly along the way for our salvation.

Indeed, Abraham's offspring would become a great nation from which the Christ of God would be born to deliver mankind from spiritual bondage. Each happening along the way, as we travel toward that God-ordained goal, is <u>never</u> merely coincidental. Each occurrence takes place in accordance with the LORD God's will and with an eye upon the resultant blessing for all humanity.

So the time had arrived for His people to leave Egypt and take the next step in God's plan for the redemption of the world through the Seed of the woman. From the tiniest detail to the most colossal miracle, the LORD God had the entire matter firmly in His benevolent hands. So let's just settle back and observe the next step.

OK, so Moses was the hand-picked vessel into whom God would pour the spiritual strength to lead His people out of Egypt toward the land that had already been given to Abraham. To prepare Moses for this daunting task of leading His people to the Land of Promise, his mother, though obviously not aware of God's enormous agenda for her son, taught him well, as godly parents do.

Moses was nurtured in the truth about the one true God. He became well acquainted with the purpose for which God had called Israel—that special mission which was theirs to accomplish. Yet, as far as Pharaoh's daughter was concerned, Moses was <u>her</u> son. He grew up with all the education and earthly benefits available. Even the people generally saw him as the son of the Princess. In fact, she gave him his name. **She called his name Moses,** (drawn out) **saying, "Because I drew him out of the water"** (Exodus 2:10).

So, how about you and me? Should we not realize that each of us is special in God's eyes? Yes, we are! Every one of us has been called by

God into His kingdom of grace. We each have a God-given purpose and place in His wondrous plan of salvation for all people. Of this we are assured by the inspired writer: **God from the beginning chose you for salvation through sanctification by the Spirit and belief in the truth, to which He called you by our gospel, for the obtaining of the glory of our Lord Jesus Christ. . . . Now may your LORD Jesus Christ Himself, and our God and Father, who has loved us and given us everlasting consolation and good hope by grace, comfort your hearts and establish you in every good word and work** (II Thessalonians 2:13,14,16,17).

Indeed, the work of the LORD's kingdom stands before all of us. His divine calling rests upon each of us. Do we, like the Prophet Isaiah, hear **the voice of the LORD, saying: "Whom shall I send, and who will go for Us?"** Do we answer and say with the prophet, **"Here am I! Send me!"** (Isaiah 6:8)?

PRAYER

Oh, LORD, Your ways are marvelous to behold. Each step I take along the way to the fulfillment of Your blessed promise first made in the Garden is filled with Your incredibly miraculous acts and blessing. Your wondrous love for us, who dwell in the midst of Your created world, is awesome to review. LORD, I pray, as I continue to travel on this majestic trip toward the fulfillment of Your promise in the Garden, please, pour out upon me the gift of Your Spirit. For with You in my mind and heart, this journey will continue to be pure joy and strengthening to my faith. This I need, for all around me I witness Satan leading hearts and minds into godless ways and fleshly pursuits. Therefore move me by the power of Your Spirit to openly confess my faith before all by word and deed. And so, may the Devil's ways be stifled and Your kingdom come to many with Your forgiving love and gracious mercy. Through the Seed of the woman, our Savior and LORD, I pray. Amen.

In keeping with this desire, may we join Isaac Watts, and sing with heart and soul:

> *Oh, bless the LORD, my soul!*
> *Let all within me join*
> *And aid my tongue to bless His name*
> *Whose favors are divine.*
>
> *Oh, bless the LORD, my soul,*
> *Nor let His mercies lie*
> *Forgotten in unthankfulness*
> *And without praises die.*
>
> *His wondrous works and ways*
> *He made by Moses known,*
> *And sent the world His truth and grace*
> *By His beloved Son. (CW 238:1.2.5)*

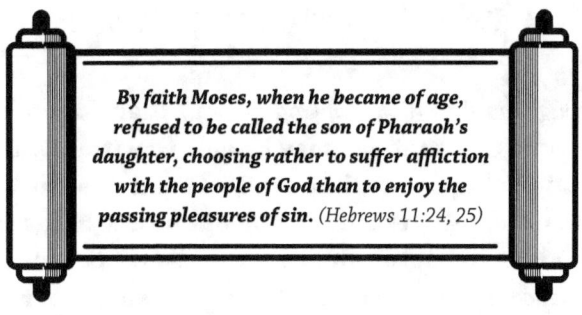

By faith Moses, when he became of age,
refused to be called the son of Pharaoh's
daughter, choosing rather to suffer affliction
with the people of God than to enjoy the
passing pleasures of sin. (Hebrews 11:24, 25)

MOSES CALLED INTO GOD'S SPECIAL SERVICE

Under the guidance of the LORD God, Moses grew up as a prince in the palace of the Pharaoh of Egypt. He became a strong and healthy young man. He was, of course, schooled in the ways of Egypt, but above all he was educated in the will and ways of the one true God of heaven and earth. As we remember, his caretaker and teacher in every facet of his life was none other than his natural mother. She quite thoroughly taught him the truth about the one true God and His long-range purpose for His people Israel.

What can we learn from this? Well, this may help us all realize that in the midst of a world of idolatry and unbelief, we can effectively raise our children to know the one true and living God of heaven and earth. The power and strength of all of those around us who oppose God and His Word are no match against the strength of God and the power of His Word of truth. The Apostle Paul was inspired by God to say it just right: **My brethren, be strong in the Lord and in the power of His might. Put on the whole armor of God, that you may be able to stand against the wiles of the devil. For we do not wrestle against flesh and blood, but against principalities, against powers, against the rulers of the darkness of this age, against spiritual hosts of wickedness in the heavenly places.** (*Note: The devil and his legions are outside of our physical reach. They can be held at* *bay only through our faithful use of God's Word.)* **Therefore take up the whole armor of God that you may be able to withstand in the evil day, and having done all, to stand. Stand therefore, having girded your waist with truth, having put on the breastplate of righteousness, and having shod your feet with the preparation of the gospel of peace; above all, taking the shield of faith with which you will be able to quench all the fiery darts of the wicked one. And take the helmet of salvation, and the sword of the Spirit, which is the word of God** (Ephesians 6:10–17).

Parents, it is our calling to not only do all we can to secure our children's physical and mental wellbeing, but above all it is our God-given privileged responsibility to vigorously care for their spiritual welfare—that is, bring them up in the fear (reverence) and knowledge of the one true God. As the Psalmist puts it so well: **Behold, children are a heritage from the LORD, the fruit of the womb is His reward** (Psalm 127:3). Pray God that He will move us to treat them as such! Yes, my friends, it is a responsibility that we may not ignore— namely, to teach our children about God, what He has said to them and us in His Word. It is all-important that they be shown His marvelous love for them in the Messiah, their Savior and Lord. That's the priceless privilege with which Moses was blessed throughout his developing years. It is the blessing of God that every child deserves and needs.

Time passed; Moses grew up into manhood and celebrated his fortieth birthday. As he grew in his relationship with God and became stronger in his faith, he was increasingly agitated by the conditions under which his brethren in the LORD labored. He witnessed the severity of the taskmasters and the miserable life to which his brethren were being subjected. Before his very eyes, day after day after day the unjust conditions and the merciless mistreatment of his people was before him. Was he to conduct himself as royalty, the son of the princess, and simply disregard the horrendous ill treatment of his brethren who were called by God for that special mission of spiritually saving all people? Sooner or later a choice had to be made.

The writer to the Hebrews was inspired to explain it this way: **By faith Moses, when he became of age, refused to be called the son of Pharaoh's daughter, choosing rather to suffer affliction with the people of God than to enjoy the passing pleasures of sin** (Hebrews 11:24, 25). Although Moses was in a position far different than most of us, God's faithful are regularly called upon to make choices as they pass through this sin-corrupted world. The contradiction between the lifestyles of the unbelieving world and the words and ways of God are before us every day. And yes, our sinful nature is only too anxious to respond positively to the Devil's lure. For that reason we spend much time in prayer to our LORD God: **"Do not lead us into temptation but deliver us from the evil one"** (Luke 11:4). That is why we as the children of God spend time regularly bowing before the Word of our LORD and drinking in the messages of guidance and forgiving love from the Spirit of our God.

So what should Moses do? How should he react to the injustices on display every day as he observed the Egyptian overseers mistreating his people? As one might suppose, finally he just couldn't take it any longer. One day as he witnessed an Egyptian taskmaster beating one of his Hebrew brethren, he snapped! He looked this way and that way, and when he saw no one watching, he killed the Egyptian and hid him in the sand (Exodus 2:12).

So there Moses was with murder on his hands. The son of the princess or not, Moses was certain that this would not go well for him—especially if this should come to Pharaoh's attention. But what if someone had seen the struggle, the murder, the burial? Very likely someone saw—someone might know. He was right, for the very next day as he tried to stop a fight between two Hebrew men, one blurted out these tell-tale words: **"Who made you a prince and a judge over**

us? Do you intend to kill me as you killed the Egyptian?" (Exodus 2:14)

There it was—no doubt about it. Since this was known by one, soon it would be known by many. As was expected, finally news of his crime reached the throne of Pharaoh. Of course, he became enraged! Although Moses was the prince of the palace and was the adopted son of Pharaoh's daughter—no matter. This was too much—this could not be tolerated! As a result: **He** (Pharaoh) **sought to kill Moses** (Exodus 2:15). And when the ruler of this mighty nation of Egypt chose to take such action, who or what would stand in his way? Forget about a trial, a judge, a jury. Pharaoh was all of those! His word was the law!

So now, what should Moses do? There wasn't much that he could do except flee for his life! But where . . . where should he go? There was no place in that country where he would be safe, so he left the only home he knew and "high-tailed" it to the east without any particular destination in mind. The desert—that was the safest place he could think of. He simply left humanity behind and journeyed to the east and then south—far from the reach of the Egyptian government.

Finally he found himself in the Sinai Peninsula, the land of Midian. There he began to relax . . . somewhat. Unknown to him, he was actually among distant relatives. (*Note: after the death of Sarah, Abraham married Keturah. Midian was one of their sons.*) In Midia Moses was unknown, and there he could finally feel free from danger and begin life anew.

One fine morning as he sat quietly relaxing by a well where shepherds and shepherdesses watered their flocks, it just so happened that a number of maidens arrived with their flocks of sheep. As they went about their task of drawing water and filling the water troughs, other shepherds arrived, barged their way in, and rudely pushed aside the shepherdesses and their sheep.

"Hey, hey, hey! Wait a minute here!" Moses could not stand by and watch as **ruffians** bullied the girls, so he stepped in, stood up for them, and helped them water their sheep. Since such intervention was rather unusual, when the girls arrived home, they just had to inform their father of this rather unique experience: **"An Egyptian delivered us from the hand of the shepherds, and he also drew enough water for us and watered the flock"** (Exodus 2:19).

It so happened that their father was the priest of Midian and given to generous hospitality. Of course, the father was upset that his daughters had not shown better manners to their new friend at the well— Egyptian or not. He felt that they should have invited him to their home for refreshments and dinner. *"Maybe it's not too late yet."* So, their father decided to set matters aright: **"And where is he? Why is it that you have left the man? Call him, that he may eat bread"** (Exodus 2:20).

Of course, nobody had a cell phone . . . so they scrambled back to the well . . . were able to find Moses, and invited him to their home. To make a long story short, Moses became part of their family and eventually married one of the daughters, Zipporah.

OK. What do you think? A stroke of luck? Some might say so, but we know better . . . don't we? The LORD God is moving things in exactly the direction that he chooses for the result that He wishes. And we know what that is, don't we? So let's just sit tight, watch and wait, and observe the hand of God moving things according to His will.

So there Moses was, far away from all the trappings of princely living. In fact, he became a shepherd working for his father-in-law. What a change—from a prince with all the luxuries of the kingdom of Egypt at his feet, to a lowly shepherd on the rocky hills and sandy plains of Sinai. Indeed, it was a transformation—but in many ways a welcome one.

His peaceful shepherding led him into many different and strange areas of the Sinai peninsula. He was away from everything and everyone—except God. That's the way the LORD God wanted it to be. As we remember, God had Moses in His sights from the day of his conception—from the day of his birth—from the day that he lay there in that home-made basket in the river among the reeds. Every day God knew where he was, what he was doing, and what he was going to do. It's amazing (isn't it?)—how the LORD God goes about His marvelous work so very patiently but with absolute determination and resolve to accomplish His preordained goals.

So, what's next? Well, after forty years of shepherding in the wilderness, (yes, forty years passed, and Moses was eighty years of age!), it was time for God to have a talk with His chosen vessel. So how was God going to accomplish that out in the deserts of Sinai? Let's just watch and see.

One day as Moses was herding his sheep in the southern part of the Sinai Peninsula, he came near to what came to be known as "the mountain of God," Mount Horeb. *(Note: Sometimes this mountain is referred to by the more familiar name of Mount Sinai.)* There on the foothills of Sinai an event occurred that became branded in the mind and heart of Moses for the rest of his life—for **the Angel of the LORD appeared to him in a flame of fire from the midst of a bush** (Exodus 3:2). *(Note: There's that expression again: **the Angel of the LORD.**)*

Fire in the midst of a bush? Rather unusual, wouldn't you say? There were no lightning strikes or storms around, so what could have caused this fire? Out of the ordinary? It surely was, and it got Moses' attention, didn't it? That's exactly what God wanted. As Moses watched the flaming bush, there was something rather strange about it. What was that? It didn't disintegrate! It just kept on burning without burning up! Moses could do nothing but just stare at it. Ah-ha! Again, that is exactly what God had planned. While Moses' attention was riveted on the burning bush (that didn't burn up), the LORD God spoke: **"Moses, Moses!"** (Exodus 3:4)

A voice called him by name! There was no one else out there in this desolate country—just Moses, the sheep and . . . this burning bush! And a voice was calling his name from the bush! It was as clear as day. Was Moses losing his mind? Was he hallucinating? Had he been out there in the sun and in the wilderness by himself just a bit too long? Though Moses likely felt that it was all somewhat surreal, he cautiously and weakly answered: **"Here I am"** (Exodus 3:4).

Now, what followed was extremely important. God's entire plan of salvation for the whole world hinged upon this rather strange encounter out in the middle of . . . nowhere. First of all, Moses needed to comprehend that this was a conversation between him and the one true, living God of heaven and earth! This was neither a dream nor a delusion. In fact, it involved an extraordinary and holy calling from none other than the LORD God.

Yes, Moses needed to realize that this was the One about whom his mother had spoken at length and in detail. This was the one true God who had called the nation of Israel for that one special purpose of producing the Savior for all people—that special Seed of the woman. So, while Moses stood before the burning bush watching the flames reach for the heavens, God clearly set the proper stage for this one very special purpose: **"Do not draw near this place. Take your sandals off your feet, for the place where you stand is holy ground. I am the God of your Father—the God of Abraham, the God of Isaac, and the God of Jacob"** (Exodus 3:5–6).

Wouldn't that be enough to cause any of us to hide our face and fall on our knees in holy awe and reverence? It affected Moses exactly like that: **He hid his face, for he was afraid to look upon God** (Exodus 3:6).

That is precisely the reaction that the LORD God wanted. He wanted the undivided, awe-stricken attention of Moses. Then the LORD laid out before him the somewhat startling purpose of this meeting.

And the LORD said: "I have surely seen the oppression of My people who are in Egypt, and have heard their cry because of their taskmasters, for I know their sorrow. So I have come down to deliver them out of the hand of the Egyptians, and to bring them up from that land to a good and large land, to a land flowing with milk and honey, to a place of the Canaanites and the Hittites and the Amorites and the Perizzites and the Hivites and the Jebusites. Now therefore, behold, the cry of the children of Israel has come to Me, and I have also seen the oppression with which the Egyptians oppress them. Come now, therefore, and I will send you to Pharaoh that you may bring My people, the children of Israel, out of Egypt (Exodus 3:7–10).

What a bombshell! Here was Moses, a contented shepherd—taking care of his father-in-law's sheep out in the desert lands of Sinai—when suddenly, the one and only LORD God was talking to him! Understandably, Moses was utterly flabbergasted. Who wouldn't be? *"Is this a mirage? Is all of this my imagination? Yet who other than God would know about these things? Clearly, this is the LORD God speaking to me! And what He is saying is terrifying,"*

Moses couldn't help but wonder: *"Why me? Here I am, a lowly shepherd. For forty years I have made a way of life for myself out here among the mountains and sandy plains of this wilderness. And now, here I am, eighty years old. I should go back to Egypt where I might still be wanted for murder? Are You kidding me? And, besides all of that, I don't have the gifts . . . I am not equipped for such an unbelievably difficult undertaking."* Valid excuses? Maybe—at least in the mind of Moses—and maybe in our minds also. But, what counted was this: THIS WAS GOD'S WILL!

And since it was God's will, Moses could rest assured that the LORD God would bless with the means to carry it through.

Indeed, how often in our own lives do we make decisions and plans for the future, but then issues grow complicated, and we know not which way to turn. Our future looks dark, and we are overwhelmed with the challenging prospects that seem to lie in our paths. Then we turn to Him who alone can strengthen, lead, and bless. Yes, all of us need to remember that God knows us better than we know ourselves. After all, He produced us, redeemed us, sanctified us, and chose us to be His very own for time and for all eternity. Therefore, we can and should confidently pray:

> *Your way, not mine, O LORD,*
> *However dark it be.*
> *Lead me by Your own hand;*
> *You choose the path for me.*
> *I dare not choose my lot;*
> *I would not if I might,*
> *You choose for me, my God;*
> *So shall I walk aright. (TLH 532:1 adapted)*

PRAYER

Thank you, LORD, for the "burning bush" in my life. My burning bush is Your inspired Word, where You speak to me, encourage me, lead me, guide me, comfort me, and forgive me. As the inspired Psalmist puts it so perfectly, **Your word is a lamp to my feet and a light to my path** (Psalm 119:105). Please, LORD, fill me with Your Spirit that I may strive to walk each day in accordance with your Word of Life. And when I fail because of my weaknesses, please do not cast me aside. Rather, pick me up, speak to me through the "burning bush" of Your Word—work true repentance in my heart—bless me and lead me in Your ways of righteousness. For the sake of the Seed of the woman, Jesus Christ, my Savior and Lord, I pray. Amen.

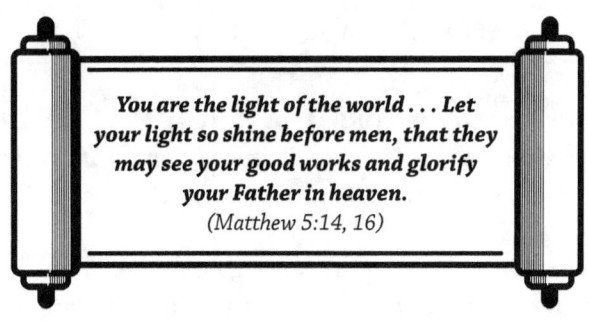

You are the light of the world . . . Let your light so shine before men, that they may see your good works and glorify your Father in heaven.
(Matthew 5:14, 16)

EXCUSES, EXCUSES, EXCUSES GALORE

Moses had all the excuses in the book . . . and then some! He came up with one reason after another why God should choose someone else to carry out this daunting task of leading His people out of Egypt to the Promised Land. So, let's see what we can learn about ourselves and our relationship with God as we listen attentively to Moses as he tries to make his case before the LORD God. Above all, we would do well to listen thoughtfully to God's responses:

Excuse #1: **"Who am I that I should go to Pharaoh, and that I should bring the children of Israel out of Egypt?"** (Exodus 3:11)

Right off, we see that Moses had to learn some very important lessons. For example, he needed to learn that God <u>never</u> asks anything of His people without His supportive blessing. Moses, like Abraham, Isaac, and Jacob before him, had to learn to trust in the LORD God with all of his heart and soul and mind. Indeed, who am I? Our Savior answered that question, once and for all, very well: **"Without Me you can do nothing"** (John 15:5).

Each of us learns and relearns that lesson every day, don't we? As we make our way through this world of sin, we hear the inspired words of the psalmist ringing in our ears: **Trust in the LORD and do good; dwell in the land, and feed on His faithfulness. Delight yourself also in the LORD, and He shall give you the desires of your heart.**

267

Commit your way to the LORD, trust also in Him, and He shall bring it to pass (Psalm 37:3–5). *"Who am I? Nobody of any importance, but God blesses my service to accomplish marvelous things—all to His glory."*

So there Moses was—out in the wilderness at the foot of Mt. Horeb. Unknown to Moses, this would become a very sacred place—for there on that mountain the LORD God would one day in the not too distant future inscribe on two tablets of stone His immortal Commandments and place them into Moses' hands. Of course, God knew that . . . but Moses didn't. Moses was spared the details, which may have been beyond his comprehension anyway. God simply assured His called servant: **"I will certainly be with you. And this shall be a sign to you that I have sent you: When you have brought the people out of Egypt, you shall serve God on this mountain"** (Exodus 3:11–12).

Note the absolute certainty of God: Not "if," not "maybe," not "there is a possibility"—but **"when you have brought the people out of Egypt"** secondly, **"you shall serve God on this mountain."**

Please remember those words of God; they will become especially meaningful as we observe how God fulfilled them later. This is simply another example of God knowing how, when, and where a preordained occurrence orchestrated by Him was going to happen in the future. Yes, God charts the days in the lives of every one of His dear children—and that of course includes us.

But what about Moses? Could he see beyond the moment? No, he couldn't, and neither can we. The answer to any possible dilemma is the same as it has ever been for us humans: Faith, faith, faith. That is what God called for then, and that is what He calls for today—faith in the certainty of God's proper action and His ultimate blessing.

(In an excellent commentary and application of this verbal exchange between Moses and God, Pastor Michael Eichstadt, President of the

Church of the Lutheran Confession, wrote the following in a monthly pastoral letter to the clergy of the CLC. It is worthy of quoting. So here it is, with his permission):

"Who am I?" That was the stunned response of Moses to the LORD's directive: "So now, go. I am sending you to Pharaoh to bring my people the Israelites out of Egypt" (Ex. 3:10). Picture Moses with a "deer in the headlights" look as the enormity of God's assignment sank in. It was an impossible mission! There were insurmountable obstacles. First, there was Pharaoh, a ruler who wielded immense power and had an ego to match. Then there were the nightmarish logistics of organizing and preparing an entire nation of two million people for a trek through uncharted wilderness. Who could accomplish that?

Moses saw the obstacles, and also had a realistic view of himself. In his younger years he may have been ready to take on the world, but his attempt at helping his people had backfired horribly, forcing him to run for his life. During the course of forty years tending sheep, he had learned patience and humility. "Who am I that I should bring the Israelites out of Egypt?"

Moses' self-assessment was correct, but he was focusing on the wrong person. Instead of gauging the chances of success on who he was, he ought to have been looking at the One who was sending him. It wasn't a matter of "Who am I?" but of the "I AM." "I will be with you," God told his reluctant servant. Success was guaranteed!

Do you ever feel like Moses? Who wouldn't when we are sent out by the LORD to preach the whole counsel of God? **"Preach the Word; be prepared in season and out of season; correct, rebuke, and encourage—with great patience and careful instruction"** (2 Tim. 4:2). The LORD warns that His Word won't always be welcomed. People don't want to hear about sin and accountability to God. They gravitate toward charismatic leaders who tell them what their "itching ears" want to hear. Our society is in denial that God has any influence or control over human history.

By nature we don't want to put ourselves in the line of fire and take a stand on Scripture. We have an Old Adam that is every bit as stubborn and hostile to the LORD as Pharaoh was. The task of proclaiming, "Thus says the LORD," in the face of the world's temptations and distractions can seem like a hopeless effort with little chance of success. After all, who are we?

But then remember God's promise: **"I will be with you."** The I AM who is always the same and always faithful to His Word of love is our confidence. It's not up to us. He gives His servants the courage to speak. He assures them His Word will not return empty but will accomplish what He desires. He gives them the message.

And what a message it is! Moses was to announce that God had seen His people's oppression. He had heard their prayers, and He had come down to deliver them. It is the same message we have been preaching throughout this Lenten season. God has seen the oppression and death sin has brought upon all mankind. He hears His people's cries for mercy. His heart goes out to them. He Himself has come down to deliver sinners. The Angel of the LORD who incredibly appeared to Moses in the burning bush wonderfully became man and spent thirty-three years here on earth as our Brother. The holy Son of God met the enemy head-on. **"The LORD has laid on Him the iniquity of us all"** (Is. 53:6). His blood is the payment for all sin of all time.

God said that through Moses He would bring His people out of Egypt to a land flowing with milk and honey. That was just the beginning. For the Savior born from Abraham's family 1500 years later would open the way to the thrilling, liberating message of hope for everyone enslaved by sin and death. To our hesitant: **"Who am I?"** the LORD, who overcome sin and death, says, "Go, I will be with you!"

But Moses wasn't convinced. He had a boat load of excuses:

Excuse #2: **" . . . and they say to me, 'What is His name?' what shall I say to them?"** He was concerned, and we understand his hesitancy about approaching the children of Israel and boldly announcing to them, **"The God of your fathers has sent me to you"** (Exodus 3:13).

What was supposed to happen then? Were they all going to embrace him and shout for joy? After all, he had been gone from his brethren in Egypt for forty years! And even while he was with them, he was the son of the Princess—so even at that time he had little to do with the people of Israel. Then, suddenly he is called upon by the LORD God of heaven and earth to approach them as their leader? No wonder that he had second thoughts.

He knew that they were bound to ask: "'Who are you, and who sent you?' How shall I answer? What shall I say? If I say, it is God who has sent me. OK, rather than they are bound to ask: **"What is His name?"** A logical question. Think about that for a moment. We know that Egypt was loaded with so-called gods, and the people were bound to wonder, *"Which one are you representing?"* God's answer was very simple and straight forward: **"I AM WHO I AM. Thus you shall say to the children of Israel: 'The LORD God of your fathers, the God of Abraham, the God of Isaac, and the God of Jacob, has sent me to you. This is My name forever, and this is My memorial to all generations"** (Exodus 3:15).

My friends, that is a name of God that we should never forget: **I AM**. Not "I was"; not "I will be"—but **I AM**. God always was and always will be. Therefore His name is **I AM**.

No wonder Moses was shaking in his boots. He was called upon to become the leader of the chosen people of the great **I AM**! And since he was chosen by **I AM**, there was no turning away from it, unable and unprepared as he thought himself to be. As Pastor Michael Eichstadt so eloquently described and as the Apostle Paul was caused by the Spirit to encourage: **If God is for us, who can be against us**? (Romans 8:31)

But Moses had to be convinced that God was really <u>for</u> him—so God laid out the plan. *"First, go and meet with the elders of Israel and announce to them that the Lord God has sent you. Make it clear to them that I am fully aware of their suffering at the hands of the Egyptians. Besides, let them know that I have sent you to lead them out of Egypt to the land flowing with milk and honey and promised to their forefathers-in-the-faith centuries ago. When they have come to realize that I am speaking through you, they will follow you."*

"Next, you and the elders of Israel shall request an audience with the king of Egypt. When he indicates his willingness to meet with you, come before him with this request:" **"The LORD God of the Hebrews has met with us; and now, please, let us go three days' journey into the wilderness, that we may sacrifice to the LORD our God"** (Exodus 3:18).

Well, that sounded pretty simple, didn't it? Is that all there was to it? Just announce to the dictator of Egypt that these couple million people—who by the way, have become the major source of the slave labor in federal work projects throughout Egypt—they will be leaving for a few days to go into the wilderness to worship their God? <u>And</u> this ruthless, egotistical Pharaoh will simply say, *"OK—I wish you well. See you when you get back."* Are you kidding? Not a chance!

But God was way ahead of Moses. He knew exactly what would happen. In fact, God told Moses that Pharaoh would, of course, say *"No."* Nevertheless, the ruler of Egypt should be given a chance to do things the easy way, and Pharaoh would be forced to understand that God does not play games. This dictator of Egypt must know that the will of the ever-living God will always be done. If there is a refusal to do it the easy way, then it will be done the hard way. Either way, what God has determined <u>will be done</u>. So Moses was to realize that when the Pharaoh would initially refuse his request, payback would follow. In God's words: **"I will stretch out My hand and strike Egypt with all My wonders which I will do in its midst; and after that he will let you go"** (Exodus 3:20).

So there Moses was in the middle of this terrible show-down. That left Moses trembling in his sandals even more! After all, he had become accustomed to living the life of a nomad for days on end, when his greatest responsibility was to care for his father-in-law's sheep. We can well understand how hard it was for Moses to come to grips with this request of God; he simply had great difficulty in wrapping his mind around it all. As a result, he continued to argue that he was not suited for this all-important task.

So here is excuse #3: **"They will not believe me"** (Exodus 4:1). *"Why should they believe me? Who am I? I won't even be able to get past Pharaoh's gates! And if I do, what if they simply disregard everything that I say?"* The LORD had an easy answer for him. **The LORD said to him, "What is that in your hand?"** (Exodus 4:2) Weakly, Moses answered, **"A rod"** (Exodus 4:2).

His rod—now that's something with which Moses was well acquainted. The rod was part of the common equipment for a shepherd. This wooden club, about three feet long, was used by the shepherd to protect his sheep from anything that would do them harm. Snakes and predators of various types were no match for the experienced and faithful shepherd with a sturdy club in his capable hands.

So the LORD instructed Moses to cast his rod to the ground. When he did so, much to Moses' surprise, it became a snake! Of course, Moses fled in fear—and to add to his astonishment, the Lord told Moses to reach down and grab the snake by the tail. Grab the snake by its tail? That in itself might have caused most of us to recoil in fright. Nevertheless, Moses followed God's instructions precisely and no doubt carefully. Much to his surprise, when he reached down and grabbed the snake by its tail, the snake turned into a rod again.

Before Moses could respond negatively, God had another exercise for him. He was instructed to thrust his hand into his bosom. When he did so, and again removed his hand from under his garments, his hand had turned as white as snow, diseased with leprosy! So God ordered him to do it again. He did, and when he withdrew it that second time, it was completely restored. These were two amazing miracles that could be used to impress Pharaoh and his advisors of Moses' divine authenticity!

The LORD God fully understood what a "hard sell" this was going to be, so He had a follow-up ready: **"And it shall be, if they do not believe even these two signs, or listen to your voice, that you shall take water from the river and pour it on the dry land. And the water which you take from the river will become blood on the dry land"** (Exodus 4:2,9).

Moses was wearing down. His LORD was equipping him for any possible scenario that might develop. But yet the factor of "Who am I?" lingered in his mind and heart—so he made one final attempt to back out of God's assignment.

Excuse #4: **"I am slow of speech"** (Exodus 4:10). The LORD had an easy and obvious answer for that one: **"Who has made man's**

mouth . . . Have not I the LORD? Now therefore, go, and I will be with your mouth and teach you what you shall say" (Exodus 4:11–12).

In other words, *"Moses, will you just go! I will take care of the details. Don't you think that I who have produced you am able to* **teach you what you shall say?"**

All of this summons up memories which I personally experienced years ago. I can't help but be reminded of myself, of course, to a much, much smaller degree than that of Moses. When I was hoping to serve my LORD in some capacity in the public ministry, I was politely told "no" by those in authority in the church. There were a number of reasons given: My formal education wasn't right, for eight years in a one-room country school were not good enough. In high school I hardly understood how the English language worked, to say nothing of Latin, German, Greek, and Hebrew.

Besides lacking in the "right" education, I was told that I was simply too old to begin schooling for the work in the ministry of our LORD. This would require at least seven years—and considering my rather meager education, it might demand even more years of preparation. Maybe they were right. After time in the military and farming for a few years, I was twenty-four years old—with a meager high school education!

Many times the thoughts crossed my mind: *"God, are You sure this is what You want me to do? Here I am on the farm—and I sort of enjoy it. Who am I? The work of Your church is the most important labor there is on this side of eternity. Your Word of forgiving love in the Messiah needs to be spread and applied to the lives and souls of our fellow man in any way we can. I know that...but LORD, I don't think I have the gifts for such a high calling— to say nothing of my rather sparse and insufficient education. Besides, many highly respected workers in Your kingdom labors have also discouraged my attempts in that direction. As a matter of fact, neither do I think that I can speak in a way that is worthy of your Word."*

But the LORD God said, *"Who has made your mouth? Have not I, the Lord? Will you just go? I will be with your mouth and teach you what to say."* Well, with the help of my fiancé and with much prayer to my heavenly Father, I finally gave in. "OK, here I am, LORD. Do with me what You wish!"

Today and every day I thank my gracious LORD for taking this weak vessel of clay and giving it the special opportunity and privilege of being a mouthpiece for Him for many years. Whatever good was accomplished in my ministry was all without a doubt, His doing. Whatever went wrong was, without question, a result of my weakness and my lacking in steadfast faith in Him and His Truth. But through it all, it can be said without hesitation and in all truthfulness: "He took this clod of clay and found a way to use it to His glory. All praise to Him alone!"

Well, Moses was running out of excuses also. He was just plain frightened to death at the prospect of accepting such a huge calling—and who can blame him? He was at his wit's end and pleaded with the LORD: **"O my Lord, please, please send someone else—anyone but me"** (Exodus 4:13, adapted). But the LORD had his eyes set on Moses already before he was in that basket floating amidst the reeds on the Nile. God was not about to give in.

If we can use such terminology, it would seem that the LORD God was maybe becoming a bit frustrated with Moses—yet He worked patiently with what He had: a person crippled by sin—a soul with a corrupted nature—an individual who was confused about life's purpose—but yet a person who needed to learn by faith and remember one all-important truth: God never asks anything of us poor mortals without guaranteeing His blessing.

So, again the LORD dealt with Moses' claimed handicap—his so-called "slowness of speech." In effect God assured him, *"I'll tell you what I'll do. Aaron, your brother, is a good speaker; right? So here's the plan: I will tell you what to do and what to say; then you will relay My words to Aaron, and he will be your spokesman to the people. He will be your mouth, and you will be like God to him. That is, he needs to be assured that I am the One who is making all the decisions and planning all the details. This will give him the necessary confidence in the face of the severe struggles that lie ahead. And don't forget your rod with which you will do miracles."* Finally Moses was out of excuses.

It's amazing, isn't it? As we watch the LORD God up close, patiently dealing with fragile and insecure humans—we really get the picture, don't we? He doesn't have much to work with, but that is what makes His works so grand and marvelous in our eyes. Once again, we remember what the Apostle Paul was moved to put so well: **That the excellence of the power may be of God and not of us** (II Corinthians 4:7). He moves things little by little, day by day, and year by year ever closer toward His final, predetermined goal. And that goal, of course, is the salvation of all mankind—the restoration of everything we lost on that infamous day in the Garden.

At this point in time, God was set on establishing a nation from which the Seed of the woman, the Messiah, the Christ would finally come to save us all from Satan's clutches and deliver us into His everlasting kingdom of grace and love for time and forever. Indeed, Christmas would finally come. There is no doubt about that—and each of these God-ordained happenings moves us ever closer to that day and to be ever more intimately connected with the LORD our God.

Also, as we continue to follow God's gentle yet rather firm words, we can learn much about our Christian activity in this our day. Let's never forget that as we continue to serve the LORD God in His kingdom of grace, the same process is going on at this very moment. God struggles with us humans day after day to motivate us to give ourselves to the privilege of carrying out the duties of His kingdom.

In order to accomplish His purposes through us, He directs and speaks to us continually through His Word. We know what He wants us to do, and we know beyond a shadow of a doubt that He will bless our God-directed labors—for as we proclaim His Word in all of its truthfulness and glory, He assures us. **"So shall My word be that goes forth from My mouth; it shall not return to Me void, but it shall accomplish what I please, and it shall prosper in the thing for which I sent it** (Isaiah 55:11).

There we have it—we know that by declaring His Word in all of its truth, He will always accomplish exactly what His will ordains. For example, He opens doors for us and invites us to faithfully step through them, that souls may be saved and that His kingdom may come to many. In the process, His name is glorified—but in order for this to take place, He wishes for us to take Him at His Word and step through those doors. He urges us to carry out His kingdom labors to the best of our God-given ability and with the power of His Word. Constantly He assures us that He will always be there to bless our activity, great or small, carried on in His name.

Our excuses don't carry any weight, for as it was with Moses, so it is with us: God is always there to make it all work out for the good of His kingdom. Actually, it is all very simple. God does not give us impossible tasks, He simply asks us to listen to Him and do what He advises, in the best way that we can. He will take care of the rest. If we feel that we are not able to speak His Word, there may well be an "Aaron" that will speak on our behalf. The undeniable fact remains, as children of the heavenly Father, **You are the light of the world. A city that is set on a hill cannot be hidden. Nor do they light a lamp and put it under a basket, but on a lamp stand, and it gives light to all who are in the house. Let your light so shine before men, that they may**

see your good works and glorify your Father in heaven (Matthew 5:15–16).

Briefly said, *"Just go in the name of the Lord God in any way that you can, and leave the rest to our living and gracious God."*

A 19th century hymn writer sums it all up rather well:

> *He His church has firmly founded;*
> *He will build what He began.*
> *We, by sin and foes surrounded*
> *Build her walls as best we can.*
>
> *Frail and fleeting are our powers,*
> *Short our days, our foresight dim.*
> *We confess a choice not ours;*
> *We were chosen first by Him.*
>
> *Though we here must strive in weakness,*
> *Though in tears we often bend,*
> *What His might began in meekness*
> *Shall achieve a glorious end.*
>
> *Onward then, without despairing!*
> *Calm we follow at His Word,*
> *Thus through joy and sorrow bearing*
> *Faithful witness to our Lord. (CW 530:2–5)*

PRAYER

LORD God, I thank and praise You for giving me the opportunity to be a co-worker together with You in the most marvelous work there is on this Earth. Of course, there are ups and downs, frustrations and oppositions on every hand. What else can we expect since we are living and working in a world where Satan is everywhere and very persistent in his activities? Every day he is busy trying to prevent Your glorious kingdom from coming into the hearts of people. Yet I know that as I proclaim Your Word in all of its truth, it shall never return to You void but it shall accomplish what You please and it shall prosper in the things for which You sent it (Isaiah 55:11). And so it is my prayer that Your kingdom will come to many, to the glory of Your holy name. Amen.

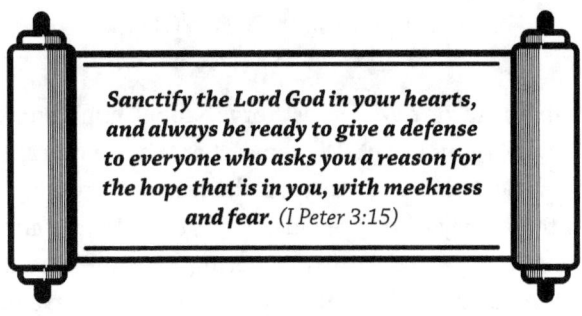

Sanctify the Lord God in your hearts, and always be ready to give a defense to everyone who asks you a reason for the hope that is in you, with meekness and fear. (I Peter 3:15)

TO THE PROMISED LAND WITH GOD'S BLESSING

Immediately Moses threw himself wholeheartedly into the God-given task at hand. What a challenge he faced—yet he was convinced that the LORD was in charge and that He would bless this monumental undertaking in spite of the obvious and undeniable challenges that lay in his path.

One lingering worry still troubled Moses. He hadn't mentioned it to God in his list of excuses, but it was there in his thoughts, nevertheless. What was it? It was the reason why he had fled from Egypt in the first place. Remember? He had murdered an Egyptian official.

Moses was well aware that forty years had passed since that fateful day—but the question that lingered in the mind of Moses was this: Were there any possible hostilities against him back in Egypt as a result of his responsibility for that death? That's why God Himself verbally assured Moses: **"Go return to Egypt; for all the men are dead who sought your life"** (Exodus 4:19).

So at least Moses could put that concern behind him. With that last detail put to rest, he was ready to go. With family and their few belongings loaded on beasts of burden, off they went toward Egypt.

And what about Aaron? We almost forgot about him, didn't we? Well, of course, he was still in Egypt. We remember that he was appointed by God to be the mouthpiece for Moses, so he was contacted by the LORD and directed to journey into the wilderness to join Moses and see what this was all about. What a delightful meeting for these brothers after forty years of separation! This must have given Moses a tremendously important boost.

After their joyful reunion, Moses laid out God's plan, point by point and detail by detail. It was a lengthy and intense meeting as Moses meticulously reviewed all of the God-given instructions and signs. Aaron soaked it all up like a sponge and became a ready and valuable asset in the marvelous but daunting task of moving this huge population of God's people out of Egypt and setting their sights on the Land of Promise—yes, and moving one step closer to fulfilling God's promise, the birth of the world's Savior.

The first order of business was, by God's design, to meet with the elders of God's people. Obviously, Israel was organized, for they likely met regularly for worship services, educating their children in the knowledge of the LORD God as well as meeting to address community issues—so calling a meeting with spokesmen of the people was not difficult to arrange. But then came the difficult part—namely, the task of convincing and organizing these millions of people for departure from the land where they had lived for more than 400 years.

Aaron did a marvelous job of relaying to the people all the words that God had spoken to Moses. Not only that, but also all of the miraculous signs that God had proposed were performed in the sight of this enraptured gathering of believing children of God. The elders accepted the words of God with believing hearts.

But then came the clincher: The people were told that the LORD their God was well aware of their extreme plight as slaves of the Egyptians.

They were assured that God had not forgotten them and that soon their slavery would be over. This melted their hearts. They bowed their heads and intently worshiped their loving and gracious LORD.

Next came that huge and daunting challenge of meeting with Pharaoh! As we know, God had already warned Moses that this mighty ruler of Egypt would vigorously deny their request to let His people go. Nevertheless, there Moses was—standing before one of the most powerful men in the entire world with that very request. So what was the God-designed petition that Moses was requested to place at the feet of Pharaoh? **"Thus says the LORD God of Israel: 'Let My people go, that they may hold a feast to Me in the wilderness'"** (Exodus 5:1).

As expected, the answer came quickly: **"Who is the LORD, that I should obey His voice to let Israel go? I do not know the LORD, nor will I let Israel go"** (Exodus 5:2). *"OK, Moses; there's your answer. Now what?"* Those were rather telling words of Pharaoh, weren't they: **"I do not know the LORD."**

Such a response is so typical . . . so basic to the labors of His people in the midst of this world of sin and unbelief. The work of His kingdom is never easy because of where we are. We are living in the midst of a **"wicked and adulterous generation,"** as our LORD Jesus described it in Matthew 16:4. We are trying to do His work in a world where most people, generally, <u>do not know the LORD</u>. And usually they have no desire to know Him; but should that prevent us from facing the odds and doing what our Savior-God asked us to do? Of course not! (But more on that later.)

First, let's watch as all this plays out in the historic happening before us. Moses and Aaron would not back down an inch from their God-given request—and Pharaoh was likewise steadfast in his refusal. In fact, the king of Egypt became so upset with their request that he decided to review his policy toward the slaves. Here was his reasoning:

"If they have all this time on their hands—if they have time to go into the wilderness to worship their God (of all things!), they must not be busy enough. I can fix that!"

The dictator in charge of the Egyptian government called his taskmasters in and gave them new orders: *"At present, straw is being gathered by others and delivered to the slaves for their brick making. But apparently they have too much time on their hands—so we will discontinue this helping service. From now on they will gather their own straw—yet their quota for making bricks will remain the same. So their request to go into the wilderness to worship their God is denied!"*

The request backfired! God's people were forced to work with even more effort than before. Besides, the needed straw was not available, so they were forced to cut the stubble down to the ground, which consumed much more time. As a result, their brick quotas for all of the construction projects around Egypt were not being met. Yet, under strict orders from the Pharaoh, his taskmasters were not at all considerate. In fact, the Egyptians mercilessly and endlessly beat the appointed Hebrew supervisors of the slaves for not meeting their assigned goals.

So, what should they do? Well, the Hebrew supervisors were forced to make a point. They brought their grievances directly to Pharaoh. His expected answer: **"You are idle! You are idle! Therefore you say, 'Let us go and sacrifice to the LORD.' Therefore go now and work; for no straw shall be given you, yet you shall deliver the quota of bricks!"** (Exodus 5:17–18)

To whom should they turn? They were laboring under impossible odds. God's people were being beaten daily for something they could not correct. In their frustration they cried out to Moses and Aaron, *"Look at the predicament that you two have engineered for us. Pharaoh hates us. The taskmasters are literally on our back ceaselessly—they are on the brink of killing us! Do you expect us to believe that this is the will of our Lord?"*

Moses and Aaron had mutiny on their hands. This was not going according to plan. Maybe they had forgotten that the Lord God had warned them that coping with the Israelites on the one hand and facing Pharaoh's hostility on the other hand was not going to be easy. Yes, more than likely they had forgotten that God had clearly informed them that Pharaoh would reject their request.

We can easily relate to forgetting what God has said, can't we? For example: Mission work in the midst of our society—declaring God's words of law and His glorious forgiving love in the Messiah for all people in the midst of a **faithless and perverse generation** (Matthew 17:17) will never be easy. Everywhere there are nominal Christians who are often loath to hear the simple truths of the living God. Such apathy abounds on every hand. As a result, we may find ourselves lost in a maze of questions from God's believing people. What should we do? How do we do it? Why should we try to carry on mission endeavors when very few seem to care about their spiritual welfare—when hardly anyone seems to be concerned about God and how His Word applies to their lives and the lives of others?

I clearly remember a rather dejected fellow pastor confiding, "Mission work is all but impossible. People really don't want what we have to give." Well, after that rather depressing remark, a rather lengthy and intense conversation followed on that all-important subject. To sum up the point of that deliberation, it was carefully pointed out that the LORD God has the answer for us. Clearly, it is not our business to concern ourselves with what appears to be the outcome of our labors.

The work that the LORD God has given to us is distinctly outlined: **Preach the word! Be ready in season and out of season. Convince, rebuke, exhort, with all longsuffering and teaching** (II Timothy

4:2). Furthermore, the Apostle Peter was moved by the Spirit to encourage: **Sanctify the Lord God in your hearts, and always be ready to give a defense to everyone who asks you a reason for the hope that is in you, with meekness and fear** (I Peter 3:15).

That's not complicated, is it? And furthermore, the LORD God never promised that it was going to be easy. We have only the simple assignment: Just declare what God has said in the best way we can, with any and every means at our disposal. Be ready to defend our faith when anyone asks us about it. Briefly put, simply confess what we believe **with meekness and fear**. Let the LORD take care of the results—that's God's business, not ours!

Well, Moses and Aaron had a much larger problem than is usually experienced by us, didn't they? And they were utterly clueless as to what to do next. The reason was this: The people were on the brink of mutiny. The only alternative—take it to the LORD in prayer. Good choice. However, have a listen to the prayer of Moses. It appears that Moses was praying not in steadfast and confident faith. Rather, it seems that the prayer of Moses was spoken out of frustration—a kind of last resort sort of thing. Besides that, it was rather accusatory; he seemed to feel that he was between a rock and a hard place—and so he was! But accusing God was not the answer, yet that is what Moses did: **"LORD, why have You brought trouble on this people? Why is it You have sent me?** (Exodus 5:22)

Sound familiar? Indeed it does. Now, we must recognize what was really happening between Moses, God's people, and the Egyptian king. Without a doubt, a verbal war was going on here—but the primary battle was not a struggle between Moses and the people of Israel, nor was it merely a disagreement between Moses and Pharaoh. The real conflict that was being waged was the same one that had begun back in the Garden of Eden. It was the war between God and Satan!

Satan knew exactly what was happening between God, Moses, and the people of Israel. Besides that, he certainly knew why it was happening. He was well aware that the promise of salvation for the whole world was tied to God's chosen people, the children of Israel. Our Savior, Jesus, made that abundantly clear when He pointed out simply, **"Salvation is of the Jews"** (John 4:22).

That, my friends in Christ, is what was hanging in the balance, as Satan fully understood. He was totally aware that this God-appointed Savior would crush his evil head, once and for all time, and deliver humanity from his evil grip of anger, hate, and eternal death. So what could be expected of him? He would fight with evil might against anything and everything that God had planned and promised. Though Satan's intentions were frustrated at every turn by the will of God, Satan never gave up—and he never will—until the end!

So, please be assured that according to the promises of God, the Christ would be born from the people of Israel. The Lord Jesus would enter the strong man's (Satan's) evil-abode and render him helpless—as our Savior explained: **"How can one enter a strong man's house and plunder his goods, unless he first binds the strong man? And then he will plunder his house"** (Matthew 12:29).

How did Pharaoh fit into this picture? Well, although he was indeed the king of Egypt, he was in fact Satan's lackey, doing the Evil One's bidding. God was fully aware of this arrangement and would deal with the ruler of Egypt accordingly.

Therefore, though the future of God's kingdom appeared to be in jeopardy—though that golden thread of faith appeared to be stretched to the limit, we can hear the voices of the faithful people of God continuing to sing with confidence and joy:

Hark the glad sound! The Savior comes,
The Savior promised long;
Let ev'ry heart prepare a throne
And ev'ry voice a song.

He comes the captives to release,
In Satan's prison held.
The gates of brass before Him burst;
The iron fetters yield.

He comes the broken heart to bind,
The bleeding soul to cure,
And with the treasures of His grace
To enrich the humble poor.

Our glad hosannas, Prince of Peace,
Your welcome shall proclaim,
And heav'n's eternal arches ring
With Your beloved name. (CW 12)

PRAYER

Dear LORD our God, as You know, the world is filled with evil. Satan is still using every evil trick in his huge arsenal to thwart the labors of Your kingdom. Nevertheless, as in days of old, the soul-saving work of Your kingdom continues. Your Word of Truth continues to break through the barriers of Satan's lies and enters into the hearts of people everywhere. Thank You, LORD, for giving me the privilege of being part of Your ongoing campaign to seek out lost souls, strengthen the weak, comfort the broken hearted, and free the captives from Satan's evil dungeon of destruction and eternal death. Your gospel of love for all, clearly portrayed in the Messiah, is alone the salvation for mankind. Therefore I pray, O LORD, inspire me with Your Spirit to do all that I can to free lost souls from Satan's ghastly grip. And by the power of Your glorious gospel of salvation in the Christ, continue to bring them into

Your kingdom of light and life. In the name of our ever gracious Savior, I pray. Amen.

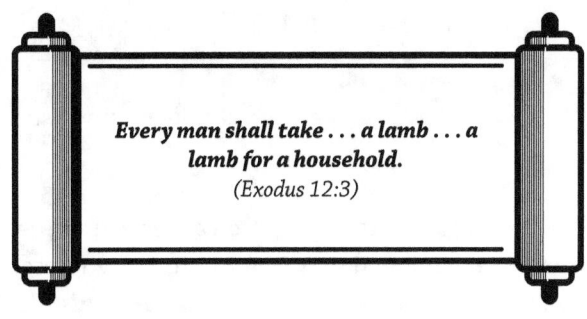

I AM THE LORD

The LORD's will will always be done. We know that . . . but the king of Egypt didn't. Pharaoh, as Satan's disciple, was definitely attempting to squelch God's will. And we know . . . that . . . will . . . never . . . happen! Nevertheless, as has been pointed out, God planned to give Pharaoh an opportunity to do things the easy way. That could have been done by granting a reprieve from the mandated work schedule of His people, but the king of Egypt had chosen to oppose God's will. Guided by the Evil One, Pharaoh had determined to do things the hard way. And, of course, God knew that would happen.

God's unchangeable covenant with His people, as you will recall, was made up of two parts. First and foremost was His promise of salvation through the Seed of the woman. So basically everything, as far as God was concerned, from the Garden of Eden until Christmas, had to do with keeping THE PROMISE. God moved everything, day by day, month by month, and year by year toward that one goal. Christmas would come—God promised it, and therefore it would happen!

The second part of God's covenant with His people had to do with the place where His people would dwell to fulfill the Promise made in the Garden. As you will remember, this was already promised to Abraham centuries earlier. To be sure, God had revealed a brief outline of the upcoming events to Abraham—but did Abraham get the point? Maybe not—at least not entirely. After all, God sometimes referred to happenings that would take place a few hundred years into the future.

Likely, few of us would have grasped and readily retained such prophetic information.

However, that we might better grasp God's preordained design, it is good for us to be reminded that God had informed Abraham centuries before He brought it to pass. **"Know certainly that your descendants will be strangers in a land that is not theirs [Egypt], and will serve them, and they will afflict them four hundred years. And also the nation whom they serve I will judge; afterward they shall come out with great possessions . . . But in the fourth generation they shall return here"** (Genesis 15:13–14,16). *(Note: "here" was the land of Canaan, where Abraham dwelt at the time.)*

So here we are, and the four hundred years in Egypt were up! Moses was commissioned by our Covenant God to lead His people out of Egypt, where they had lived as strangers for 430 years. As we know, the king of Egypt refused to hear of it! Moses was in a difficult place, to say the least. Not only was Pharaoh obstinately opposed to losing his slave-labor force, but the people of God were angry with Moses as well. As far as they were concerned, their intolerable work load was a result of what they considered to be the faulty leadership of Moses.

Things had gotten so bad that the people of Israel would no longer listen to Moses at all. In their weakness of faith they were afraid that any further conversations between Moses and the Egyptian Pharaoh could only make matters worse for them. Nevertheless, God instructed Moses that he had to go back—he had to meet with Pharaoh a number of times and request that he let God's people go.

Why must Moses do this? Simply put, because the king of Egypt had chosen the "hard way"—so the "hard way" it would be! Isn't it interesting how patiently God deals with unbelievers, giving them the opportunity to submit to His will, even though He knows they won't?

(Examples of that truth are everywhere around us today. I'll leave it to you to make those connections)

In order to demonstrate to Pharaoh that he was dealing with Someone much more powerful than himself, the LORD God of heaven and earth triggered a series of plagues that would strike the nation of Egypt. From first to last, there were the scourges of bloody water, of frogs, lice, flies, disease on the beasts, boils on man and beast, hail, locusts, and darkness. (For details see Exodus: 7–11.) In spite of all of the suffering among the people brought about by these powerful afflictions, God knew that Pharaoh would harden his heart and stubbornly refuse the request of Moses.

One after another, the plagues ran their destructive courses, inflicting misery on the Egyptians—while God's people were generally spared. In the midst of these God-sent devastating punishments, at times Pharaoh seemed to "give in" a bit—and then God would remove the plague. With things back to normal, Pharaoh would change his mind and continue in his stubborn obstinacy. Then the judgment of God in the form of another plague would fall upon the nation.

Finally the inevitable happened. Because Pharaoh continually rejected God, the judgment of the Almighty fell upon him. The Evil One tightened his grip upon the king so that any possible capacity for compassion for the people of Egypt withered and died—he was incapable of feeling sorry about the devastation all around him and the misery of his own people.

But the last scourge was the clincher: The plague of death would fall upon every Egyptian home. Every firstborn male of Egyptian humans (and animals), including the first born of Pharaoh himself, would fall under the curse of God. Faced with this inevitable plague of death and with his own son dead in his arms, the heart of this lackey of Satan remained hardened—firmly unmoved. He had become so possessed by the Evil One that he would not give up his slave laborers—no matter what!

We need to stop here for a moment, take a deep breath, and carefully observe the workings of God in this final national scourge. We need to recognize how God protected His people in the midst of this nation-wide catastrophe. To carry out this final plague in an orderly fashion and protect His believing children, the LORD God created something so special that His people would remember it for generations; He established the "pass-over."

What a remarkable picture was portrayed by the LORD God when He instituted this very significant event! Let's listen carefully to the words of God as He clarified every detail of the procedure that His people were to follow: **"Every man shall take . . . a lamb . . . a lamb for a household. . . . Your lamb shall be without blemish, a male of the first year. . . . The fourteenth day of the same month . . . the congregation of Israel shall kill it at twilight. And they shall take some of the blood and put it on the two doorposts and on the lintel of the houses where they eat it. . . . I will pass through the land of Egypt on that night, and will strike all the firstborn in the land of Egypt, both man and beast; and against all the gods of Egypt I will execute judgment: I am the LORD. Now the blood shall be a sign to you on the houses where you are. And when I see the blood, I will pass over you; and the plague shall not be on you to destroy you when I strike the land of Egypt"** (Exodus 12:3,5–7,12–13).

God's people would be spared from this plague of death via faithful obedience to His directives. By faith in the instructions of the LORD, they were to apply the blood of a perfect lamb upon the door posts, on each side of the door, and across the lintel above the door. The Passover was ordered by God, first of all to save His people from the plague of death . . . and secondly to finally deliver them from the wicked captivity of Pharaoh, the Devil's servant.

But there was another purpose for this miraculous sign. It was a forecast of what was to take place centuries into the future. Like Abraham's potential sacrifice of Isaac, the Passover was all tied together with God's promise to redeem humanity—the promise which He had made in the Garden of Eden. The very sinless Seed of the woman, born to crush the head of Satan, would one day be that perfect "Lamb" chosen by God to be sacrificed for the sins of the world. That is what the Apostle Peter was inspired to point out when he was moved to write: **You were not redeemed with corruptible things, like silver or gold, . . . but with the precious blood of Christ, as of a lamb without blemish and without spot** (I Peter 1:18–19).

Yes, way back then—centuries before the Christ was born—the Passover lamb was a prophetic picture of God's perfect Lamb, His Son and our Savior. This specific Seed of the woman would pour out His life-blood on the cross as a sacrifice for the sins of the world. Therefore by faith we "paint" His sacrificial blood upon the "doorposts" and "lintels" of our hearts and lives. And we cry out confidently with the Apostle Paul: **We have redemption through His blood, the forgiveness of sins, according to the riches of His grace** (Ephesians 1:7).

So it was, hundreds of years after Moses, that the Apostle Paul was moved by the Spirit of God to point to the connection between the Passover and the Lamb of God who takes away the sins of the world— when he was inspired by God to proclaim: **Christ, our Passover, was sacrificed for us** (I Corinthians 5:7b).

It is good for our faith-life to note that there are numerous examples throughout Scripture where future actions and signs of God were clearly predicted. As we observe this, we will fully recognize that God always clearly sees and knows exactly what the future holds. I suppose this should be no surprise, for the future is created by Him! As a result, He directs things accordingly, and graciously gives us a glimpse, now and then, into future events.

A few basic examples come to mind: By God's grace, Noah, as an instrument of God, preached for 120 years of the coming flood. Very few listened, and nobody beyond Noah's family believed—but the Flood happened exactly as God had predicted.

God urged the prophet Jeremiah to warn His people of their upcoming captivity by a foreign nation from the north—Babylon. This would take place because of their unbelief and idolatry, as the prophet clearly pointed out. It took decades before the captivity finally happened, but it took place exactly as God had foretold through His prophet.

Centuries before the birth of the Messiah, the LORD God moved the prophet Micah to specify that the Christ, the Seed of the woman, would be born in Bethlehem as **ruler in Israel, whose goings forth have been from of old, from everlasting** (Micah 5:2). The Wise Men from the East were guided accordingly: **And when they had come into the house, they saw the young Child with Mary His mother, and fell down and worshiped Him** (Matthew 2:11).

Indeed, we celebrate our "Passover" as we recognize the full blessing of the birth of the Seed of the woman, our LORD and Savior Jesus Christ. The angels of God announce to everyone: **"There is born to you this day in the city of David a Savior, who is Christ the Lord"** (Luke 2:11).

Jesus points all the way back to the raising of the brazen serpent in the wilderness and shows us that this is a forecast and vivid portrayal of His crucifixion: **"As Moses lifted up the serpent in the wilderness,**

even so must the Son of Man be lifted up, that whoever believes in Him should not perish but have eternal life" (John 2:14–15).

Jesus spoke to His disciples of His upcoming condemnation, torture, death, and resurrection: **"Behold, we are going up to Jerusalem, and the Son of Man will be betrayed to the chief priests and to the scribes; and they will condemn Him to death, and deliver Him to the Gentiles to mock and to scourge and to crucify. And the third day He will rise again"** (Matthew 20:18–19).

Did His disciples understand the enormity of it all? No, they did not. Even while it was happening exactly as our Savior predicted, they had a very difficult time accepting it. But there it was before them, in all of its glorious truth, exactly as our Savior had predicted! Yet doubt remained. Remember the words of Thomas? **"Unless I see in His hands the print of the nails, and put my finger into the print of the nails, and put my hand into His side, I will not believe"** (John 20:25).

But notice—with kind and gentle patience our Savior dealt with this weak faith: He said to Thomas:

"Reach your finger here, and look at My hands; and reach your hand here, and put it into My side. Do not be unbelieving, but believing." And Thomas answered and said to Him: "My Lord and my God!" Jesus said to him: "Thomas, because you have seen Me, you have believed. Blessed are those who have not seen and yet have believed" (John 20:27–29).

Furthermore, the Savior promised His disciples that His Father would send the Holy Spirit to them: **"These things I have spoken to you while being present with you. But the Helper, the Holy Spirit, whom the Father will send in My name, He will teach you all things, and bring to your remembrance all things that I said to you"** (John 14:25–26).

Not until the Spirit was poured out upon them on Pentecost did they remember that Jesus had promised this enormous blessing. Further, we celebrate our "Passover" each time we come before our LORD and hear those forgiving words of our Messiah spoken to His disciples then and now: **"Take and eat, this is my body. Drink from it, all of you. For this is My blood of the new covenant, which is shed for many for the remission of sins"** (Matthew 26:26–28).

We rejoice in our "Passover" as the Lord God's Son arose from the dead, victorious over sin, death, and the power of Satan. And IT'S ALL FOR US: **"Because I live, you will live also"** (John 14:19).

Yes! Through the fulfilled promise of the Seed of the woman, we celebrate the crushing of Satan's head and everything that the Evil One stands for! This is the "Passover" victory God has given to everyone in this sin-racked world. It becomes our own possession simply by faith. **For God so loved the world that He gave His only begotten Son, that whoever believes in Him should not perish but have everlasting life** (John 3:16).

Each time we sing those timeless words of Thomas Kingo, we are focusing upon our "Passover."

> *Like the golden sun ascending,*
> *Breaking through the gloom of night,*
> *On the earth its glory spending*
> *So that darkness takes to flight,*
> *Thus my Jesus from the grave*
> *And death's dismal, dreadful cave*
> *Rose triumphant Easter morning*
> *At the early purple dawning.*
>
> *Thanks to You, O Christ victorious!*
> *Thanks to You, O Lord of life!*
> *Death has now no power o'er us.*

You have conquered in the strife.
Thanks because You did arise
And have opened paradise!
None can fully sing the glory
Of the resurrection story.

You have died for my transgression;
All my sins on You were laid.
You have won for me salvation;
On the cross my debt was paid.
From the grave I shall arise
And shall meet You in the skies.
Death itself is transitory;
I shall lift my head in glory.

For the joy Your advent gave me,
For Your gospel's great reward,
For Your baptism which has saved me,
For Your Supper and Your Word,
For Your death, the bitter scorn,
For Your resurrection morn:
Lord, I thank You and extol You,
And in heav'n I shall behold You. (CW 147:1–3,5)

Indeed, it's a long way from Eden to Bethlehem, yet we know where our road leads. That's why we keep on traveling. What a blessed journey—what wonderful traveling companions—what a soul strengthening mission! It is a marvelous blessing to observe as our loving LORD moves everything that stands in His way so that He may finally deliver to us that wonder-filled "Passover" that we cherish and adore in heart and soul every day of our lives.

PRAYER

Lord God, I thank and praise you for the blessing of Your Word—for through it I have the privilege of seeing the depths and greatness of Your holiness and merciful grace toward all. In Your Word You stoop down to me and all mankind and show the majesty of Your merciful love for all of us lowly beings. Lord, I pray, fill me and all Your believing children with a full measure of Your Spirit that we may gladly hear You speak to us in Your Word of life and thus draw ever closer to You in our living. May we ever heed the words of our Savior, who directs us to **"search the Scriptures, for in them you think you have eternal life; and these are they which testify of Me"** (John 7:39). Amen!

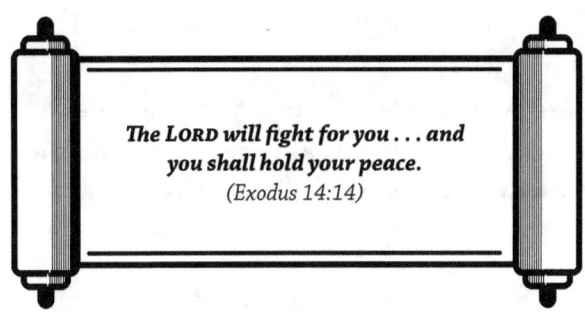

FAITH PUT TO THE ULTIMATE TEST

The final plague that befell Egypt is almost beyond words to describe; God outlines it for us with all of the shuddering but necessary God-ordained horror: **And it came to pass at midnight that the LORD struck all the firstborn in the land of Egypt, from the firstborn of Pharaoh who sat on his throne to the firstborn of the captive who was in the dungeon, and all the firstborn of livestock. So Pharaoh rose in the night, he, all his servants, and all the Egyptians; and there was a cry in Egypt, for there was not a house where there was not one dead.**

Then he called for Moses and Aaron by night, and said, "Rise and go out from among my people, both you and the children of Israel. And go, serve the LORD as you have said. And take your flocks and your herds, as you have said, and be gone; and bless me also" (Exodus 12:30–32).

This was too much for even the heart-hardened Egyptian leader to swallow. With his godless, human mind working, he might very well have reasoned, *"Well, the first nine plagues were simply coincidental. Some of them were maybe acts of nature. Others were probably just unusual phenomena that happen from time to time."* But then the final disaster hit; everywhere throughout the land the firstborn of man and beast—dead! Coincidental? An act of nature? IT HAD TO BE AN ACT OF THE LORD GOD. It was all so overpowering that the king even requested a blessing from the departing people of God—**"and bless me also."** Even **the Egyptians urged the people, that they might send them out of the land in haste. For they said, "We shall all be dead"** (Exodus 12:33).

What a daunting operation was suddenly dropped into Moses' lap! The population of the people of God was huge, estimated to number in the millions. Their flocks and herds were extensive. Everything had to be prepared to move out quickly! All the wagons and carts that they could lay their hands on were loaded to overflowing. And let's not forget, **the children of Israel had done according to the word of Moses, and they had asked from the Egyptians articles of silver, articles of gold, and clothing. And the LORD had given the people favor in the sight of the Egyptians, so that they granted them what they requested. Thus they plundered the Egyptians** (Exodus 12:29–33, 35–36).

What was it again that the LORD God had predicted hundreds of years previously? **"Know certainly that your descendants will be strangers in a land that is not theirs, and will serve them, and they will afflict them four hundred years. And also the nation whom they serve I will judge; afterward they** (Israel) **shall come out with great possessions"** (Genesis 15:13–14).

Again and again we are totally amazed as one happening and then another jumps out before us in accordance with God's prediction. On the other hand, we shouldn't be surprised, for these happenings were all preordained. The LORD God sees them all centuries before they happen. The reason, of course, is obvious: the future is God's domain. He knows what He will cause to happen long before it actually takes place. In short, God alone determines the future! That is why we can so confidently relax as we take each step into our tomorrows. We and our future are solidly in the gracious hands of our loving God. What can be better than that?

Finally, the children of Israel were on their way, heading toward the Promised Land . . . but not via the shortest route, and for good reason. The simplest and closest route would have been across the river of Egypt and into the land of the Philistines. But God vetoed that route. Why? Well, for one thing, God knew that His people were not ready. Entering the Promised Land the most logical way would bring them head to head—spear to spear—sword to sword with the Philistines. And the army of Philistia was well known to be fierce in battle. God was concerned that His people might become demoralized when facing such odds and turn back to Egypt. Besides that, they needed training—they needed to flex their muscles of faith a bit.

There was another important purpose for traveling south. Remember (way back) when the LORD spoke to Moses as he stood barefooted at the base of Mount Sinai before the bush that burned but never disintegrated? It was then and there that God spoke these words of prophecy to Moses: **"I will certainly be with you. And this shall be a sign to you that I have sent you: When you have brought the people out of Egypt, <u>you shall serve God on this mountain</u>"** (Exodus 3:12).

How would Moses serve God on that mountain? We shall see, won't we? At this point we simply need to know that there was a great deal of work to be done to prepare this huge nation for what lay ahead.

We must never forget that God was dealing with some rather frail material: People—weak, fragile, sinful people—like us! Considering their natural propensity for weakness of faith, God had a great deal of preparatory work to do: mostly, their faith needed to be strengthened. This needed to be done before they were ready to face the difficult task of entering the Promised Land. Their travels were not going to be easy. The LORD knew that—so this would be a time for teaching—learning—growing in absolute faith. They had to learn to trust Him with all of their heart, soul, and mind! So they were guided southward through a barren wilderness toward the Red Sea.

The presence of the LORD was unmistakable. What a glorious sight! What a faith strengthening, spectacular display stood before the people of God daily as the LORD went before them, guiding them in a pillar of cloud by day and a pillar of fire by night. There could be no doubt, the LORD God was with them every inch of the way as He directed Moses to lead the children of Israel southward to camp by the Red Sea. We must remember, none of this was accidental. Even camping by the Red Sea would serve God's design. It was all according to His master plan.

Yes, God always sees the big picture. Remember? The LORD God knew that Pharaoh would change his mind . . . again. So, what's new? Of course, in desperation he had let God's people go—BUT his knee-jerk reaction to the terrible death toll staring him in the face throughout the land soon subsided. Rather quickly he reverted back to his old, God-defying, Satan-driven state.

Yes, we remember that the LORD had hardened his heart. And that, my friends, is a condition that is beyond serious. The inspired writer of Hebrews puts it like this: **It is a fearful thing to fall into the hands of the living God** (Hebrews 10:31), but that is exactly where Pharaoh was. Rejection of God's will again and again and again may finally result in God's judgment of everlasting condemnation. From that absolute decree of God there is no escape!

This is true today and every day. Indeed, our LORD warns us all through the same writer of Holy Scripture: **How shall we escape if we neglect so great a salvation, which at the first began to be spoken by the Lord, and was confirmed to us by those who heard Him, God also bearing witness both with signs and wonders, with various miracles and gifts of the Holy Spirit, according to**

His own will? (Hebrews 2:3–4) Indeed, today—every day, the LORD God cries out to all through His inspired writer:

"Today, if you will hear His voice, do not harden your hearts" (Hebrews 4:7).

The king of Egypt had brought God's damning judgment upon himself. He had refused to walk according to God's will and do things the easy way. He had hardened his heart against God's advice, so now he would be forced to do God's will . . . but the hard way!

So the king of Egypt was totally frustrated. When reality "kicked in," he finally realized that his primary labor force was gone. The progress in his entire country had screeched to a devastating halt. All of his huge plans and ideas for the country stopped dead in their tracks. Yet spiritually he had learned absolutely nothing!

After all, he was this big, powerful ruler of the nation of Egypt— wasn't he? As such, he simply couldn't let this happen. He could only see what was directly before him. The futility of trying to preserve his own little worldly kingdom without his slave labor was beyond his grasp. He could only cry out: **"Why have we done this, that we have let Israel go from serving us?"** (Exodus 14:5)

In other words: *"Our country is empty of slaves. Our building projects are at a standstill. No workers, no building materials, no construction, no field work. What are we going to do without them? What have we done? This will not do!"* His total frustration resulted in a snap judgment: *"Alert the army! Ready the horses and chariots!"* Six hundred choice chariots were commandeered and sent out in hot pursuit of the slaves. It wasn't long before they spotted God's people in the distance. *"There they are, camping on the banks of the Red Sea. What a break. We've got 'em now."*

In that sparse desert, even without telescopes or binocular, the children of Israel could detect objects quite some distance away. They could hardly believe what they saw, for it appeared that the entire Egyptian army, with horses and chariots, was frantically heading in their direction. The dust of the desert swirled behind them as the Egyptians bore down upon their prey.

The people of Israel were beside themselves with fear. A feeling of utter terror and helplessness overtook them. What could they do? The Red Sea was before them—and behind them the entire Egyptian army was bearing down. Of course, they cried out to the LORD for help. Good! That's exactly what God wanted!

The appointed leaders of Israel went scampering about to search out Moses while the distressed people vehemently accused: *"Were there not graves in Egypt to bury us? We're going to die! We're going to lose our lives out here in this God-forsaken no man's land. Didn't we tell you when we were back in Egypt:* **'Leave us alone that we may serve the Egyptians'?** (Exodus 14:12) *But no, you had to drag us out here to die in this desert wilderness!"*

Nevertheless, Moses stood his ground. Why? Because he was constrained and strengthened by the Word of the ever-living God. Indeed, the LORD God was the One who had directed this journey, and Moses was positive that the LORD would not forsake them, regardless of the formidable odds that were bearing down upon them.

What an example for every one of us who from time to time find ourselves struggling with threatening and overwhelming odds in the midst of this world of sin. Moses, with faith in the words of the living, gracious, and Almighty God, stood solid and sound in the face of the apparently insuperable Egyptian forces charging down upon them. Astonishing, isn't it? He didn't waver for a second but rather defended his God-ordained decisions before all the people. He didn't need Aaron to speak for him this time! Fearlessly he stood before his fellow Israelites and made one of the finest, faith-filled, yet shortest sermons ever delivered: **"Do not be afraid. Stand still, and see the salvation of the LORD, which He will accomplish for you today. For the Egyptians whom you see today, you shall see again no more forever. <u>The LORD will fight for you, and you shall hold your peace</u>"** (Exodus 14:13–14).

In other words, *"The LORD will take care of everything—He will protect you— He will deliver you—and what will you do? You shall shut your mouths and quit complaining!"* Couldn't be much simpler and more to the point than that, could it?

What a tremendously powerful statement—what a blessing—what a stimulant for every child of God for all time! Think about that for a moment. The LORD will <u>always</u> fight for His people. Yes! Always— continually—without fail, for our struggles are not merely physical but above all spiritual.

Remember Satan? Of course you do. Who of God's children can forget him? Every move that God made to finally bring about the fulfillment of His promise made in the Garden of Eden is countered by Satan. And from that day forward he has engineered opposition to God in any and every way he could. From enticing Cain to murder his brother Abel down to this very day, Satan and his army of evil angels worked and still labor tirelessly to somehow and in some way side-track God's plan of salvation for the world.

In our day, the efforts of the Evil One are spent trying to convince people that the Bible has it all wrong. *"It's just an old, outdated book. Pay no attention to it. Live it up! The Savior of the world didn't really come to save you. God is dead! You need to live your life any way you choose—take advantage of every opportunity that seems good to you. You, you, you— that's all that is important in life. If it feels good . . . do it. Pay no attention to those who are continually pointing you to what they say is God's Word. Don't listen when they say: 'God is speaking to you every day in His Word.' After all, you are the master of your fate; you and you alone are the captain of your soul."*

Without question, the greatest battle in life for each of God's believing children, then and now, is our struggle with Satan and his evil forces. Will this ever subside? The answer to that is easy and undeniable—not as long as we are breathing on this side of eternity. Doubtless, this struggle will continue until this world has run its course and will finally be swallowed up in the judgment of God's wrath. Until then, we are urged by the Holy Spirit through the Apostle Paul: **My brethren, be strong in the Lord and in the power of His might. Put on the whole armor of God, that you may be able to stand against the wiles of the devil. . . . Therefore take up the whole armor of God, that you may be able to withstand in the evil day, and having done all, to stand. Stand therefore, having girded your waist with truth, having put on the breastplate of righteousness, and having shod your feet with the preparation of the gospel of peace; above all, taking the shield of faith with which you will be able to quench all the fiery darts of the wicked one. And take the helmet of salvation, and the sword of the Spirit, which is the word of God** (Ephesians 6:10–11 & 13–17).

And so, my steadfast traveling companions, as we have witnessed again and again on this splendid journey from Eden to Bethlehem, it is a long way. Nevertheless, we clearly see that every inch that His people progress on this marvelous sojourn toward the Promised Land is a steady march toward victory that will finally culminate in the birth of the Savior for every human being on the face of the earth. Besides that, on this trip with our LORD we recognize again and again that **the LORD will fight for you** (Exodus 14:14).

He fought for you and me from that first promise in the Garden to when the Christ sacrificed Himself on Calvary's hill. Beyond that, He fights for you and me every single day of our lives. Why? We are His own; we have been bought with the price and paid for in full on Calvary's cross. As the Apostle Paul is inspired to assure you and me: **You were bought at a price, therefore glorify God in your body and in your spirit, which are God's** (I Corinthians 6:20). Praise the LORD!

On our day-to-day march through the spiritual obstacles of this life, a seventeenth-century hymn writer speaks to us with this encouragement:

> *Rise! To arms! With prayer employ you,*
> *O Christians, lest the foe destroy you,*
> *For Satan has designed your fall.*
> *Wield God's Word, a weapon glorious;*
> *Against each foe you'll be victorious;*
> *Our God will set you o'er them all.*
> *Fear not the prince of hell—*
> *Here is Immanuel! Sing hosanna!*
> *The strong ones yield*
> *To Christ, our shield,*
> *And we as conqu'rors hold the field. (CW 455:1)*

PRAYER

Thank you, thank you, thank you, LORD! I am filled with joy and thankfulness, for You have once again made it clear to me that when I am confronted with obstacles that seem impossible to overcome, You will never forsake me. In fact, You have made it very clear to me, Your dear child, that You will always fight for me. So with You at my side I can face any and every trying difficulty. I can confidently declare: **If God is for us, who can be against us?** (Romans 8:31) Fill me with Your Spirit, O LORD, that I may accept every challenge in life, knowing that You are there to fight for me. Please, LORD, my God, move me to celebrate my peace and joy each day, trusting alone in You. In our Savior's name I pray. Amen!

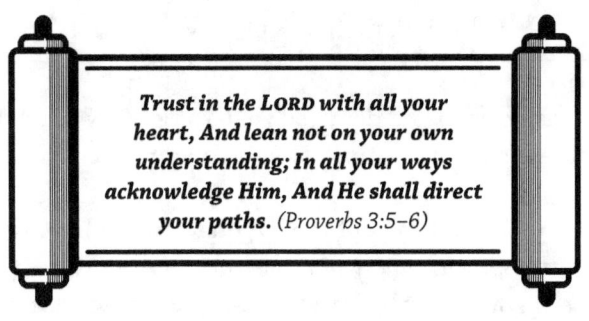

A MIRACULOUS LESSON IN FAITH AND OBEDIENCE

So here came the Egyptian army with clear and concise orders from the Egyptian Pharaoh, "Bring my slaves back!" So what was the first thing that God did to prevent what appeared to be certain disaster for His people? With the entire Egyptian army threatening to overtake them, and with the waters of the Red Sea before them, something extraordinary was called for. Human reason says, *"It's a hopeless situation. Nothing can be done. We are at the mercy of the Egyptian army."* But the LORD God asks: "Did you forget who I Am? Please remember, **'I am the LORD'** (Exodus 12:12).

Do not overlook the fact that **My thoughts are not your thoughts, nor are your ways My ways. For as the heavens are higher than the earth, so are My ways higher than your ways, and My thoughts than your thoughts** (Isaiah 55:8–9).

So permit me to ask you, dear reader: When you were in Sunday School or Christian Day School, do you remember the lesson about the pillar of cloud and the pillar of fire that God created to guide His children on their divine journey by day and by night? We fully understand how these magnificent blessings assured God's people every day of His continual presence. Besides, these God-created miracles served as perfect guides for His people who were making their way into and through the barren and deserted wilderness. Now watch how the LORD used these special creations to serve a very specific need.

To cope with the real threat of the Egyptian army, **the Angel of God,** *(There's that very special name again which may very well refer to the Son of God Himself)* **who went before the camp of Israel, moved and went behind them; and the pillar of cloud went from before them and stood behind them. So it came between the camp of the Egyptians and the camp of Israel. Thus it was a cloud and darkness to the one, and it gave light by night to the other, so that the one did not come near the other all that night** (Exodus 14:19–20).

Before the Egyptian army arrived, and while the people of Israel were shaking in their sandals, the Angel of God moved behind them with that dense wall-cloud. How extensive that cloud-pillar was, we don't know, but it was large enough to stop the Egyptian legions dead in their tracks.

They were dumb-founded by this strange, unexplainable shield of total darkness in the midst of day! There was no recourse; the Egyptian legions simply had to "cool their heels" and wait for the air to clear. So what was going to happen next? Well, nothing was going to happen until the time was right on God's timetable. And that perfect time came after God put into motion the next installment of His miraculous work to save His people.

Let's not forget, these people had witnessed God's miracles dozens of times before, including the ten plagues that ended with that marvelous, inspirational feast of the Passover. Such extraordinary workings of God had to be fresh in their memories—but we know how that goes, don't we? After the LORD has brought us through one seemingly disastrous predicament in our lives, we too often forget. Rather than calmly approaching the next obstacle with confident expectation of the LORD's blessing, we too often get all tied up in worrisome knots. As a result, many times in dire situations we suffer, simply because of our lack of faith and trust in the LORD God and His loving solutions.

Anxious anticipation of what God would do in this fear-filled circumstance was palpable everywhere among this vast gathering of the Israelites. They were certainly aware that their LORD God had protected them and blessed them up to this point—but this was different . . . wasn't it? A solution was simply beyond their comprehension, and that is exactly how God wanted it to be. Why? The academy of God . . . remember? **Trust in the LORD with all your heart, and lean not on your own understanding; in all your ways acknowledge Him, and He shall direct your paths** (Proverbs 3:5–6). It's simple to say, isn't it? It's even easier to hear, but it was and is so very difficult to practice . . . for them and for us.

Then finally the answer from God came, as it always does, in all of its divine glory. God spoke to Moses, **"Tell the children of Israel to go forward. But lift up your rod, and stretch out your hand over the sea and divide it. And the children of Israel shall go on dry ground through the midst of the sea"** (Exodus 14:15–16).

Now, there's an unexpected resolution to the problem, isn't it? It sounded simple enough . . . but how can this possibly work? Human reason says, *"There's a raging sea out there! Walking on dry ground through the midst of it? Are you kidding me? We've experienced miracles before. But this . . . this is simply . . . beyond reason."* Indeed it is—so what was required? The solution, as has been pointed out again and again, was very simple: Faith—faith—faith! Trust in the mighty arm of God. This was just one more lesson in that on-going school of God as He continued to prepare His people for what He would bring to pass in the future.

Let's ponder a bit on another rather important aspect of this lesson. Notice how God was about to use Moses and his shepherd's rod in a very special way. Could not God have simply commanded the seas to divide? Of course, He could have. But watch: God chose to use a human and a human tool to accomplish miraculous happenings. Lesson: Let no one think or say, *"Such activity is foolishness—it's just not reasonable! Therefore, I'm not going to do it."*

When God tells us, in His Word, what to do and how to do it, promising that He will bless it . . . only an unbelieving fool will refuse. Of course, we will do it, reasonable or not! Right? We know by faith that God's blessing will absolutely follow! That's how God chooses to work even to this very day. He chooses to employ His people in actions that they may not reasonably understand in order to carry on His kingdom work <u>to His glory</u>!

The Apostle Paul reminds God's people of their special and unique calling when he was inspired by the Spirit to speak to all of us: **We then, as <u>workers together with Him</u> also plead with you not to receive the grace of God in vain** (II Corinthians 6:1). In other words: *"Listen carefully as the LORD God speaks to you, His chosen people—**His workers together with Him**. Walk, work, and carry on your duties. Labor diligently according to what He has said."* That's it! In fact, that's as far as we can go.

The result is God's business. And we are assured by God Himself, **"For as the rain comes down, and the snow from heaven, and do not return there, but water the earth, and make it bring forth and bud, that it may give seed to the sower and bread to the eater, so shall My word be that goes forth from My mouth; it shall not return to Me void, but it shall accomplish what I please, and it shall prosper in the thing for which I sent it** (Isaiah 55:10–11).

So it was with God's people as they camped on the shores of the Red Sea. With certain danger bearing down upon them, they were obliged to do one thing—listen carefully to God's instructions and do exactly what He said. Once again we must remember that they were being prepared for the miracle of miracles. They were God's chosen people who were being readied, first of all, to take possession of the land that had been promised to them already in Abraham's day.

Secondly, and more importantly, the fullness of time in God's grace would one day come. There, in the Land of Promise, the grandest miracle ever to take place on the face of this Earth was going to happen. And you know what that was—the God-promised birth of that particular Seed of the woman—the Messiah—born to save the world from its sin, death, and Satan's evil grip.

So what's going to be the next step in this enormous undertaking? Well, somehow the people had to be prepared for this . . . this God-designed, faith-required episode. Moses and his helpers must have gotten busy with meetings and explanations with as many of the people as possible. Quickly the word spread about this remarkable solution to what seemed to be an impossible conundrum. Finally it was done—at least as well as possible. The people had been alerted as to what was about to take place. There was nothing left to do . . . but wait.

Then it happened; as the people of God stood on the banks of the Red Sea, filled with anxious anticipation, **Moses stretched out his hand over the sea** (Exodus 14:22), and suddenly a very strong east wind began to blow. It grew more intense and unceasing until before their very eyes, the gusts of forceful winds captured the sea waters and divided them. The intensity of the prevailing wind continued for some time, sucking every drop of moisture from the bed of the sea. The waters were held at bay, creating a marvelously inviting passageway through the very midst of the waters, **and the waters were a wall to them on their right hand and on their left** (Exodus 14:22).

It was happening—just as God had said—before their very eyes! The people of Israel didn't need any coaxing. As soon as the sea bed was dry enough, into the midst of the sea they marched. There must have been much relieved cheering and laughter as the elderly, the handicapped, the pregnant women, the fathers, the mothers, the little children— all ventured into that vast God-created corridor for life. Their beasts of burden—the livestock—their carts filled with tents, food, and clothing—all moved along between those huge walls of water held at bay by the "arm" of God as if a concrete barrier were damming the flow of the sea. Hour after hour they marched—steadily progressing—in steadfast trust in the living God. Finally . . . the last soul had made its way through that God-produced passageway to safety and freedom.

But now watch as the next phase of that miraculous working of God developed. When the last of God's people, together with their cargo, had scampered up the opposite banks of the sea, the cloud was lifted— the curtain was raised—the darkness dissipated so that the Egyptians finally could see what was happening. We can imagine their response: *"No . . . no . . . no! Our slaves are slipping away through this . . . this unbelievable passageway. It doesn't make sense—but there it is—a pathway through the waters of the Red Sea. We thought we had 'em. They were ours. They couldn't escape . . . but there they go."*

Might they be moved to see the hand of the Almighty and come to realize that the LORD God of Israel was the one true God of the world and the universe? Could they possibly recognize this to be a miracle that only the Almighty could produce? One would like to think so— but remember, Satan was controlling their hearts. All they could see was that the unthinkable was taking place before their very eyes. The Israelites were escaping! Their slaves were getting away through the midst of the sea!

"CHARGE!" came orders from the Egyptian general. The warriors plunged into the God-engineered passageway. With horses and chariots the soldiers mindlessly pursued the nation of God's people. But wait! What was happening? The wheels were flying off their chariots right and left. As a result their horse-drawn vehicles were colliding with each other—soldiers were thrust from their two-wheeled carts—wreckage and bodies were violently crushed together under the pounding hooves

of frantic horses. This was so unreal that some of the soldiers fearfully cried out in dismay, **"Let us flee from the face of Israel, for the LORD fights for them against the Egyptians"** (Exodus 14:25).

You think? Yes, some couldn't help but recognize the hand of the LORD God of Israel in these bizarre happenings. Obviously, their words indicated a recognition of the activity of none other than the Almighty God of Israel—but unfortunately it appeared to be a recognition sponsored by terror rather than promoted by faith.

Nevertheless, the LORD God was preaching a powerful sermon to the Egyptians as well as to His people—then and now. The message was clear: **God reigns over the nations; God sits on His holy throne. The princes of the people have gathered together, the people of the God of Abraham. For the shields of the earth belong to God; He is greatly exalted** (Psalm 47:8–9).

Servants of Pharaoh and Satan . . . take note: To use a rather colloquial expression: "You ain't seen nothin' yet!" Here came the final devastating act of God: Under the LORD's direction Moses stretched his hand over the sea again—and while the people of God stood safely on the far shore, observing the devastating wreckage in the midst of the Red Sea . . . God's dam broke!

The waters sloshed together like a giant tsunami. The massive, powerful waters completely crushed what was left of the man-made "toys," and every living thing was drowned in a giant, watery grave. Nothing remained but slivers of broken wood and dead bodies of soldiers and horses surfacing upon the waters.

It was a sad end for those who defied the voice of the living God, but it was a joyous victory for the LORD God and His people. The promises of God spoken to Abraham continue to echo in our ears: **"I will bless those who bless you, and I will curse him who curses you; and in you all the families of the earth shall be blessed"** (Genesis 12:3).

With that in mind, **then Moses and the children of Israel sang this song to the LORD,**

> **"I will sing to the LORD,**
> **For He has triumphed gloriously!**
> **The horse and its rider**
> **He has thrown into the sea!**
> **The LORD is my strength and song,**
> **And He has become my salvation"** (Exodus 15:1–2a).

Then Miriam the prophetess, the sister of Aaron, took the timbrel in her hand; and all the women went out after her with timbrels and with dances (Exodus 15:20).

What a soul-strengthening lesson in faith and trust to be remembered! God's inspired writer in the Book of Hebrews is moved to record it all very simply in one sentence: **By faith they passed through the Red Sea as by dry land, whereas the Egyptians,**

attempting to do so, were drowned (Hebrews 11:29). A giant leap for God's people had been made toward freedom. Finally they could say, *"At last Egypt is behind us. We are free—free from the wretched beatings, free from the heartless taskmasters, free to live without the back-breaking labor and the heartless grind of slavery."*

Indeed, they were free, but maybe they were not aware that freedom has its price. Even with God watching over them, they had to learn how to cope with things that slavery had never required. Slavery had its problems, but sudden freedom also had many unexpected challenges. The only tried and tested method to be used to face every obstacle was very simple: Faith . . . faith in the promises and care of their loving God.

The message was clear: No one—absolutely no one would be permitted to stand in opposition to God and His people as He carried out His plan of redemption for the world in the Seed of the woman, the Messiah. Christmas was going to happen—it was going to come, regardless of the opposition. Satan was already under the curse of God . . . and he knew it. Now, anyone who would be moved by Satan to defy the will of the living God and stand in His way would fall under the same curse.

Can we assume that those same blessings of God rest upon His people to this very day? Yes, we can . . . and we should. He has chosen us to be His by pure grace (undeserved mercy) through faith in His Son, the Seed of the woman. He has selected us out of the vast multitude of people on this Earth to be His very own. The very Christ of the living God is speaking to each of us when He simply explains, **"You did not choose Me, but I chose you and appointed you that you should go and bear fruit, and that your fruit should remain, that whatever you ask the Father in My name He may give you"** (John 15:16).

Therefore He wishes for us to live with Him and for Him each day, as though we will die tomorrow . . . for we may. But He also encourages us to live each day under His guidance and love as though we will live forever . . . for we will! With that in mind, let us join all believers down through the centuries in singing:

> Lord, 'tis not that I did choose You;
> That, I know could never be,
> For this heart would still refuse You
> Had Your grace not chosen me.
> You removed the sin that stained me,
> Cleansing me to be Your own;
> For this purpose You ordained me,
> That I live for You alone.
>
> It was grace in Christ that called me,
> Taught my darkened heart and mind,
> Else the world had yet enthralled me,
> To Your heav'nly glories blind.
> Now I worship none above You;
> For Your grace alone I thirst,
> Knowing well that, if I love You,
> You, O Father, loved me first.
>
> Praise the God of all creation;
> Praise the Father's boundless love.
> Praise the Lamb, our expiation,
> Priest and King enthroned above.
> Praise the Spirit of salvation,
> Him by whom our spirits live.
> Undivided adoration
> To the great Jehovah give. (CW 380)

PRAYER

LORD, my God, many are the times that I find myself in situations of distress. I know not which way to turn or what to do. I am embarrassed to admit it, but when life's problems flood my life, only too often I fail to look to You for the solution. I find myself to be miserable, and sometimes I weep and moan and wonder how this will all end. Then I remember, **"The LORD will fight for you"** (Exodus 14:14). *"Yes, the LORD will fight for me! He loves me and I belong to Him. I will confidently turn it over to the LORD. Quiet down, my soul, and observe as the LORD eliminates the most horrendous obstacles in life. Yes, I will take the God-inspired words of the Psalmist to heart,"* **Wait on the LORD; be of good courage, and He shall strengthen your heart; wait I say, on the LORD!** (Psalm 27:14) Amen.

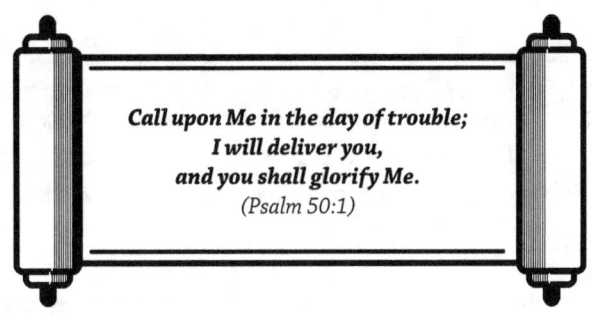

Call upon Me in the day of trouble;
I will deliver you,
and you shall glorify Me.
(Psalm 50:1)

WHAT SHALL WE EAT? WHAT SHALL WE DRINK?

So here they were out in the desert—yes, literally desert! Vegetation for the animals was sparse—water sources were nearly non-existent. And what are the necessities to maintain life . . . both for man and beast? The requirements were the same then as they are today—food and water . . . right? Well, the food that they managed to bring with them was quickly diminishing—but you might say, *"They had their livestock . . . didn't they?"* Yes, they did—but meat, meat, and more meat was far from a satisfactory diet. They needed vegetables, fruits, grains, and breads as well as water; but all such were literally gone!

Three days went by . . . no streams, no wells, no pools—no water! Things were getting critical. We're talking about a huge number of people and animals all parched to the core! Then came an unexpected surprise. *"What is that up ahead? It appears to be . . . could it be . . . yes it is! It's water."* There in the midst of the desert appeared a pool of water. What a discovery!

The people ran to the site, jostled and shoved as they anxiously crowded around that life-saving find. Most were ready to drink, drink, drink, and fill all of their water containers to the brim! But there were others who were properly suspicious of this unexpected discovery in the midst of the desert. Wisely they stepped in to sample the waters—

and what did they find? *"Oh, no! Something is wrong with it. It's bitter! It's not fit to drink!"* They looked at each other with the heart-sick question: *"What do we do now? Moses, where is Moses?* **Moses . . . what shall we drink?"** (Exodus 15:24)

Of course, Moses knew that God's people were seriously dehydrated with nothing in sight to curb this life-threatening dilemma. Finally they found water, but their hopes were dashed into a thousand pieces as the water was discovered to be unusable. What could Moses do? By himself . . . nothing. But remember? **The LORD will fight for you** (Exodus 14:14).

That promise of the LORD God applied to every condition and situation in the life of the children of God then . . . and yet today. So Moses took this critical matter to the LORD in prayer. That is exactly what God wanted. Our loving God certainly doesn't enjoy it as His people endure hardships in life, yet lessons in faith-life often can be learned only through the avenue of extreme sufferings.

Could the LORD have instantly purified the water? Of course, He could have—but as we have witnessed, God often chooses to involve His children in carrying out His answers to their prayers. Do you remember the Red Sea episode? Just as God had used Moses and his rod to part the Red Sea, so here He chose to use a special means through which He would answer His people's request.

So God directed, "Here is a tree. Cut it down and cast it into the waters." What might their and our reason say to that? *"A tree tossed into the water? C'mon! What possible good will that do? Everyone is thirsting to death, and we're supposed to spend time and energy cutting down a tree and dropping it into this bitter pool of water? What is the sense in that?"* Reasonably . . . none! But you see, God was testing them (Exodus 15:25), and what does faith in the instructions of God say? *"Do it! Do it with faith in the words of God, and be assured that it will result in God's blessing!"*

Did they do it? Yes, they did. Trusting in God's directive . . . they did it! Then and there a miracle happened before their very eyes as the bitter waters were made sweet and ready to drink. Who would have predicted that? But it happened exactly as God wanted. Once again, they were being taught to take the LORD at His words, no matter what their reason suggested. That is such an important lesson to learn . . . both then and now.

Then and now? Absolutely. Our LORD God is performing miracles every day for us. "Really?" Yes, really. "Give me an example," you might say. I thought you might say that, so I have prepared some examples, entitled: BE STILL AND KNOW THAT I AM GOD (Psalm 46:10).

What are these things called miracles?
Are they part of our lives?
Should we pray for a miracle
When desperation cries?

God's miracles are everywhere,
Around us every day.
But we may often miss them 'cause
We're looking the wrong way.

God urges us to pause a bit,
Amidst life's busy day.
"Be still and know that I am God,"
His miracles convey.

Yet, reoccurrence of a thing,
May rob it of our awe,
Then we may not appreciate
A miracle we saw.

When Jesus spoke to Lazarus,
As he lay cold and dead,
And raised him up to live again,
"A miracle!" it's said.

But is the pow'r of God no less
In miracles of birth?
Or when a lifeless looking seed
Is planted in the earth?

There life springs forth all fresh and new,
A miracle each day.
We can't explain this mystery,
But look, it's on display

For everyone to view by faith
And see God's glory pure.
"Be still and know that I am God,"
His miracles assure.

God's Word is filled with miracles,
That's simply how He works.
His ways are far above our ways,
As heav'n above the earth.

We clearly see at Christmas, why
God's people celebrate,
Rejoicing in the miracles,
As God's Word indicates:

"The virgin shall conceive and bear
A Son," Isaiah writes.
And God sends angels to explain,
In heaven's glorious lights:

"For unto you is born this day,
A Savior from your sin."
This little child belongs to you
And you salvation win.

So also when Christ gave His life
In payment for our sin,
A miracle then followed as
Our Lord arose again.

His Holy Supper He prepares,
invites in love to us,
"This is My body and My blood
Shed for your righteousness."

He bids us use a simple thing
Like water to baptize.
The Spirit then works miracles
Before our very eyes.

These miracles of power and love
With joy we celebrate.
For in them we find peace with God,
That's why we must relate

His miracles to everyone,
That all by faith may know
The love of God for all of us,
Who serve Him here below.

So let your faith soar to the heights,
Behold what eyes can't see.
"Be still and know that I am God,"
His miracles believe!

(Poems of Prayer & Praise pp. 55–56)

Graciously, our LORD still involves His people today, just as He did at the pool of Marah. By faith His dear children simply <u>do</u> as He directs with confidence in His gracious love. The result is that God continues to work saving miracles through and for us, His children, every day!

Jesus Christ, true God from eternity, continued this practice throughout His ministry. The Apostle John reminds us, **And truly Jesus did many other signs (miracles) in the presence of His disciples, which are not written in this book; but these are written that you may believe that Jesus is the Christ, the Son of God, and that believing you may have life in His name** (John 20:30–31).

And so it was, there by the pool of water in the midst of the desert, the LORD God gave His people clean, fresh, wholesome water to drink—and He gave them far more than that. He gave them a real lesson in faith and confidence in His love for them. Everyone was thankful, and with joy they filled their water containers to the brim with that precious gift of God. Then they were ready and prepared to move on.

But the LORD wasn't finished with His demonstration of love for them. They had traveled only a couple of days in the direction of Mount Horeb *(sometimes referred to as Mount Sinai)*, when the LORD God provided them with a wonderful respite. There, in the most unlikely place on Earth, a special gift from their loving God came into view. It was practically unbelievable. What was it? Was it a mirage in the midst of the desert? They hadn't ever seen anything so beautiful and so inviting. They just couldn't get there fast enough.

As they drew closer, what seemed to be an optical illusion became a reality. There in the midst of that desolate desert were not seven but SEVENTY PALM TREES SURROUNDING TWELVE WELLS OF WATER! Talk about a sight for weary eyes and a picture-perfect place to pitch their tents, rest, and relax—a spa in the midst of . . . nowhere . . . nowhere else but right here!

All was well, right? They had learned their lesson. From this moment on they would carry on, knowing that the LORD God was with them every inch of the way. After the previous experiences they would trust implicitly in God for their well-being with absolute faith and confidence in His abiding care. Oh, my, wouldn't it be nice if that were the actual reality, both then and now?

Our sinful natures are extremely tough and a spiritual affliction with which we must deal every single day. That is exactly how it was with His people in the wilderness—their egos wouldn't give them any rest and peace. Besides that, Satan never "misses a beat" in his on-going, flesh-provoking symphony orchestrated to capture the minds and hearts of God's people, then as well as now. For that reason we continually pray:

> *How can I thank you, Lord,*
> *For all Your loving kindness,*
> *That You have patiently*
> *Borne with me in my blindness!*
> *When dead in many sins*
> *And trespasses I lay,*
> *I kindled, holy God,*
> *Your anger ev'ry day.*
>
> *It is Your work alone*
> *That I am now converted;*
> *O'er Satan's work in me*
> *You have Your pow'r asserted.*
> *Your mercy and Your grace*
> *That rise afresh each morn*
> *Have turned my stony heart*
> *Into a heart newborn.*
>
> *Lord, You have raised me up*
> *To joy and exultation.*
> *And clearly shown the way*
> *That leads me to salvation.*
> *My sins are washed away;*
> *For this I thank You, LORD.*
> *Now with my heart and soul*
> *All evil I abhor. (CW 460:1–3)*

PRAYER

LORD, my God, I know by faith that my life is filled with miracles which You carry on constantly on my behalf. As You were with Your people of the Old Testament, so You are with me every day in my life. Yes, I know that You my Savior have promised unconditionally, **"I am with you always, even to the end of the age"** (Matthew 28:20). As a result I am confident, by faith, that I am in Your loving care every minute of every day and night. I thank and praise You for Your undeserved goodness and love. Already when I was a child, You miraculously welcomed me into Your kingdom of grace through Your sacrament of Holy Baptism. Besides being born again by the power of Your Spirit, You have given me the privilege of serving You in Your kingdom of grace in many ways. Fill me with Your Spirit, LORD, that I may always remember that my primary labor in this life is to serve You in body and spirit. For only then will my life be filled with the purpose for which I was created and redeemed. In my Savior's name and to Your everlasting glory I pray. Amen.

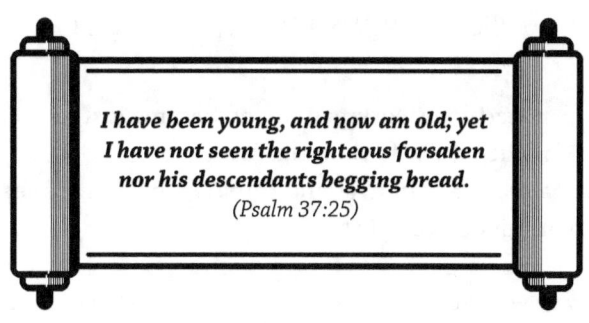

*I have been young, and now am old; yet
I have not seen the righteous forsaken
nor his descendants begging bread.*
(Psalm 37:25)

MANNA FROM HEAVEN

Six weeks was a long time for that huge nation of God's people to be trudging through the desert. It seemed to many of them that they were mindlessly following their leaders without an end in sight, like a "wild goose chase." On top of that, many could not forget their days in Egypt.

According to the way human nature functions, it was easy for them to remember the good but conveniently forget the bad. Under the strain of this seemingly endless trip through the desert, they became an easy target for Satan. Urged on by the Evil One, the people became more and more dissatisfied. Finally their steady dirge of lament became a complaint to Moses and Aaron, **"Oh, that we had died by the hand of the LORD in the land of Egypt, when we sat by the pots of meat and when we ate bread to the full! For you have brought us out into this wilderness to kill this whole assembly with hunger"** (Exodus 16:3).

That wondrous special assignment for God's people in His entire long-range vision for the world's salvation was all but lost amidst the trials and troubles of this hapless journey. In spite of the promises and blessings of the LORD God, their corrupt human nature surged up in their minds, hearts, and voices: *"Here we are, out in the desert. We are all going to starve to death out here. Why did we ever choose to follow this Moses guy? Why did we ever leave Egypt? What are we doing out here? Did we come out into the desert to . . . die? What were we thinking!"* Indeed, how soon the miraculous workings of God became lost in their warped perception of reality. Their faith in the providence of God withered beneath the pain of their hunger and thirst. Hopelessness seemed to dominate their minds and spirits.

So let's try to get the picture: There they were—this nation of God's people out in the desert. Of course, their LORD had accomplished marvelous things on their behalf in the past. They were safe and sound; the Egyptian armies had been miraculously conquered by the unmistakable hand of God; the bitter waters at Marah had been sweetened by the supernatural works of God; Elim had provided a wonderful respite as they lingered among the palm trees and drank from the fresh waters—yet Elim was not their destination. Moses was looking ahead when he directed them to leave Elim, that pleasant oasis of beauty.

Moses was well aware that their LORD God had a mission for them to accomplish. Yes, they were being prepared for the grandest God-ordained miracle that this world has ever known—namely, producing the Messiah, the Son of the living God. That was their one and only God-given mission and the reason for all of this. Of course, they didn't fully grasp it all. Besides, they still had a ways to go in the school of faith conducted by God Himself.

So as they continued south under the leadership of Moses and Aaron toward Mount Sinai, they found themselves in what was called the Wilderness of Sin (Note: Perhaps a reference to Sin, a man-created moon deity), a parched desert-land where hardly anything grew. It was dry and mercilessly hot. They were hungry and thirsty; their livestock were suffering, and the miraculous happenings of the past month became a distant memory as the harsh desert terrain sapped their strength and will. In fact, however, all was under God's direction as part of His schooling to strengthen His people for what lay ahead.

How is it with us? Yes, it's easy to "trust" in God when everything is going well, isn't it? When we pass through periods of pleasant times—when our life seems good, and our future appears to be all set and without serious problems, what happens? We tend to take things for granted, don't we? *"Yeah, of course I believe in God. But I have it all under control. All is well. God is good."* Of course God is good! He is <u>always</u> good—but sometimes we lose sight of that in the midst of difficult times. So let's listen to the wisdom of an 18th century hymn writer as he "brings us up short" with this reminder:

> *In <u>ev'ry</u> condition, in sickness, in health,*
> *In poverty's vale, or abounding in wealth,*
> *At home and abroad, on the land, on the sea—*
> *The LORD, the Almighty, your strength e'er shall be. (CW 416:2)*

My friends in Christ, many are the times that we need a jolt in life to bring us down on our knees before the LORD our God to plead for His forgiveness, mercy, strength, and blessing. And God knows how to do that and when to do it! Indeed, God is always good . . . even in trying times. Therefore the Psalmist encourages us every day, regardless of our state of affairs or the trials that we are suffering:

> **Make a joyful shout to the LORD, all you lands!**
> **Serve the LORD with gladness;**
> **Come before His presence with singing.**
> **Know that the LORD, He is God;**
> **It is He who has made us, and not we ourselves;**
> **We are His people and sheep of His pasture.**
> **Enter into His gates with thanksgiving,**
> **And into His courts with praise.**
> **Be thankful to Him, and bless His name,**
> **For the LORD is <u>good</u>;**
> **His mercy is everlasting,**
> **And His truth endures to all generations (Psalm 100).**

OK, back to our grumpy friends out in the desert sands of Sinai. Of course, God was not going to let His people down; He never forsakes His own. The Psalmist David was inspired by the Spirit of God to give us some personal advice: **I have been young, and now am old; yet I have not seen the righteous forsaken nor his descendants begging bread** (Psalm 37:25). Though God's people might forget who they were called to be and what they were called to do, God never forgets! So the LORD God spoke to Moses with this answer to the prayers of His children: **"Behold, I will rain bread from heaven for you"** (Exodus 16:4).

"What? Raining bread from heaven? That sounds like an impossible promise! OK, the Egyptians were drowned in the sea, a tree was cast into the waters at Marah to make them drinkable, an oasis appeared in the midst of the desert...but raining bread from heaven? That's got to be a miracle of miracles!" Then while Aaron was trying to convince God's people of the need to trust the promises of the LORD, suddenly the people's attention was drawn to a distant cloudy apparition in the sky: **The glory of the LORD appeared in the cloud** (Exodus 16:11b). It was unmistakable.

Then out of the cloud came the thundering voice of God. And what did God say to Moses? **"I have heard the murmurings of the children of Israel. Speak to them, saying, 'At twilight you shall eat meat, and in the morning you shall be filled with bread. And you shall know that I am the LORD your God'"** (Exodus 16:12).

When God's people are in need, both then and now, the LORD

God <u>always sees</u> and <u>always answers</u>. What a tremendous blessing: God would provide meat in the evening and bread in the morning! It seemed too good to be true . . . but yet the LORD God had said so! It had to be true, for **"I am the LORD your God"** (Exodus 16:12).

We should never forget that divine proclamation! In those few words the LORD God was speaking volumes! He packed a great deal into that self-designated name LORD. What the LORD God is saying is this: *"Please, don't forget that I am the one true God of heaven and earth. I am the One who created everything out of nothing. I am the One who watched the destruction of My perfect creation. Yes, it was I who made the promise of redemption for all mankind already in the Garden of Eden. <u>I am your one and only Covenant God</u>. You, my people, have been called to be My very own with one ultimate and primary divine purpose—one world-saving mission— namely, to produce the Seed of the woman. Through Him salvation in My forgiving love will be poured out upon the entire world."*

And do you know what? By faith in His redeeming love in <u>the</u> Seed of the woman—His only Son Jesus the Christ, the promised Messiah, you and I have become part of the family of the LORD! That is what He means when He caused His holy writer to describe us like this: **You are a chosen generation, a royal priesthood, a holy nation, His own special people, that you may proclaim the praises of Him who called you out of darkness into His marvelous light; who once were not a people but are now the people of God!** (I Peter 2:9)

When we take time to concentrate upon the meaning of the name of God (*Jehovah*, translated LORD in our Bibles), it's breath-taking, isn't it? It should be! May it ever be so with each and every one of us throughout our lives!

Once again let's observe how the one-and-only Covenant God fulfilled His immediate miraculous promise to His people out there in the midst of the Desert of Sin! **"At twilight you shall eat meat, and in**

the morning you shall be filled with bread." So when the evening shadows began to form, and twilight settled down upon the desert, everyone watched and waited. Their eyes were glued to the heavens. What, how, where, when would this wonder take place?

They didn't have long to wait. As the sun set, and the shades of night settled across the sandy floor of the desert, the cool evening air was filled with . . . birds! Thousands of quail, yes, multitudes of winged foul appeared out of nowhere and settled down in the midst of the camp of God's people! The entire nation of Israel went into a frenzy as those plump little birds were snatched up and prepared for a feast of all feasts. They ate and ate and ate. What a glorious evening! What a night of blessing to remember . . . blessings directly from the LORD their God!

A gentle peace settled down across the nation of God's people as their appetites were entirely satisfied and their spirits were lifted. Another lesson of faith in God's constant love for His people was taught. How quickly their attitude improved as they looked toward the future with renewed strength and trust in their gracious, all-caring God.

As they closed their eyes in contented rest and sleep, we hope they uttered a prayer of repentance for their lack of trust and confidence in their merciful Benefactor. As they drifted off into restful sleep, how could they help but do so with heartfelt thankfulness for the miraculous and divine favor they had experienced! How can we do any less?

God was not yet finished. Remember—bread from heaven? The people didn't forget. As the darkness of night was gradually swallowed up by the beams of morning light, the people of God peeked out of their shelters. Strangely, across the sandy plains lay a heavy dew. Was that it? If so, where was the "bread?" But then, as they watched with rapt attention, the dew lifted, and there it was. Something strangely different lay on the ground. **It was a small round substance, as fine as frost on the ground** (Exodus 16:14). Moses helped them out:

"This is the bread which the LORD has given you to eat" (Exodus 16:14&15).

It lay everywhere; the ground was covered with it! Knowing human nature as we do, we might suppose that immediately they prepared to gather up huge quantities of this miraculous bread—but hold on just a minute! The LORD had something to say about that! God wished for them to practice a little frugality as well as build some trust in the merciful hand of God.

Yes, the LORD attached an interesting condition to this blessing. He placed a limit on the amount they could gather. A limit? Absolutely! This was their rather generous, God-allotted quota: According to the number of people in their tent, they were to gather one omer for each individual in a given household. *(Note: Omer=2.087 qt.)* After eating, there were to be no leftovers. Nothing was to be kept overnight for a morning breakfast; period!

Do you see the purpose in this lesson? Each and every day they were obligated to look to God for His daily blessing with firm confidence in His never-ending goodness. A good lesson to learn, isn't it? Yes, it is that way with us also as we carry on our lives in our "houses of plenty." Each time we make that heart-felt request that our Savior taught us, that's what we are asking, isn't it? **Give us *this day* our daily bread** (Matthew 6:11). Tomorrow—next week—next year and so on—we need to leave our every need in the hands of our miracle-working God.

But with manna lying all over out there on the surface of the ground, it was just so utterly tempting! Some among the Israelites thought: *"I'll just put a little portion aside until morning and have it for another meal. After all, who knows if this will ever happen again!"* Sorry. Evidently, some weren't carefully listening to what God had said. If they were listening, they were not trusting. Sound familiar? But they quickly learned, for by the next morning the manna they had stored had turned rotten and wormy. So much for that lesson!

Yes, the LORD had ordained that it was to be a **daily** task. There was always plenty for everyone. In fact, it was so plentiful that each morning, after everyone had gathered their allotment, there was bountiful bread left on the sandy desert floor. What happened to that? Well, when the sun arose, the ungathered manna melted and was gone. The next day would be another day of faith and blessing.

But there was one other important matter connected with the daily gathering of the bread. There was one exception to the daily routine of collecting only one omer per day for each member of the household. That exception was the day preceding the Sabbath Day. *(Note: A weekly day of rest was already introduced at the time of creation, when God rested on the seventh day. **Then God blessed the seventh day and sanctified it,** (set it apart as special and holy) **because in it He rested from all His work which God had created and made** (Genesis 2:3). However, the Sabbath Day is not specifically referred to again by God in His Word until at this particular time and place.)*

In all likelihood, during their stay in Egypt, God's people reserved the seventh day in the week (Saturday) as a special day for physical and spiritual rest—so it all made perfect sense to them when the LORD God instructed them in this manner: **"Tomorrow is a Sabbath rest, a holy Sabbath to the LORD. Bake what you will bake today, and boil what you will boil; and lay up for yourselves all that remains, to be kept until morning."** So they laid it up till morning, as Moses commanded; and it did not stink, nor were there any worms in it. Then Moses said, **"Eat that today, for today is a Sabbath to the LORD; today you will not find it** [the miracle bread] **in the field. Six days you shall gather it, but on the seventh day, which is the Sabbath, there will be none"** (Exodus 16:25–26).

The double portion of manna kept just fine for their nourishment on the Sabbath Day. But human nature being what it is, some in foolish lack of faith tested God's instructions and went out on the Sabbath Day to gather more of those nourishing morsels. Of course, there were none to gather, for it was the Sabbath!

Curiosity often begs an answer to this question: "What was the nature of this 'bread,' this manna?" It appears that this miracle food from God had amazingly versatile culinary qualities. Manna could be eaten without any preparation—just as it was. It could also be baked into loaves, cakes, or biscuits. For a variety it might be cooked into mush. In many ways it seemed a lot like oatmeal or cream of wheat. But whatever its qualities might have been for physical nourishment, there was a greater lesson to be learned here—namely, the spiritual one. The spiritual one? What might that be?

Well, let's stop and think about that aspect. In the midst of the physical hunger of His people, God inserted the spiritual element of the Sabbath Day—the God-ordained day for soul nourishment as well as physical rest. Why was that important?

In my childhood I learned a lesson that may help us relate to this all-important feature. Growing up on the farm is still quite fresh in my mind. I clearly remember how our constant and direct dependence upon the elements of God's creation seemed to draw us close to Him in our everyday activities. As some of you remember, years ago most of the work was done by hand and with horses, while tractors were making a noisy debut. I remember like it was yesterday, when Sunday, our Sabbath Day, arrived, there was an eerie quietness on the farms—all was silent. Only maybe the bleating of sheep, the squealing of hogs, or the mooing of the cattle was heard.

The fields might be filled with dry shocks of grain awaiting their final trip to the threshing machine and the granary—or harvested fields inviting fall plowing—or stacks of hay out in the meadows stood ready to be moved to the hay-loft in the barn—while gutters, pens, and stalls of the animals needed cleaning and given fresh bedding (the work was endless!)—yet when the Sabbath Day arrived, no noisy machinery was heard in fields or yards. Necessary labor for livestock care was done in silence. All was done quietly, as though everyone in our little world were saying: **"The LORD is in His holy temple. Let all the earth keep silence before Him"** (Habakkuk 2:20).

I can still hear my father speaking about working on Sundays like any other day: *"The LORD has wondrously provided all of these blessings. It is only right that we should stop, tend only to the necessities on this day, and thank Him for His wondrous goodness. Besides, especially on this day, we need to hear Him speak to us from His Word. He who has provided well for us will see to it that we harvest and accomplish every other necessary task another day."*

Basically, that is what the LORD was saying to His people out there in the Wilderness. *"Physical needs? Yes, I will adequately supply them. Spiritual needs? Absolutely, I will continue to provide for you abundantly. But please . . . please do not forget the latter in favor of the former. Set aside a time to be silent and concentrate upon My love for you, my dear children. Use this day especially to hear Me. Receive My guiding hand to be used in your daily activities with My blessing. The Sabbath Day has been set aside for you. Use it wisely for your much needed physical and spiritual strength and rest."*

Yes, my friends in Christ, each happening experienced along this wondrous journey that we are taking with God and His people has a divine purpose. Every incident in the lives of God's people served and serves a need for His children in His kingdom of grace. They speak to each of us as we make our way through this life, focusing on Him and

His love for us all. Let's enjoy it all and drink and eat heavily of His nourishment with hearts of faith.

PRAYER

LORD my God, You have blessed me abundantly—spiritually and materially. Above all else You have blessed me with Your undeserved mercy in calling me into Your kingdom of grace through the gospel of Your love for me in the Christ, Your beloved Son. So as Your very own child, I depend upon You for needed "manna" every day, both spiritual and physical. Your wonderful means of grace in Word and Sacrament are precious gifts without which I cannot live. Each and every day I am dependent upon sustenance for mind, body and soul that You so generously provide. LORD, fill me with Your Spirit that I may not take these gifts of Your love for granted but daily recognize that all good things come from Your bountiful hands of love for me and for all of your people. LORD, give me humility and thankfulness in the day of plenty and constant faith in You for my needs in times of scarcity. So, I pray, in the words of an 18th century poet:

> *O God of Jacob, by whose hand*
> *Thy people still are fed;*
> *Who thro' this weary pilgrimage*
> *Hast all our fathers led,*
>
> *Thro' each perplexing path of life*
> *Our wand'ring foot-steps guide;*
> *Give us each day our daily bread*
> *And raiment fit provide.*
>
> *Oh, spread Thy covering wings around*
> *Till all our wanderings cease*
> *And at our Father's loved abode*
> *Our souls arrive in peace. Amen. (TLH 434:1,3,4)*

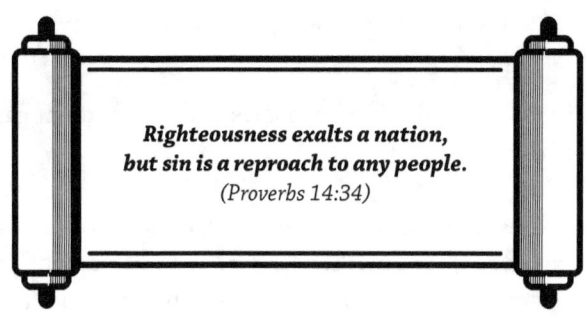

Righteousness exalts a nation,
but sin is a reproach to any people.
(Proverbs 14:34)

A THEOCRATIC GOVERNMENT

An acquaintance of mine sounded much like a libertarian when (in frustration with political gridlock) he made this assertion: "The best government is no government!" OK, that's what you say, but what does God say? God says: **Let every soul be subject to the governing authorities. For there is no authority except from God, <u>and the authorities that exist are appointed by God.</u> Therefore whoever resists the authority resists the ordinance of God, and those who resist will bring judgment on themselves. For the rulers are not a terror to good works, but to evil. Do you want to be unafraid of the authority? Do what is good, and you will have praise from the same. For <u>he is God's minister</u> to you for good. But if you do evil, be afraid; for he does not bear the sword in vain; for <u>he is God's minister</u>, an avenger to execute wrath on him who practices evil** (Romans 13:1–4).

My friends in Christ, the bottom line is this: It is God's will that every nation have a civil government—democracy, republicanism, dictatorship, monarchy, oligarchy, theocracy etc.—whatever it is, every nation needs a civil government! Why? Well, basically because we are not yet in heaven . . . not yet! Clearly, it is only through the acts of a civil government that some semblance of order is maintained in this messed-up-world. Sinful people dwell here where Satan, the father of lies and the murderer of souls, continues to con individuals into following his lead. How else but with laws and government can some type of order be maintained?

So I suppose questions might be asked: "Are the statutes of any given government always fair and without error?" Of course not. "Is law enforcement perfect?" No, it is not. After all, the very ones appointed to create and uphold the laws are sinners like those whom they serve. "Will they make mistakes?" Absolutely! "Do they have biases like everyone else?" No doubt! "Do some misuse their authority and position to harass rather than help?" Without question! "Are politicians and government officials always totally dedicated to the service of the people under their jurisdiction?" Sad to say—often times not.

Our LORD God puts it all into a "nutshell" when He declares: **Righteousness exalts a nation, but sin is a reproach to any people** (Proverbs 14:34). When all is said and done, it is absolutely true that every nation needs to be governed. However, it must also be said: If a government governs with righteous laws and if those who are given the authority to enforce those statutes do so properly, that nation will be blessed. If not, the entire population of that nation suffers.

While in Egypt, Israel lived under the dictatorship of Pharaoh. He was the supreme authority in whom all governmental powers were vested. Israel carried on in everyday living and working under that regime for hundreds of years. But then suddenly when they left Egypt, they were free from all man-made governmental rules and laws. Their ruler was God—and though He had appointed Moses as His earthly manager, they were still functioning under the rule of God—and thus their government was a theocracy.

The LORD God left some details of government to Moses, who was totally dedicated to the cause and calling of God. And, no doubt about it, administering the day to day affairs of a nation the size of Israel was mind-boggling to say the least. As we know, the total number of people in Israel had grown substantially during their 430 years in Egypt. Before they entered the Land of Promise, God directed the leaders to **take a census of all the congregation of the children of Israel from twenty years old and above, by their fathers' houses, all who are able to go to war in Israel** (Numbers 26:2). The result indicates that there were more than 600,000 males, aged 20 years old and older, in the nation of Israel. On that basis, the population of Israel has been conservatively estimated to have numbered about two million, five hundred thousand (2,500,000) souls. With that kind of population in mind, we can well understand the difficulty of governing. Obviously, this was a very trying and difficult task for Moses.

Enter . . . Jethro. Do you remember him? Sure, you do. He was the father-in-law of Moses. As you recall, Moses fled from Egypt after that serious altercation with an Egyptian which resulted in the Egyptian's death. In his hurried escape, Moses traveled all the way to Media, where he met and lived with Jethro, a priest in Media, for forty years. While staying with Jethro, Moses married one of Jethro's daughters, and they were blessed with two sons.

It appears that Jethro **had heard of all that God had done for Moses and for Israel His people—that the LORD had brought Israel out of Egypt** (Exodus 18:1). It's kind of amazing, isn't it? News traveled faster than one might think . . . even in those days. Remember, there were no newspapers, televisions, or telephones *(not even the "crank up" kind with a wooden wall-box)*. Some have wondered, *"How did they ever live without a telephone?"* Well, they lived just fine, thank you! Apparently, they communicated with distant family, friends, and acquaintances <u>only when necessary</u>!

In spite of the total lack of any modern message exchange system, Jethro got the word that Moses and the nation of Israel were encamped near Mount Sinai. Now, that's at least a 150 mile jaunt from Media, where Jethro resided—no small distance to travel by donkey or camel, yet Jethro was determined to make the trip in order to reunite Moses and his family. *(Note: It appears that the wife and children of Moses returned to the safety of Jethro's home maybe sometime during the plagues in Egypt. Cf. Exodus 4:20 with Exodus 18:6.)*

Jethro sent word to Moses that he was coming: **"I, your father-in-law Jethro, am coming to you with your wife and her two sons with her"** (Exodus 18:6). A joyful reunion took place as they hugged and kissed and briefly discussed the happenings of the previous weeks. They reviewed how the LORD God had miraculously delivered them from the armies of Pharaoh and how He had continually and miraculously saved them and preserved them on that long, dangerous, and faith-strengthening journey through the wilderness. Jethro capped the celebration very properly with a worship service of thanksgiving to the LORD God. Aaron invited all the elders of Israel to join Moses' family in this wonderful, God-centered celebration of thanksgiving.

The next day—back to work. As the God-appointed leader of Israel, Moses was kept very busy, to put it mildly. Anything of any magnitude whatever in the nation of Israel came to rest on the shoulders of Moses. There were some elders under Moses who carried out various counseling chores on behalf of their leader, yet the major judgments—the "heavy lifting" was exclusively under the jurisdiction of Moses alone.

One can hardly imagine the vast amount of administrative and judicial work that came before Moses daily. Given the fact that the people of Israel were sinful humans like us, it isn't difficult to realize the gravity and the voluminous amount of intensive labor that rested on the shoulders of Moses each and every day. As a result, from early morning until late at night, he carried on as Israel's judge on behalf of God, guiding and leading His people to live together in a godly fashion.

Jethro studiously watched as Moses labored intensely, day after day after day. Finally he got the picture very clearly. Apparently, Moses' father-in-law was a no-nonsense, right-to-the-point kind of man, so rather bluntly he approached Moses with this question: **"What is this thing that you are doing for the people? Why do you alone sit,** (as judge) **and all the people stand before you from morning until evening?"** (Exodus 18:14)

And Moses said to his father-in-law: "Because the people come to me to inquire of God. When they have a difficultly, they come to me, and I judge between one and another; and I make known the statutes of God and His laws" (Exodus 18:15–16).

Well, now, that sounded like a fairly good explanation. However, given the number of people involved, it was without a doubt an overwhelming task and maybe an impossible work load, so Jethro, who obviously was a very smart and observant father-in law, clearly saw a problem with this arrangement. He didn't spare any words but brusquely came to the point, **"The thing that you do is not good"** (Exodus 18:17).

That got the attention of Moses immediately! Indeed, maybe it sounded a bit harsh—yet what he was driving at was this: **"Both you and these people who are with you** (your deputies) **will surely wear yourselves out. For this thing is too much for you; you are not able to perform it by yourself"** (Exodus 18:18).

Of course, that's easy to say, as we all well know. It's not difficult to point to a problem, but the solution to the problem is usually the difficult part. But Jethro was not just a critic; he also proposed a possible remedy for the obvious overload that Moses and his lieutenants were bearing.

Briefly he made it clear: *"Get more people involved in your organization! You're doing well with counseling the people according to God's will, and that should continue, but you need more help. You need to select a number of God-fearing men from among the people to carry out some of this responsibility.*

As your subordinates they will function among the people and advise them according to the will of God. Some will be governors over thousands, others over hundreds, some will have fifty in their jurisdiction, while others may have as few as ten people to counsel" (Paraphrase of Exodus 18:19–23).

Jethro was right, and Moses knew it. Immediately he heeded the wise counsel of Jethro. It took some doing and some time, but Moses learned to delegate more of his responsibilities to well-chosen subordinates while he continued to handle only the most difficult cases. As a result, government offices and departments were slowly emerging, and the nation of God's people was beginning, more and more, to function as a working theocracy—a nation under God's rule.

We must remember that the establishment of the nation of Israel was not an end in itself. Israel was God's chosen nation with one wonderful purpose and reason for existing—namely, the task of producing the Child of Hope for all of sinful humanity. When that would stand accomplished under the leadership of that God-appointed Savior of the world, the rule of God would be established in the hearts of people everywhere. Yes, under Shiloh—the Christ—God's Son from eternity, all believers would be gathered together **as a chosen generation, a royal priesthood, a holy nation, His own special people. For what purpose? That you may proclaim the praises of Him who called you out of darkness into His marvelous light** (I Peter 2:9). As Jacob put it so well: **To Him** (Shiloh) **shall be the obedience of the people** (Genesis 49:10b).

Sad to say, national Israel as it exists today is a shell without the kernel—the husk without the corn—the straw without the grain. Modern day Israel has thoroughly rejected the Messiah who was the **glory of . . . Israel** (Luke 2:32). Indeed, the Apostle John spells it out clearly when moved by the Spirit of God he reports concerning the Christ of God: He **was the true Light which gives light to every man who comes into the world. He was in the world, and the**

world was made through Him, and the world did not know Him. He came to His own, and His own did not receive Him (John 1:9–11).

Today's Israel is just another nation among other nations of the world. Nations will rise and nations will fall. Governments will rise and then they will fail. History attests to this fact century after century after century. But that one nation, that spiritual Kingdom of the ever-living LORD God, established under the leadership of God's Son, Jesus Christ, will grow and continue to flourish in the midst of all of the dust and debris of the falling kingdoms of men. The kingdom of the living God will continue to carry on its work of delivering salvation, life, and peace in the name of Shiloh, the Prince of Peace, throughout the world.

Finally, the remains of this world's kingdoms will be swept away in the fire of God's judgment—but God's kingdom of grace, functioning in the midst of this sin-sick world, will melt into His eternal kingdom of heavenly glory. As our resurrected Savior promised while still on this earth: **Let not your heart be troubled; you believe in God, believe also in Me. In my Father's house are many mansions; if it were not so, I would have told you. I go to prepare a place for you. And if I go and prepare a place for you, I will come again and receive you to Myself; that where I am, there you may be also. And where I go you know, and the way you know** (John 14:1–4).

Yes, my friends, it is a long way from Eden to Bethlehem—but as we continue on this joyous journey, we are thrilled again and again as we recognize that the LORD God is always in command, causing all things to work together for the good of His people and toward the fulfillment of His promise made in the Garden. Yes, that promise will be fulfilled— His promised Messiah will come. In Him, God's ultimate goal of establishing one elect nation under God would be accomplished.

My friends in Christ, we are living in that glorious time right now. Christ's kingdom is flourishing throughout the world. Listen! What do we hear? We hear God's children everywhere as they are singing:

When Jesus enters land and nation
And changes people with His love,
When, yielding to His kind persuasion,
Our hearts His truth and blessing prove,
Then shall our life on earth be blest;
The peace of God on us shall rest.

When Jesus comes—O blessed story—
He works a change in heart and life;
God's kingdom comes with pow'r and glory
To young and old, to man and wife.
Through sacrament and living Word
Faith, love, and hope are now conferred.

Oh, may He soon to ev'ry nation
Find entrance where He is unknown,
With life and light and free salvation,
That Satan's pow'r be overthrown,
And healing to all hearts may come
In heathen land and Christian home! (CW 32:3–5)

PRAYER

Dear LORD, I thank and praise You every day for calling me by the power of Your Spirit into Your kingdom of grace. There I rest in peace governed by You, for there my Shiloh has come to give me rest and peace for time which will be perfectly experienced in the joys of eternity. But while I am still here, I also have a responsibility toward the civil powers of this world. The governing authorities in this world are ordained by You for the blessing of all. Since we all have a sinful nature, order must be maintained for the good of all. Gross crime must be held in check in this world where Satan rules the hearts of many. For the blessing of good civil government I pray and I thank You for it. Yet above all, I thank and praise You for the blessing of being a part of Your earthly kingdom. I pray that I may pass through life with You guiding and leading me unto that perfect day. There I will be with You forever in the glories of eternity ruled by You in love. In Your holy name I pray. Amen.

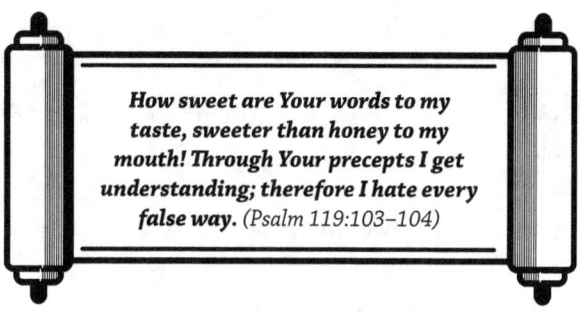

How sweet are Your words to my taste, sweeter than honey to my mouth! Through Your precepts I get understanding; therefore I hate every false way. (Psalm 119:103–104)

PREPARATIONS FOR GOD'S ONCE-AND-FOREVER SERMON

So here we are at the foot of Mount Sinai. God's people had no idea why they were there. Moses was their God-appointed leader—but neither was he privy to the reason why this huge nation of God's people were camping at the foot of Mt. Sinai. Most importantly, however, God knew . . . for He had led them there.

Three months had passed since the children of Israel had left Egypt and begun their God-directed journey to the Land of Promise—but they were going the wrong direction, weren't they? At least that is how it might appear. They had traveled southeast about 200 miles—into the desert plains of the Sinai Peninsula. Why? Well, there were a few reasons—but only God knew what they were.

We are aware that the LORD God had a great deal of ground to cover in preparing His chosen people for what lay ahead. Drawing them closer to Himself in their faith was certainly all important. Some progress had been made in that respect in the past three months—but that was only the beginning. Now it was time to expose them to the next stage in their development as a nation under God. In order to accomplish this enormous happening, an occasion far beyond their wildest dreams was about to unfold before their very eyes.

In preparation and by way of introduction for this once-in-a-lifetime, spectacular occurrence, Moses was called by God to make his way up into the mountain—Mount Sinai. So, very obediently and carefully this centenarian servant of God slowly made his way up and through the crevices and crannies of that famous mountain . . . when suddenly, the very voice of God sounded loud and clear with these directions:

"Thus you shall say to the house of Jacob, and tell the children of Israel: 'You have seen what I did to the Egyptians, and how I bore you on eagles' wings and brought you to Myself. Now therefore, if you will indeed obey My voice and keep My covenant, then you shall be a special treasure to Me above all people, for all the earth is Mine. And you shall be to Me a kingdom of priests and a holy nation.' These are the words which you shall speak to the children of Israel" (Exodus 19: 3–6).

What a tremendous introduction to that which was to follow! First the LORD God, through His servant Moses, pointed His people to the happenings of the last three months. There they could see and should realize beyond question His continual presence—His constant and committed relationship to them and His unfailing love for them: The pillar of fire and the pillar of a cloud—the crossing of the Sea between walls of water—the LORD God destroying His people's enemies, the Egyptian army, in that watery grave—making the bitter waters sweet at Marah—providing rest and peace by the bubbling fountains and shade under the giant palms of Elim—giving them Manna to eat every morning and quail every evening. He had carried them every inch of the way as on eagle's wings. They were invited to remember, recognize, and sing:

Praise to the LORD,
Who o'er all things is wondrously reigning,
And, as on wings of an eagle, uplifting, sustaining.
Have you not seen,
All that is needful has been
Sent by His gracious ordaining? (CW 234:2)

Most importantly and above all, God reminded them of that one special and grand assignment which He had given them—**"obey My voice and keep My covenant."** Yes, they would be the soul possessors of His **"covenant"** which had been promised many millennia earlier in the Garden of Eden and affirmed to their father Abraham when God promised: **"In you all the families of the earth shall be blessed"** (Genesis 12:3).

No doubt about it, the LORD God would be with them every inch of the way because they were His **treasure**. In the midst of all of the godless, unbelieving corruption of a sin-filled world, they would be tied to Him with His golden chain of love. They would be His **kingdom of priests and a holy nation**. "Remember—and don't forget," said God, **"all the earth is mine**, and you are called to be my **priests**—my mouth-pieces unto the ends of the Earth."

With these blessed words from the LORD God Himself, God's devoted servant slowly made his way back down the mountain and brought these wonder-filled words of affirmation and promise from God to the elders assigned to their various sections of soul-care among the nation of Israel. They in turn likely met with their constituents and delivered God's reminder, blessings, and encouragement. The answer from God's chosen children came back loudly and clearly. In one accord—they whole-heartedly affirmed, **"All that the LORD has spoken we will do"** (Exodus 19:8).

What a concise and faith-strengthening proclamation from the living God! Yes, and what an apparently heart-felt answer was given by His people!

Moses was filled with joy as he made his way back up the mountain to relay the people's reply of devotion and dedication to the LORD God. Finally it was revealed—namely, the primary purpose for this meeting with God at Mount Sinai. To begin, the LORD God said to Moses, **"Behold, I come to you in the thick cloud, that the people may hear when I speak with you, and believe you forever"** (Exodus 19:9).

What was going on here? What was God saying? Well, the LORD wished to confirm something very important to His people. They needed to realize once and for all time, that as long as Moses lived, he stood before them in the place of God. He was the mouthpiece of God—he was the promoter of God's will. To rebel against Moses was to oppose God Himself. So before He went any further, God wanted this understood by the people, absolutely . . . that they might **"believe you** (Moses) **forever."**

This had to be a frightening and anxious moment for God's people. They clearly remembered the tremendous power and merciful kindness of God unmistakably demonstrated over the past three months. Now, suddenly they were to prepare themselves to hear the LORD God Himself speaking to His appointed leader, Moses, as well as to them.

The people understandably were shaken. *"What should we do? How should we get ready? What must we do in preparation?"* The LORD had anticipated such a frightened reaction from His people, so He gently instructed Moses to help them in their desire to properly prepare for this once-in-a-lifetime experience: **"Go to the people and sanctify them today and tomorrow, and let them wash their clothes. And let them be ready for the third day. For on the third day the**

LORD will come down upon Mount Sinai in the sight of all the people" (Exodus 19:10,11).

OK! We are acquainted with "getting ready" for special occasions, aren't we? Attending worship services is a good example. We bathe and put on clean and appropriate clothing. We try to remember any important items we need to complement our special visit with God.

How is this different than when we talk with God regularly every day as we go about our activities as His children? Why should attending a worship service be a particularly special event in our lives? In short, we prepare ourselves physically, mentally, and spiritually—for we are about to enter a place especially prepared for hearing and worshiping none other than the LORD God of heaven and earth!

On such special occasions we have the privilege of hearing our loving LORD God speak to us in His very own words about life and living with Him and with one another—repenting of our sins in thought, words, and deeds—gratefully receiving His forgiving love and His assurances of our eternal salvation in His Son, our Savior, Jesus Christ. Besides all of that, we are given the privilege of supporting His work in this world by prayers, offerings, and by accepting responsibilities in His kingdom labors. Yes, what a marvelous privilege it is—to gather with fellow believers—to speak with Him in our prayers—to raise our voices and sing praises to Him for all of His blessings. Absolutely, for these particular times in our lives we should make genuine, heartfelt preparations—physically and spiritually.

What faced the people of God on that very rare occasion at the foot of Mount Sinai was infinitely and intensely different, wasn't it? At that especial designated day they were directed to diligently prepare themselves to literally (physically as well as spiritually) stand in the very presence of the Living God of heaven and earth and hear Him speak to them—personally. Think about that for a moment! How would you prepare? Each of us must ask ourselves: *"What would I do to ready myself for such an unbelievable event?"* One thing is certain; we could prepare ourselves through prayer:

> *Come, Holy Spirit, come!*
> *Let Thy bright beams arise;*
> *Dispel the sorrow from our minds,*
> *The darkness from our eyes.*

> *Revive our drooping faith,*
> *Our doubts and fears remove,*
> *And kindle in our breasts the flame*
> *Of never-dying love.*

> *'Tis Thine to cleanse the heart,*
> *To sanctify the soul,*
> *And pour fresh life into each part,*
> *And new-create the whole. Amen. (TLH 225:1,2,4)*

PRAYER

Dear LORD, what a marvelous privilege it is to gather together with fellow believers to worship You. As You know, during the week I pray privately and/or with family. I read from Your Word as well as from prepared devotions written to guide me in matters of life and living for You. These provide an everyday blessing. But it is so very special to worship with fellow believers—pray with them—sing hymns with depth of meaning—and above all hear Your inspired Word of life and the message prepared and delivered for me and the other worshipers. So on those special days and evenings in the Church Year, I pray, bless these spiritually invigorating services. Decorate our lives, hearts, and minds with Your messages of grace and mercy as we come before You to be reminded of Your entire plan of salvation for me and for all people. Thank You for this blessing in our Savior's name. Amen

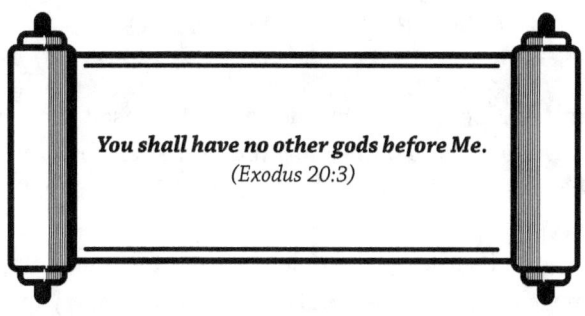

You shall have no other gods before Me.
(Exodus 20:3)

GOD REQUIRES FAITHFULNESS TO HIM ALONE

Suddenly, intense thundering reverberated from the heavens—bright lightning flashes filled the sky—Mount Sinai was abruptly wrapped in a thick, dark cloud—the ear-piercing blare of trumpets filled the air. And in the midst of it all God Himself descended upon the mountain in a stream of fire—thick smoke engulfed Mount Sinai—the trumpet blasts became louder and louder—the entire mountain quaked as the Creator of all touched down upon the highest peak. From this majestic pulpit, the voice of the LORD God of heaven and earth thundered from the mountain top across the plains below: **"I am the LORD your God, who brought you out of the land of Egypt, out of the house of bondage"** (Exodus 20:2).

"I am the LORD your God. *I am Jehovah, your God who made that saving covenant with your first parents already in the Garden of Eden. I am your LORD God, who confirmed My covenant with your father Abraham and poured out My blessings upon you, Abraham's offspring. I am the One who favored you with abundance during your 400 year stay in Egypt. Yes, I am the One who delivered you from the slavery of that nation."*

God didn't need a microphone or amplifying system of any kind. His majestically profound affirmations clearly echoed from the mountain top and reverberated down to the very souls of His people who stood in rapt attention. Then, from the voice of God Himself came these words—His will proclaimed in simple terms that all could understand: **"You shall have no other gods before Me"** (Exodus 20:3).

So here we stand with God's people at the foot of that holy mount and hear Him speak to His people—His people then . . . and you and me, His people now.

In the first place, He was speaking to His children in the nation of Israel—His people who had one holy and distinctive calling. And what was that special destiny for Israel again? They were to stand as that one glorious light—that one and only bright beacon of salvation and restoration for the entire world. In the center of their God-given purpose was the production of the Messiah—the Savior for all mankind through whom God's wondrous salvation would be accomplished.

Now, we must bear in mind that God intended this nation of His people to live where He called them to be . . . where again? Smack-dab in the midst of a grossly idolatrous people in this sin-darkened world— Canaan! So the question arises: How could they meet God's objective? How could they be God's lighthouse lighting the way through all the man-made and Satan-encouraged idolatry that was everywhere in that territory where they were about to dwell?

God's people must know from the outset—in the very first commandment—that the LORD God allows no challenges posed by false gods. His people must realize that giving any worshipful credence whatever to anyone or anything other than the one true LORD God would be a terrible contradiction to the purpose for which they were called. Therefore, clearly and simply: **"You shall have <u>no other gods</u> before me"** (Exodus 20:2).

In other words, *"You shall not give your heart, your soul, your very life into the care and keeping of make-believe gods concocted by the sinful minds of others."* Clear enough; right?

As we stand together with our brethren at the foot of Mount Sinai, we are forced to ask ourselves, *"Do these words speak to us today?"* Of course they do! We are all the children of God by faith in the God-appointed Savior of us all—namely, the LORD Jesus, the Seed of the woman, our Savior and LORD. The entire moral code of God delivered from that mountain top will stand even 'till the end of time. <u>For, contrary to the belief of society, God's written moral code shall never be dissolved</u> but will continue to be the one absolute, perfect law for moral conduct among all humanity until this world comes to an end!

Sinful humans have the silly notion that <u>they have the ability</u> to determine what is right and what is wrong—that <u>they are able to</u> determine what constitutes life and living—that they are able to determine what is moral and what is not! It's worse than silly; it's ridiculous, isn't it? Yet it's one of Satan's lies! In fact, it's one of his best! Why? Look at the results . . . this lie prospers everywhere!

This lie of the Evil One has been adopted by the vast majority of the people the world over! Everywhere sinful people have the audacity to assume that they can determine what is best for them—how they should live—how they are to function with their neighbors—how they should behave with their spouse, children, etc. How did this ridiculous scenario happen? You remember, don't you? Yes, it all began in the Garden.

Yes, this very Law of God was originally inscribed in the heart of man at creation, for God <u>implanted a perfect knowledge of right and wrong into human souls</u>. Although the fall of Adam and Eve into sin ruined their perfection, humans still retain a meager sense of right and wrong. We often refer to that indwelling awareness of right and wrong in mankind as *conscience*. Even though that inner voice may be beaten, battered, and bound, it's still there in the human soul.

The Apostle Paul points directly to that fact when God caused him to write about the evidence of the Law of God found even in unbelievers, **who show the work of the law written in their hearts, their conscience also bearing witness** (Romans 2:15). We often refer to that obvious phenomenon in mankind as the "natural knowledge of God."

So now, there on Mount Sinai, the LORD God would clearly and graciously spell out His moral Law, to stand absolutely for all time for all humanity. It was a very dramatic and awesome moment for Israel, and it is a tremendously important moment for each of us.

Let's try to get the picture here. As was mentioned, His people were about to enter into a land where Satan controlled the hearts, minds, and bodies of the inhabitants. As a result, idolatry was everywhere. It had saturated everything that they thought, said, and did. The Canaanites of the land had created gods and goddesses representing everything imaginable—from earthly creatures to heavenly bodies. Their work, their family life . . . even their entertainment and sex lives were woven into the fabric of their idolatry.

Worship facilities for carrying on their "religious" services were located everywhere. Of course, the LORD God knew what was in store for His people, and therefore He was preparing their hearts and minds for the moral challenges they were about to experience firsthand. For that reason God further explains:

"You shall not make for yourself any carved image, or any likeness of anything that is in heaven above, or that is in the earth beneath, or that is in the water under the earth; you shall not bow down to them nor serve them. For I, the LORD your

God, am a jealous God, visiting the iniquity of the fathers on the children to the third and fourth generations of those who hate Me, but showing mercy to thousands, to those who love Me and keep My commandments" (Exodus 20:2–6).

The list of false gods that spiritually depraved souls create has no end. The reason why is clearly underlined in each generation. We need to review it once again. When people who have been created to worship the LORD God alone and serve only Him lose sight of Him in their hearts and minds, they are as lost as lost can be. As a result, their lives are without meaning and purpose. They wander about trying to invent something—anything in an attempt to create a cause or a purpose in life—a reason for living—something to believe in. Why? To fill the void that is so keenly felt—to try to give a meaningless life some meaning!

Thus, humans have concocted a multiplication of gods in the world. Down through the generations there have been all types of "supreme beings" created by the minds of man: Animals, trees, mountains, rivers, heavenly bodies and whatever! Any and all become possible candidates for divinity in the corrupted minds of humanity. It is still happening regularly in this day and age.

As stark examples: In the 20th century during World War II, the world witnessed kamikaze pilots carrying out suicide attacks upon given targets *in the name of their man-created gods*. In this 21st century young men and women are recruited by religious terrorist organizations to blow themselves up—and in the process kill innocent bystanders. Prisoners are beheaded in public because they are considered to be infidels—people who do not accept the man-created, Muslim god Allah! Why? Idolaters carry out such atrocities in the mistaken belief that their "god or gods" will be pleased and will reward them in a supposed afterlife!

And, by the way, does any of us believe that we are exempt from the dangers of idolatry? I hope not! For it is lying at the doorstep of every one of us. Think about it. With Satan's engineering, the blessings of God can easily become our idols! Things and stuff can become our objects of worship! Isn't that a contradiction? Indeed, it is! The LORD God blesses—and then the blessings may become one's god? What? How can that be possible?

Let's give that some thought for a minute. Isn't it true? The object upon which one sets one's heart and around which one builds one's life and upon which one depends for security and happiness is a type of a god—isn't it? It might be wealth; it could be prestige; maybe it is buildings, houses, self-glory, things—things—things. Indeed, we all need to ask ourselves and be reminded daily, "Who has given me that wealth—Who has blessed me with this home—Who has given me that special ability to achieve outstanding accomplishments?" We know the answer to those questions, don't we?

That's why Martin Luther very properly and simply explains God's first commandment in this way: "We should fear, love, and trust in God above all things!" For if God's blessings become the center of our lives and our reason for living, they may very well have supplanted God! The blessing may well have become the central purpose in our lives and our reason for living and our basis for happiness. To put it bluntly: The blessing becomes all important . . . rather than the Blesser! Are we guilty? Sad to say, only too often we are.

That is why we need to repent often—again and again and again. We need to flee for refuge to His infinite mercy, seeking and imploring His gracious, forgiving love, for the sake of our LORD Jesus Christ. Yes, my friends in Christ, we need to be assured often by our loving LORD: "*For the sake of the Seed of the woman, Jesus Christ, My Son, your Savior, your sins are forgiven. Go in peace—avoid sin—walk with me.*" What a glorious purpose the Law of God serves! And what gracious blessings we enjoy in His forgiving-Gospel-love!

Yes, we ought never forget: Just as Israel was called to be a blazing light of godliness in the midst of the sin-darkened world, we too as God's own people have that same privileged responsibility. May we never forget that soul-inspiring description of each of us: **"You are the light of the world. A city that is set on a hill cannot be hidden. Nor do they light a lamp and put it under a basket, but on a lampstand, and it gives light to all who are in the house. Let your light so shine before men, that they may see your good works and glorify your Father in heaven"** (Matthew 5:14–16).

Yes, my friends in Christ, just as the children of Israel were chosen to reflect God's bright and glorious light of God in the midst of their sin-darkened world, so we, the called children of the living God in Christ, are privileged to reflect Him in the midst of our world. Our Savior said it all in just a few chosen words: **"Let your light so shine before men, that they may see your good works and glorify your Father in heaven"** (Matthew 5:16).

But there is one other description of God that we have not addressed here. The question is this: Is God jealous? The response might be surprising, but the God-given answer is, "Absolutely!" There is no question about it—and He is not ashamed to admit it.

The LORD God who created mankind—He who watched as His special creations, Adam and Eve—the crowns of His creation, walk away from Him to follow Satan—He who pledged to rescue mankind from that wretched fall—He who promised to send One who would destroy Satan and his work—He who chose Abraham through whose offspring all the nations of the earth would be blessed by that special Child—Shiloh—the Messiah—Jesus, the Christ: He alone has the right to expect unfettered and unconditional, heartfelt devotion and dedication from the people that He called to deliver His plan of salvation to each and every soul in this sin-benighted world.

And yes, He who has blessed us with abiding faith in His promises fulfilled in the Messiah, our Savior and LORD—He has every right to expect undying and continued praise to Him alone from every one of us every single day of our lives. Absolutely, our God is and has a right to be a jealous God! He will not share us with anyone or anything!

To that end may we join that gifted 17th-century hymn writer in thanking and praising our LORD for His wondrous salvation in the Christ:

> *From eternity, O God,*
> *In your Son you did elect me.*
> *Therefore, Father, on life's road*
> *Graciously to heav'n direct me;*
> *Send to me your Holy Spirit*
> *That his gifts I may inherit.*
>
> *Born alive but dead in sin,*
> *Lost to all good things by nature,*
> *I was found and changed within*
> *And became a newborn creature.*
> *Sinful flesh works ruination,*
> *But the Spirit works salvation.*
>
> *Drive away the gloomy night*
> *Of my darkened mind's reflection.*
> *Quench all thoughts that are not right;*
> *Hold my reason in subjection.*
> *For your truth may I be yearning,*
> *Heav'nly wisdom ever learning. (CW 461:1–3)*

PRAYER

My dear LORD, each day that I live is filled with Your blessings. The refrigerator is filled with food. My living quarters are pleasant, warm, and cozy. You have provided medical care when it is needed. You have given me family, friends, acquaintances, and neighbors who fill my life with joy and pleasantness. Your wonders of creation are all around me every day, and they cause me to constantly marvel as I view the works of Your miraculous creative hands in the things that we have been privileged to uncover. The list is endless as I think of the many gifts You have given to me, wondrously providing for my spiritual growth, strength, and care. But suffice it to say, O LORD—THANK YOU—Thank You for Your undeserved goodness! May Your blessings to me serve as a bright light showing the way into Your kingdom for other souls. In the name of my Savior and Lord, who is the Gift of all gifts. Amen.

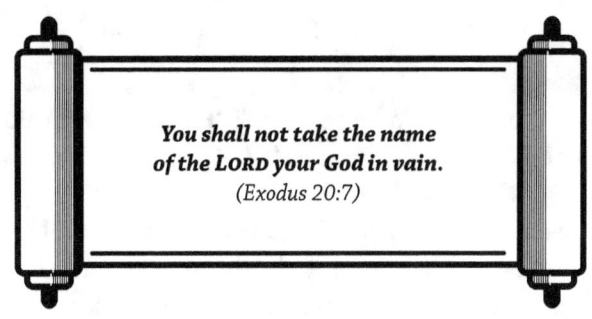

*You shall not take the name
of the LORD your God in vain.*
(Exodus 20:7)

GOD REQUIRES THAT WE RESPECT HIS HOLY NAME

The thunderous voice of God sounded again from the mountain top and filled the sandy plains below. The subject: God's holy name. To misuse or abuse God's name is absolutely unacceptable to God, period!

Maybe we might ask: *"What is meant by God's name?"* We all have names. But it's more than that, isn't it? Yes, it is. As a matter of fact, His name is everything that God is—everything that He does—everything that He says. Without question, everything that God is, does, and says (His entire being and reputation) is to be held in the highest regard by every one of His believing children.

You likely remember when Moses was called by God to return to Egypt for that special assignment of rescuing His people and leading them to the land of promise. In response to God's call, Moses produced a ton of excuses. He was trying to demonstrate that he was not the man for that extraordinarily high calling. With one of his excuses, Moses pleaded with God, **"Indeed, when I come to the children of Israel and say to them, 'The God of your fathers has sent me to you,' and they say to me, 'What is His name?' What shall I say to them?"** (Exodus 3:13)

Do you remember how God responded? **"I AM WHO I AM. Thus you shall say to the children of Israel, 'I AM has sent me to you.'"**

Here we have a phenomenally clear identification of God by which He reveals His very essence to Moses and to us—namely, the LORD God is—was—and always will be our eternal, unchangeable, ever-present Creator, Redeemer, and Sanctifier. Besides, He is our covenant God. Moses said it best when he put pen to parchment in the 90th Psalm: **LORD, You have been our dwelling place in all generations. Before the mountains were brought forth, or ever You had formed the earth and the world, even from everlasting to everlasting, You are God** (Psalm 90:1–2).

What is so amazing is this: The LORD God who is, was, and ever shall be—the Creator of you, me, and all mankind—the LORD and Maker of every creature that walks on the earth, every bird that decorates the sky, every aquatic creature that dwells in the waters, the world and the entire universe—the very One who watched as His perfect, creative love was crushed beneath the faithlessness of our fore-parents—He, the LORD God of all, the King of the universe, stooped down to us lowly and guilty beings and in His gracious mercy proclaimed: *"I will fix it all! That is why I promised to send you a Savior, that special Seed of the woman. He will come to restore you to be My children, for time and forever. Besides, knowing that you are blind, deaf, and dead in your trespasses and sins, I will send My Spirit to open your blind eyes, unstop your deaf ears, breathe life into your lifeless soul that you may see, hear, and believe that I love you and have 'fixed it all.' I have made you spiritually well again in the Messiah, the Seed of the woman. By faith in Him you have become My children for time and forever."*

Yes, my friends, after God has shown His pure, forgiving, and unadulterated love in the Messiah—having sent His Spirit to open our blind eyes and unstop our deaf ears that all might know how much He loves us all . . . how can anyone ever consider misusing His name?

Rather, how can His chosen people help but stand in reverent awe of everything He is, does, and says. It should hardly need to be said: **"You shall not misuse the name of the LORD your God"** (Exodus 20:7 NIV).

Furthermore, my friends, think about it. Our LORD God tells us everything that we need to know about Himself—what He has done, what He is doing, and what He will do even into eternity. Indeed, God has opened Himself for all to read. Why does He do so? Because He wishes for every human being on the face of this planet to know Him and experience His constant love for everyone. That is why we are making this joyful journey through the pages of His diary as inspired by His Spirit. We get to know Him better and better, don't we? We are privileged to see up close how He graciously, lovingly, and continually cares for His dear, believing children.

So it should go without saying: No human being has the right, nor should we have the desire, to side-step His Word nor manipulate what He has said in any way. To do so is to misuse and abuse His holy name! Maybe a few inspired examples from His thankful children are called for. Here are a couple:

1. In the midst of a world of spiritual darkness and confusion, the Psalmist was inspired to describe God's Word to us in this way: **"Your word is a lamp to my feet and a light to my path"** (Psalm 119:105).

2. In this sin-ridden world where falsehoods and outright lies everywhere threaten our faith in Him, our Savior prays to His and our heavenly Father for us: **"Sanctify them by Your truth, Your word is truth."** (John 17:17).

3. When mankind becomes enthralled with getting and having everything imaginable in this world is the ultimate lifestyle, God

reminds everyone that **man lives by every <u>word</u> that proceeds from the mouth of the LORD** (Deuteronomy 8:3).

4. To sum it up, Isaiah was moved by the Spirit to say rather poetically: **"The grass withers, the flower fades, but the <u>word</u> of our God stands forever"** (Isaiah 40:8).

My friends, without His Word we would lead a hopelessly fruitless life—going nowhere—**strangers from the covenants of promise, having no hope and without God in the world** (Ephesians 2:12).

What joy it is—what a privilege we have—to be standing with our fellow children of the living God at the foot of Mount Sinai and there hear the LORD God speak with us and to us—for we too in these New Testament times are traveling a journey in His name; aren't we? As we make our way through the obstacles and trials of this godless world, we too are looking toward the blessings and the joys of another Promised Land. That perfect place toward which we are traveling is the **new heavens and a new earth in which righteousness dwells** (II Peter 3:13).

Yes, we are walking *(and sometimes running)* every day, hand-in-hand with our Messiah, our Shiloh, toward that final goal. **And this is the testimony: that God has given us eternal life, and this life is in His Son. He who has the Son has life; he who does not have the Son of God does not have life. These things I have written to you who believe in the name of the Son of God, that you may know that you have eternal life, and that you may continue to believe in the name of the Son of God** (I John 5:11–13).

What a tremendous gift of God's grace it is—to be counted among the saints of God, now and forever! The words of Johann Mentzer (from the 17th century) help us to personalize our heartfelt thankfulness to our Savior-God very well. We join him in this meaningful prayer:

Oh, that I had a thousand voices
To praise my God with thousand tongues!
My heart, which in the Lord rejoices,
Would then proclaim in grateful songs
To all, wherever I might be,
What great things God has done for me.

Dear Father, endless praise I render
For soul and body nobly joined;
I praise You, Guardian kind and tender,
For all the daily joys I find
So richly spread on ev'ry side
And freely for my use supplied.

I praise You, Savior, whose compassion
Has brought You down to ransom me.
Your pitying heart sought my salvation;
You bore the cross triumphantly,
Brought me from bondage full release,
Made me Your own, and gave me peace.

Glory and praise, still onward reaching,
Be Yours, O Spirit of all grace,
Whose holy pow'r and faithful teaching
Give me among Your saints a place.
Whatever good by me is done
Is worked by grace divine alone.

Shall I not then be filled with gladness?
Shall I not praise You ever more
And triumph over fear and sadness,
Although my cup of woe runs o'er?
Though heav'n and earth shall disappear,
Your endless love is ever near. (CW 194)

PRAYER

LORD God, as I consider everything that You are and everything that You do for me every day, words fail as I attempt to express my gratitude for Your merciful kindness poured out so generously upon me and all of mankind. I can only join Your servant David in deep heartfelt praise and beg of You: **"Let the words of my mouth and the meditation of my heart be acceptable in Your sight, O LORD, my strength and my redeemer"** (Psalm 19:14). In the name of Your Son whom You sent to "fix it all" and redeem me to be Yours for time and forever I pray. Amen.

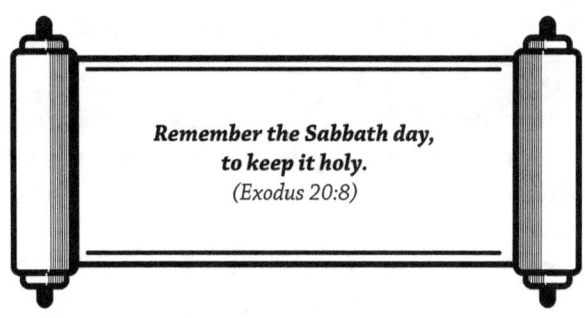

*Remember the Sabbath day,
to keep it holy.*
(Exodus 20:8)

GOD REQUIRES THAT WE WORSHIP HIM IN SPIRIT AND TRUTH

The clear, robust voice of the LORD God continued to rumble down the mountain side and across the desert floor. The people stood in stunned attention, attempting to mentally and spiritually digest every last word spoken by their faithful Leader and LORD.

As has been mentioned, after creation was completed, a day of rest followed. **Then God saw everything that He had made, and indeed it was very good. So the evening and the morning were the sixth day. Thus the heavens and the earth, and all the host of them, were finished. And on the seventh day God ended His work which He had done, and He rested on the seventh day from all His work which He had done. Then God blessed the seventh day and sanctified it, because in it He rested from all His work which God had created and made** (Genesis 1:31—2:3).

Yes, when all of those marvelous and miraculous works of creation were finished, God took a break—He relaxed a bit as He beheld the glorious works of the previous six days. As a result, the seventh day was referred to by God as the "Rest Day" or the Sabbath Day. *[Note: No further mention of the Sabbath occurs in God's Word until in Exodus 16 when God caused Manna to rain from heaven.]*

With this particular commandment, the LORD God was once again emphasizing the need for their regular spiritual rest and worship as well as a weekly day for physical rest.

The LORD was well aware that it was important that His people relax to recharge the body at least once a week. And if the body needed rest and refreshment, their soul certainly needed a special time to restore and rehearse God's ongoing love, care, forgiveness, and guidance.

Out of fatherly concern for His people, God directed that one specific day each week was to be set aside by His children for their body and soul-rest. On that one day in the week they were to separate their mind, their heart, their life from the work-a-day world and concentrate particularly on the fact that they belonged to God for His special purposes and blessing. That special Sabbath-rest was to be carefully observed by His people for their spiritual and physical welfare.

So why do we worship on Sunday, the first day of the week, rather than on Saturday, the last day of the week, as God specified? Well, the early Christians <u>did</u> keep the seventh day as a particular day of rest and worship . . . initially, but since the promised Messiah—Shiloh came and fulfilled God's law for us perfectly . . . since He paid the wages of sin for the whole world by dying on Calvary's cross . . . and since He arose from the dead on the first day of the week, completing the work of redemption for all mankind, it seemed only fitting and proper for God's people to set aside the first day of the week <u>also</u> as a day for God's faithful to gather for worship.

After a time, as the early Christian Church grew, and as the believing children of God became more confident in their religious freedom in the Christ, they gradually dropped worship services on Saturday and centered on Shiloh, the promised Savior, in whom they found complete rest and peace with God for time and for eternity. After all, as our Savior, Himself, pointed out: **"The Sabbath was made for man, and**

not man for the Sabbath. Therefore the Son of Man is also Lord of the Sabbath" (Mark 2:27).

In other words, the Sabbath Day designation was prescribed by God for the needed spiritual and physical welfare of His people. That weekly rest for body and soul is still every bit as important today. But we must also realize that the special Sabbath Day designation was originally established by God to serve His people's needs as they waited for the Messiah to come. After the Christ had come, the Apostle Paul (by inspiration of God) made it abundantly clear to all who beheld the living Christ by faith: **Do not let anyone judge you by what you eat or drink, or with regard to a religious festival, a New Moon celebration or a Sabbath day. These are a <u>shadow of the things that were to come; the reality, however, is found in Christ</u>** (Colossians 2:16–17 NIV).

The Messiah is our Sabbath—He is our rest—our peace—our life— our Shiloh. The various <u>ceremonial</u> laws and requirements, including the Sabbath Day regulations, were absolutely necessary to govern God's people and keep them close to Himself <u>until</u> the Christ would come. When that would take place, then all hearts and minds would find their rest and peace in Him, the Savior and Lord of all mankind. We remember the inspired words of Jacob, don't we? When **Shiloh comes; . . . to Him shall be the obedience of the people** (Genesis 49:10).

And so today what a spiritually uplifting and joyful experience it is to come together with fellow believers, in the midst of this sin-torn world, and be assured of God's forgiving love, mercy, and steadfast guidance. Yes, that is why we raise our voices and with heart and soul join with fellow saints in singing such hymns of joy as this:

> *This is the day the Lord has made;*
> *He calls the hours His own.*

Let heav'n rejoice; let earth be glad
And praise surround the throne.

Today He rose and left the dead,
And Satan's empire fell;
Today the saints His triumphs spread
And all His wonders tell.

Blessed is Jesus Christ, Who came
With messages of grace,
Who came in God the Father's name
To save our sinful race.

Hosanna in the highest strains
The Church on earth shall raise;
The highest heav'ns, in which He reigns,
Shall give Him nobler praise. (CW 225:1,2,4,5)

PRAYER

What a joy it is, O LORD, to come into Your house on those special days set aside to hear You speak to me from Your very own Word of life. Besides, I and my fellow believers get to talk to You through the privilege of prayer and joyously singing hymns of praise to Your holy name. Indeed, what a special joy fills my heart as I watch children and grownups received into Your kingdom through the washing of regeneration and renewing of the Holy Spirit in the Sacrament of Holy Baptism. And, yes, what an exceptional gift it is to receive Your very body and blood, remembering Your ultimate sacrifice for me through which You bless me with the assurance of the forgiveness of all of my sins. O, LORD, continue to pour out Your merciful love to me. For without You and Your gifts of grace, I would die in my sins and be condemned to eternal death. But with You in my life and heart, I have every reason to live a life of joy and peace every day. Fill me with Your Spirit, that Your love for me, proven in Your Word and Sacraments, may ever be the center of my life. Then, saturated with Your Spirit, may I be moved to do all that I can to share Your merciful love with others. In Your holy name, I pray. Amen.

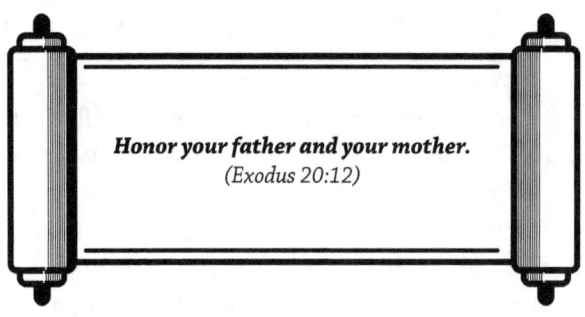

Honor your father and your mother.
(Exodus 20:12)

GOD REQUIRES THAT CHILDREN RESPECT THEIR PARENTS

The voice of the LORD God continued unabated from the mountain top, filling the desolate plains below. The people could hardly believe that the LORD God of the universe was actually speaking to them about their everyday relationship with Him. Then while they stood below listening attentively, experiencing this once in a life-time happening, they noticed a sudden switch in subject matter. Until this moment God's immortal edicts were centered upon the relationship that existed between Him and His people. But then God made a sudden transition to the intimate, God-created relationship within human families.

So in order to get the word-picture that the LORD is meticulously drafting for His people, let's back up a bit to the day that the LORD God carefully and lovingly created man and woman in His own image. It is obvious that the God-centered home was a matter of intense importance to the LORD. In fact, it was a supreme priority. As you know, Adam and Eve were the crowns of His creation. And according to God's creative wisdom, they were naturally attracted and drawn to each other. The man and the woman were bound together in an intimate and indissoluble bond. From that day forward **a man shall leave his father and mother and be joined to his wife, and <u>they shall become one flesh</u>** (Genesis 2:24).

This God-created relationship is the most wonder-filled union in existence among human beings. It supersedes every other human involvement—even our close connection with our mother and father—and yes, even our loving ties with our children. Together, husband and wife are to share their lives of joy, love, and care with each other every day . . . until they are parted by death. This thought is capsulized in God's inspired words in this way: **Wives, submit to your own husbands, as to the Lord. . . . Husbands ought to love their own wives as their own bodies; he who loves his wife loves himself** (Ephesians 5:22&28).

Besides that, what a grand gift was granted to them when God graciously provided them with a miraculous result of their love for each other: **God blessed them, and God said to them, "Be fruitful and multiply; fill the earth and subdue it"** (Genesis 1:28).

Tremendous . . . isn't it? Besides that, the LORD God inspired the Psalmist to remind us that **children are a heritage of the LORD. The fruit of the womb is His reward** (Psalm 127:3). Conception and child birth seem to happen so regularly and automatically that this blessing of God may easily be robbed of the miraculous work of God that it is. These wonderful God-created "rewards" are each so very special. Each one is uniquely different, inheriting a blend of genetics—features and abilities from both their father and mother.

But of course, we must never forget that our offspring do not automatically inherit faith and trust in the LORD God. To put it another way, the father's and mother's close relationship with the one true God of heaven and earth is not transferred to their children at birth. Just as we were born sinful beings of sinful beings, so it is with our children. Spiritually speaking, they are born in our human image—sinful flesh of sinful flesh. That is why our Savior specifically pointed out: **"You must be born again!"** (John 3:7)

Likewise, He clearly points out the reason for this transformation: **"That which is born of the flesh is flesh, and that which if born of the Spirit is spirit"** (John 3:6).

As you remember, Nicodemus was deeply perplexed by that assertion of our LORD: **"You must be born again!"** (John 3:7) Every one of us might ask a similar question like that of Nicodemus: **"How can a man be born when he is old? Can he enter a second time into his mother's womb and be born?"** (John 3:4) It might seem like a ridiculous question, but our Savior caringly and patiently dealt with Nicodemus and in the process guides us and leads us to grasp the point. Indeed, it is with love for us, our children, and for all mankind that our Savior invites: **"Let the little children come to Me, and do not forbid them; for of such is the kingdom of God. Assuredly, I say to you, whoever does not receive the kingdom of God as a little child will by no means enter it"** (Mark 10:14–15).

Our Savior is pointing to a number of very important spiritual values here. In the first place our Lord wishes for us to realize that our little children have perceptions far beyond our understanding. Our Savior is speaking of very young children here—diaper age—those who are not yet walking—who spend much of their time gurgling and grunting in the crib. These tiny gifts from God need to grow up continually seeing and hearing their God-given parents function as examples of love, care, and godliness.

So when the LORD graciously blesses us with these marvelous gifts of children, we are filled with joy as we hold our new-born son or daughter in our arms—God's wondrous blessing—His gift to us. But our LORD God wishes to make it crystal clear that this blessing carries with it a huge, God-given responsibility. Moses was inspired by God to speak very clearly regarding our privileged responsibility as parents. First of all: **"You shall love the LORD your God with all your heart, with**

all your soul, and with all your might. And these words which I command you today shall be in your heart" (Deuteronomy 6:5–6).

Not only are we obliged to faithfully hold those precious treasures of God's Word in our heart, but **"You shall teach them diligently to your children, and shall talk of them when you sit in your house, when you walk by the way, when you lie down, and when you rise up"** (Deuteronomy 6:7).

In other words, our children should grow up recognizing that godliness is our life-style. They can sense it. It should be obvious in our attitude, our actions, our words—our entire life. Our little ones perceive it when we talk with them, when we change their diapers, when we take them for a walk, when we rock them to sleep, when we lovingly lay them into their cribs.

Besides, our Savior urges us to learn from our children. We are to learn from our children? Yes, we are! We can learn much from our little children if we will but pay attention. As a matter of fact, our Savior makes it all crystal clear when He points to our children and says: **"Such is the kingdom of God. Assuredly, I say to you, whoever does not receive the kingdom of God as a little child will by no means enter it"** (Mark 10:14–15).

What makes God's little children examples of godliness? They simply believe—they totally trust their parents . . . right? They are confident that their parents love them and will do whatever is necessary to care for them and keep them safe. When little children are uncomfortable or need something, they may whimper or cry. Why? That's the only way they have to get their parents' attention. They fully believe that their parents are the only ones who can help them. There it is! That is at the heart and core of the Kingdom of God. Faith—trusting in the loving care of our living LORD God in all matters of life!

Rearing our children to see the LORD God in their lives every day is one of the most necessary and important tasks that we as God's people have been given. Nurturing and caring for our children both physically and spiritually are our primary God-given responsibilities. We may be blessed with a Christian Day School, Sunday School, good friends, etc. But we must remember that all of these blessings are "helps." They are not substitutes for a God-centered home and godly living by God-revering parents.

So also, with this commandment the LORD God was instructing children to realize that they have a God-given responsibility to their caring and loving parents. And what might that be? Very simply, they are to recognize their father and mother as gifts from God who deserve their honor, respect, love, and esteem. Therefore, the LORD God approached this very important matter by giving the children this special mandate: **"Honor your father and your mother that your days may be long upon the land which the LORD your God is giving you"** (Exodus 20:12).

The LORD made this very clear to children—young and old: Fathers and mothers are to be seen as representatives of God and are to be honored as such. So you might ask, *"Are there perfect parents in existence"*? The answer: No, there are not! *"Are there perfect children in existence"*? The answer: No, there are not! That is the very reason that our Savior reminds parents and children alike: **"Lo, I am with you always, even to the end of the age"** (Matthew 28:20).

Let's not forget that! It is all-important that we continually pray for the LORD's guidance as we carry on that vital, God-given task of being loving, caring, and dedicated parents and children.

This is a challenging assignment, to say the least. And the Evil Foe does everything possible to encourage resentments, anger, and loveless attitudes. Besides, the unbelieving world everywhere around us and our children is constantly used by Satan to lure us all away from this God-given task and away from His loving Word. Indeed, it is a struggle, but one that we can fight and win. How do we know this? Listen to the God-breathed words of David: **I would have lost heart, unless I had believed that I would see the goodness of the LORD in the land of the living. Wait on the LORD; be of good courage. And He shall strengthen your heart; wait, I say, on the LORD!** (Psalm 27:13–14)

My friends, the bottom line is this: God knew, and it shall ever be true, <u>the home is the foundation of all social and godly living</u>. A stable society required this godly philosophy in the evolving nation of Israel, and it is basic to a solid society in our day as well. So, as God's people stood before Mt. Sinai, whether they knew it or not, God was forming a nation—a theocracy *(rule of God)* wherein His people could thrive in the land He was giving them. Good, solid, godly family life was absolutely essential as they fulfilled their God-given responsibility.

Indeed, my friends in Christ, there is no greater earthly treasure placed into our possession and care by the God of all grace than the blessing of children. They might become our children as adopted, foster, or natural—but there is one certainty: It matters not how elderly we become and what age our children have grown to be—they will always continue to be our precious gifts from God. Then, by the grace of God, grandchildren and great-grandchildren are presented to us—all precious blessings from the LORD God. Indeed, to our final breath we will continue to pray:

Bless our loved ones, Holy Father;
Hear our anxious prayer;
By your mercy keep them always
In your care.

Jesus, Savior, let your presence
Be their light and guide;

Keep, oh, keep them in their weakness
At your side.

Holy Spirit, let your teaching
Sanctify their life;
Send your grace that they may conquer
In each strife.

Father, Son, and Holy Spirit,
God forever true,
Bless them, guide them, save them, keep them
Close to you. (CW 504:1,2,5,6)

PRAYER

Dear LORD, You have made it abundantly clear that Your creation of families is the backbone of any society. Please help me to not take such a gift as this for granted, as though this precious blessing requires no special attention on our part. Rather, cause me to realize that our families require constant vigilance, care, love—and above all our prayers. LORD, please fill me with Your Spirit that I may do everything possible to foster the blessing of family life. Please, LORD, inspire our children and parents to listen carefully to Your words of guidance: **Children, obey your parents in the Lord, for this is right. "Honor your father and mother." Which is the first commandment with promise: "that it may be well with you and you may live long on the earth." And you, fathers, do not provoke your children to wrath, but bring them up in the training and admonition of the Lord** (Ephesians 6:1–4). So may we too be beacons of light, in the midst of this sin-wracked world, leading always to Your kingdom of grace and peace for time and for eternity. In the name of our LORD and Savior I pray. Amen.

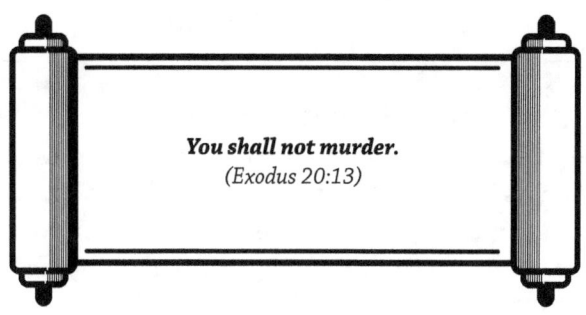

You shall not murder.
(Exodus 20:13)

GOD REQUIRES THAT WE RESPECT HUMAN LIFE

The thundering words of God's moral code continued as the people stood frozen at attention on the hot, desert sands of Sinai. It should have been self-evident, shouldn't it? The malicious and purposeful murdering of one human being by another at any time from conception onward is simply unacceptable to God and ought never to be a prerogative of man. Life and death are God's business . . . not ours!

Down through the generations God's people have always known that their lives were in the hands of God—as David was caused to confess so well: **But as for me, I trust in You, O Lord; I say, "You are my God. My times are in Your hand"** (Psalm 31:14–15a).

The people of Israel needed to bear that in mind each and every day of their lives and especially in the times that lay before them, for under God's directive they would be struggling to occupy territories held and occupied by others. Lives would be lost—homes would be shattered—business operations would be torn to shreds—all in the name of the Lord God!

Some of you may wonder—and indeed some devout believers have asked: *"Under God's plan, which called for His people to occupy a territory where there would knowingly be intense opposition, was God here advocating war—disrupting families—taking the lives of people in order to accomplish His purpose? Indeed, was God advocating murder?"* The answer to the first three questions is Yes. The answer to the last question is CERTAINLY NOT! His commandment to His people regarding the life of others stood and stands absolute to this day: **"You shall not murder"** (Exodus 20:13).

So let's examine this a bit. First off, let me ask you, do you remember what the LORD God spoke to Abraham? **"I will bless those who bless you, and I will curse him who curses you; and in you all the families of the earth shall be blessed"** (Genesis 12:3).

Unfortunately, having followed the path that Satan designed, most people of that day walked the walk of Cain and cast God aside in favor of their idolatrous lifestyle. In short, they rejected God, His promises, His love, and His people. As a result, the redemption and salvation that God promised for them and the entire population of the world were rejected, and in unbelief they treated it as though it were worthless. As we heard our LORD clearly explain in the first commandment: **"I, the LORD your God, am a jealous God, visiting the iniquity of the fathers on the children to the third and fourth generations of those who hate Me, but showing mercy to thousands, to those who love Me and keep My commandments"** (Exodus 20:5).

It is sad to say, but we have to say it anyway because it is true: These people as well as their children and the generations who walked in their path fell under God's curse—so for them to fight against God's people, hoping to destroy them and their God-given purpose of bringing salvation to the world was to fight against God and His promise of mercy and love for all people the world over.

What was the alterative? Should the Canaanites have welcomed God's people into their midst? Should they have done everything in their power to be hospitable and generous in helping them establish their lives—their homes—their families? If they in their hearts and minds had known the LORD God and His merciful love for all people, THEY WOULD HAVE DONE EXACTLY THAT. What a marvelous blessing would have been theirs! But when they rejected the LORD God, they likewise rejected His people as imposters. Those who carried the promise of God's mercy and love for all were rejected and considered to be nothing but a threat to their idolatrous lifestyle.

But let us not forget that by God's grace some individuals from outside the nation of Israel would come to know and believe in the one true and living God. Such were welcomed into God's kingdom of grace and mercy. As prominent examples we could point to Ruth, Rahab, Naaman, Uriah the Hittite as well as citizens of Ninevah, to mention a few. Many others found life and redemption in the LORD God of Israel, but the vast majority of those outside of this nation of God's people denounced the God of Israel and His chosen people. They chose the rule of Satan rather than the grace of the LORD God. They were in Satan's camp and would do anything to destroy the words and actions of the LORD God and His kingdom of gracious love.

How is it today? We are children of the fulfillment of God's promises, God's people in the midst of a world of unbelief. How should we function? Answer: Our Lord has clearly outlined our M.O. (mode of operation) in His inspired words to His servant Timothy: **Preach the Word! Be ready in season and out of season. Convince, rebuke, exhort, with all longsuffering and teaching. For the time will come when they will not endure sound doctrine, but according to their own desires, because they have itching ears, they will heap up for themselves teachers; and they will turn their ears away from the truth, and be turned aside to fables. But you be watchful in all things, endure afflictions, do the work of an evangelist, fulfill your ministry** (II Timothy 4:2–5).

Yes, my friends, here we are in this sin-laden world surrounded by unbelief. The Savior of all people has come as God promised, and the LORD God's kingdom in the Messiah has been established—but we must remember that today as in days gone by, God does not try to force people into His kingdom of grace and mercy. He does not approve of trying to "convert" people at the point of a bayonet, the threat of a grenade, or with a loaded AK-47 pointed at their head.

Rather, God's love and forgiveness are freely given to all. His Spirit works through His words and acts of mercy to bring souls into His kingdom. On the other hand, all who reject God's salvation and obstinately reject the Spirit's pleading and God's bountiful love fall under His curse here in time and forever in eternity. Again, that is God's business—not ours. Our privileged responsibility is **to proclaim liberty to the captives, and the opening of the prison to those who are bound** (Isaiah 61:1b).

So, is that it for this commandment of God? Not quite! We cannot leave this particular Word of the LORD God without recognizing that the catastrophic, man-created epidemic of the MURDER of unborn infants falls directly under this commandment: YOU SHALL NOT MURDER. Clear enough . . . wouldn't you say? But a vast number of people are not listening and/or do not care what God requires.

Politicians flood the airwaves with propaganda in favor of so-called "women's rights." In effect they are saying: WOMEN HAVE THE RIGHT TO COMMIT MURDER AND KILL THEIR OWN UNBORN BABIES! *(Note: Review chapter twenty-five of these devotions.)* But God says, "NO! You do not have that right. That's My province. I will give life, and I will take life."* However, the legislators of our land have simply caved in to the cries and jeers of our depraved society. As a result, the sad, selfish, and sinful song of a godless generation is learned and sung with gusto— while the words of God are despised, unsung, and unheard by most!

Even the Declaration of Independence of the U.S.A. guarantees certain basic rights to all humans in this country. "LIFE, LIBERTY, AND THE PURSUIT OF HAPPINESS" is a well-known phrase from our country's founding document. These clear and simple words specify the unalienable rights which the Declaration says have been given to all human beings by their Creator. Our government was created to protect such rights. Correct?

But the Satanic, godless forces of evil are openly at work and crying out: *"But that doesn't apply to defenseless, unborn infants. They don't have any rights! They simply don't have any say in the matter of life or death. Mothers may authorize murdering them at will!"* In other words, if a mother wishes to abort her baby, it is <u>not</u> considered to be a human being, for it is treated as human only <u>if she wants to deliver it safely into the world</u>. What kind of selfish, perverted, and godless thinking is that?

Oh, LORD God, have mercy and free us from this horrendous onslaught of godless, murderous action concocted by the selfish, self-indulgent, Satan-guided minds and hands of sinfully corrupted humanity. Remember? **The time will come when they will not endure sound doctrine, but according to their own desires, because they have itching ears, they will heap up for themselves teachers; and they will turn their ears away from the truth, and be turned aside to fables** (II Timothy 4:3–4).

However, there is a lesson that we must learn and relearn every day. That lesson is—leave human life in the hands of God! Declare His Word. Pray, pray, pray that our merciful LORD will move hearts to lift this Satan-incited, man-created scourge from this nation—yea, from this world. But at the same time, in the words of Holy Scripture, **Repay no one evil for evil. Have regard for good things in the sight of all men. If it is possible, as much as depends on you, live peaceably with all men. Beloved, do not avenge yourselves,**

but rather give place to wrath; for it is written, "Vengeance is Mine, I will repay." says the Lord. . . . Do not be overcome by evil, but overcome evil with good (Romans 12:17–19). To that end we continue to heed and confess with that prolific 17th century hymn writer, Isaac Watts:

> *The man is ever blest*
> *Who shuns the sinners' ways,*
> *Among their counsels never stands,*
> *Nor takes the scorners' place*

> *But makes the Law of God*
> *His study and delight*
> *Amid the labors of the day*
> *And watches of the night.*

> *He like a tree shall thrive*
> *With waters near the root.*
> *Fresh as the leaf his name shall live;*
> *His works are heav'nly fruit. (CW 475:1–3)*

PRAYER

LORD God, Your love and gracious goodness are before me every day. I see it in nature all around me—I hear it in Your Word of Life—I experience it with fellow believers—I rejoice in it with my family. LORD, Your love and mercy make life and living a joyful experience. I wish to share this blessing of life with everyone that I meet. Yet I feel so incompetent—so lacking—so unable to give away that treasure—that key to life and living that You have mercifully given to me. Throughout the review of Your Commandments, above everything else, I see Your love for me and for all mankind. Yes, these are laws, but they are laws of love, laws of guidance, laws of life with You and with all people. It is my fervent prayer that You will forgive my shortcomings and fill me with Your grace that I may be a joyful advocate of Your merciful kindness for me and for all people. In the name of Jesus Christ, who is love personified, I pray. Amen.

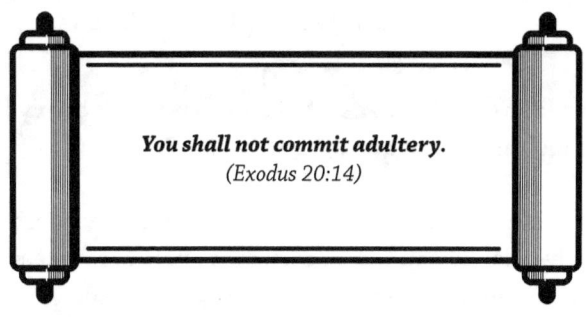

You shall not commit adultery.
(Exodus 20:14)

GOD REQUIRES THAT WE RESPECT MARRIAGE

Another moral pronouncement echoed across the sandy plains of Sinai, filling the ears and hearts of God's people. The subject: Adultery! To begin, we must realize that reproduction of every living thing on Earth was an integral part of God's creative design from day one. From the vast species of vegetation in the fields to the multiple creatures in the seas—from the scores of land animals, birds, and insects all the way upward to the design of mankind—all were created through the infinite wisdom of God—and each was created to reproduce **according to its kind** (Genesis 1:12).

Regarding the plant kingdom, God directed: **"Let the earth bring forth grass, the herb that yields seed, and the fruit tree that yields fruit according to its kind, whose seed is in itself, on the earth"** (Genesis 1:11).

Concerning the sea creatures and birds, the Creator directed: **"Be fruitful and multiply, and fill the waters in the seas, and let birds multiply on the earth"** (Genesis 1:22).

With respect to mankind, the LORD God directed: **"Be fruitful and multiply; fill the earth and subdue it; have dominion over the**

fish of the sea, over the birds of the air and over every living thing that moves on the earth" (Genesis 1:28).

It's obvious, isn't it, that reproduction was an integral part of God's perfect creative plan? Each time a corn stock produces an ear of corn—or a bird hatches her eggs—or fish are moved to lay and germinate their ova—or an animal gives birth to its offspring—yes, each time a pregnancy occurs among us humans, the miraculous, reproductive power of God is on display for all to witness and for all to praise the LORD God for His infinite wisdom and creative power.

Sad to say, sin changed all of that. As a result of man's rebellion against God and walking with Satan, the natural reproductive blessings of God for mankind were no longer governed by God's intention, love, and blessings. Rather, under the Evil One's guidance, human sexual cravings ran rampant and became Satan's playground. What God created as a wholesome relationship between a man and a woman became adulterated under the plight of sin. Everywhere among humanity, lustful desires replace the pure, joyful, and natural love relationship that God had created for husband and wife.

The saddening and revealing words of Holy Scripture describe the extent to which sexual sins have enveloped humanity and show God's reaction to this sinful, sad state: **God gave them up to vile passions. For even their women exchanged the natural use for what is against nature. Likewise also the men, leaving the natural use of the woman, burned in their lust for one another, men with men committing what is shameful. And receiving in themselves the penalty of their error which was due. And even as they did not like to retain God in their knowledge, God gave them over to a debased mind, to do those things which are not fitting** (Romans 1:26–28).

God's people, the children of Abraham, were chosen for one primary purpose—namely, to restore that once perfect relationship with God and with each other that God had created. Through faith in the Seed of the woman promised in the Garden of Eden, that flawless, loving bond with God would be regained, and the lives of all faithful humanity would be restored. Remember what our Savior promised? It must be repeated: **"I have come that they may have life, and that they may have it more abundantly"** (John 10:10).

God's chosen people were about to enter a land where carnal lust, godless sexual orgies, acting out sin-sick urges and desires were common. Wholesale carnality was on display everywhere—resembling animal behavior. Obviously, the LORD God was doing everything possible to prepare His people for entering a land where sexual immorality was the way of life, and their man-created religion embraced sexual licentiousness as "approved" by their gods and goddesses.

In contrast, God's prohibition was plain and simple: **"You shall not commit adultery"** (Exodus 20:14).

God's people were called to be a bright beacon of morality and godliness. It is as though God were saying, *"You are my people; your conduct will speak thousands of words, **for you were once darkness, but now you are light in the Lord. Walk as children of light"*** (Ephesians 5:8).

And how about us? We too are the children of the living God. We too live in a world that has been dominated by sex appeal. EVERYWHERE—from advertising—to movies—to books—to television—to clothing—to the internet etc. etc.—sex is flaunted to trigger the desire to want, to have, to experience. The unbelieving world, with Satan as its chief salesman, has taken a very special and blessed gift of God and dragged it into the gutter!

This was pointed to directly in a recent, well-written article in the Lutheran Spokesman: "Sex sells, is sold, and enslaves human hearts. Businesses use sexual messages and imagery in their advertisements to sell their products. Human bodies are sold for sex in the age-old trade of prostitution. With the proliferation of pornography, especially on the internet, countless victims are enticed and ensnared. Satan, the chief enemy of our souls, has found sex to be an effective device to enslave human hearts for his kingdom—since, as Jesus reveals, **out of the heart proceed evil thoughts, murders, adulteries, fornications** (Matthew 15:19). None of us are immune to the devil's attempts to reclaim us through the use of immoral sex." (Pastor Mark Gullerud, *Lutheran Spokesman*, Vol 58, #11—May 2016)

We have heard it before—but here it is again: Our Lord and Savior Jesus Christ speaks to each one of us whom He has called out of the darkness of this sin-drenched world and informs each one of us: *You are it! I have chosen each one of you for a very special mission. Please remember and don't forget:* **"You are the light of the world. A city that is set on a hill cannot be hidden. Nor do they light a lamp and put it under a basket, but on a lampstand, and it gives light to all who are in the house. Let your light so shine before men, that they may see your good works and glorify your Father in heaven"** (Matthew 5:14–16).

This is our calling—this is our primary purpose in life in the midst of a sin-darkened world. The key to successfully carrying out this God-given mission is clear and simple: **Watch, stand fast in the faith, be brave, be strong. Let all that you do be done with love** (I Corinthians 16:13–14). Yes, as our friend of the 17th-century said so well:

> *He canceled my offenses,*
> *Delivered me from death;*
> *He is the LORD who cleanses*

My soul from sin through faith.
In Him I can be cheerful,
Courageous on my way;
In Him I am not fearful
Of God's great Judgment Day.

My heart for joy is springing
And can no more be sad,
'Tis full of joy and singing,
Sees only sunshine glad.
The Sun that cheers my spirit
Is Jesus Christ, my King;
The heav'n I shall inherit
Makes me rejoice and sing! (CW 419: 4,7)

PRAYER

LORD my God, as You know, sin has so effectively invaded Your marvelous creation that even Your design of the miraculous reproductive system has become an instrument of the Evil One. Minds have been so captivated by the misuse of this blessing that the world is openly and shamelessly saturated with sexual overtones and appeal. Everything from selling automobiles to bathing apparel is caught in its grip. Satan enjoys every second of it. Indeed, our sinful nature happily absorbs it all. Please, LORD, in the face of this misuse of Your marvelous creative goodness, create in me a clean heart—renew a right spirit within me. And as I walk through Your created world, which I know has been corrupted by evil, grant that I always recognize Your marvelous creative design and Your gracious goodness in it all. In the name of Your Son, the Seed of the woman, our Savior Jesus the Christ. Amen.

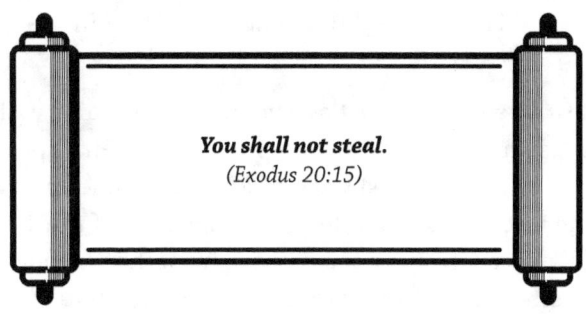

You shall not steal.
(Exodus 20:15)

GOD REQUIRES THAT WE RESPECT OTHERS' PROPERTY

There was no intermission in the giving of God's immortal moral code. God's voice did not weaken one tiny decibel as His voice filled the air and engulfed the millions of Israelites.

With the stirring words of the seventh commandment, the LORD our God wants His children to understand something very basic: EVERYTHING belongs to God. He created it all, and He preserves it all according to His will. Yes, He wants every one of us to realize that as we discover and uncover the wonders of His creation, He thereby gives us the privilege of using all things for our blessing and to His glory. But we must never forget that since God created it all, of course it all belongs to Him.

We put two and two together . . . and what do you know . . . something new and exciting has been uncovered. It has always been there. We just learned of its existence! Let's see . . . who should get the glory and praise? Us or God? That's an easy question to answer, isn't it? Who else? God, of course! It has always been there. God created it. We just discovered it!

The wonders of God's marvelous creation that we have been permitted to uncover and use during the last hundred years is astounding, and we sincerely believe that we have only scratched the surface. I clearly remember, that as a young boy, standing with my father in our farm-yard and hearing a propeller-driven airplane roaring across the crystal-clear, blue sky above. My dad dropped everything, stood up, and just gazed at this aerial phenomenon of the day gliding overhead. I'll never forget the comment of my father. "Would you just look at that: Effortlessly flying through the air like a bird. What could we possibly discover or invent that would top that?" (That, my friends, was about 75 years ago.) The answer to my Dad's question seems rather obvious because of all that has been discovered, uncovered, invented, and utilized since that day.

Yet there is so much more to uncover—so much waiting to be revealed—so many blessings lying in wait for us to discover and use. The interaction of mankind with creation again and again confirms the inspired words of the Apostle Paul, **What can be known about God is plain to them, because God has shown it to them. For His invisible attributes, namely, his eternal power and divine nature, have been clearly perceived, ever since the creation of the world, <u>in the things that have been made</u>** (Romans 1:18–20 ESV). Electrical applications, medical discoveries, agricultural advancements, space travel, etc. etc.—there's no end to the wonders that can be found and utilized in God's wondrous creation.

As long as God permits us to dwell on this side of eternity, more and more unknowns will come to light—more and more "miraculous" discoveries produced by God's creative hands will be revealed. At the discovery of this or that, our collective jaws drop in utter surprise. We repeat: the makings for this or that invention have always been here . . . just waiting for us to expose and use them. <u>But it's all God's. He created it all</u>. We just get to use and enjoy these things with thankful minds and hearts while we are here. Again, we hardly need to ask: Who should get the glory, thankfulness and praise—us or God? The answer is obvious.

In another context the Creator of all clarifies this very well when He affirms: **"Every beast of the forest is Mine, and the cattle on a thousand hills. I know all the birds of the mountains, and the wild beasts of the field are Mine"** (Psalm 50:10 &11).

So it is nothing but sinful, satanic foolishness to jealously steal what someone else is using. IT'S NOT THEIRS EITHER—IT BELONGS TO GOD!! If He wishes for us to have and use certain blessings, He certainly knows how to supply them to us. That's God's business. Our business is to **seek first the kingdom of God and His righteousness, and all these things shall be added to you** (Matthew 6:33).

The people of Israel would soon be entering upon a new phase in their lives. During their time in the wilderness, they would be attending the same school that we all attend every day—the "Academy of God." These basic lessons in morality, which our forbearers would learn at the foot of Mount Sinai, were to be applied in their everyday lives. The problem was that the unbelieving world that would be surrounding God's people had never gone to that school, and as a result, they did not think and function like God's people. And do you know what? Things haven't changed.

The world around us is governed by a totally different "School of Thought." Satan is the leading professor in this school. Unbelief fills the classroom. The corrupted nature of mankind sits in rapt attention as ingenuity and self-esteem are engineered and praised. *"Look what you can do! See what you have accomplished! Cast your eyes upon what you have invented. Just look at all the money you can make! If it is all accomplished by taking advantage of one's fellow man—misrepresentation, deception or underhandedness—That's just good business; that's using your head. That's how to make an impression on the boss. That's how to get ahead."*

Contrary wise, and in accordance with what is taught in the "Academy of God," an 18th-century hymn writer puts it perfectly well:

405

All depends on our possessing
God's abundant grace and blessing,
Though all earthly wealth depart.
They who trust with faith unshaken
In our God are not forsaken
And e'er keep a dauntless heart.

He who to this day has fed me
And to many joys has led me
Is and ever shall be mine.
He who ever gently schools me,
He who daily guides and rules me,
Will remain my help divine.

Many spend their lives in fretting
Over trifles and in getting
Things that have no solid ground.
I shall strive to win a treasure
That will bring me lasting pleasure
And that now is seldom found. (CW 421:1–3)

Yes, God's people, Abraham's children, were to keep their eyes focused upon the marvelous grace of God and His wondrous blessings given to them. As their past experience had shown them, God never let His chosen down and He never would.

So it is with every one of us. We are dwelling in the midst of a world filled with godlessness, but yet we are living in the kingdom of the ever-living God. Job said it perfectly when he was moved by the Spirit to recognize that all things we are using and enjoying, including our lives, are gifts from God. Therefore, when the expected pattern of things in Job's life was interrupted, he was caused by the Spirit of God to remind those around him and us:

"Naked I came from my mother's womb, and naked will I depart. The LORD gave, and the LORD has taken away; may the

name of the LORD be praised" (Job 1:21 NIV, 1979). And so it shall ever be true, whether we are in plenty or in need—whether we are living or dying, the constant refrain of the child of God should always be **"Blessed be the name of the LORD"** (Job 1:21).

PRAYER

How gracious You have been to me, O LORD. While working my way through life in this world, time and again I have faltered in my faith. I have failed to trust You as I ought. Too often I have fallen into making the mistake of thinking that my ideas, my goals, my plans, my decisions were all-important. How wrong I was! **Blessed is the man who trusts in the LORD, and whose hope is the LORD** (Jeremiah 17:7). I must learn this and relearn this every day. Therefore, LORD God, I earnestly pray that You will not give up on me. Rather, each day **create in me a clean heart, O God, and renew a steadfast spirit within me** (Psalm 51:10). In the name of the Lord my Savior, I pray. Amen.

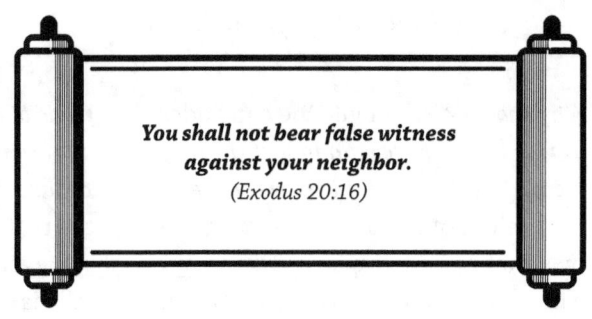

*You shall not bear false witness
against your neighbor.*
(Exodus 20:16)

GOD REQUIRES THAT WE PROTECT THE REPUTATION OF OTHERS

God's holy will continued to flow down the mountain side and automatically forced His hearers to answer one simple question: "Who is the father of all lies?" The answer was easy, wasn't it? Of course, the Devil has that infamous title all to himself because **he was a murderer from the beginning, and does not stand in the truth, because there is no truth in him. When he speaks a lie, he speaks from his own resources, for <u>he is a liar and the father of it</u>** (John 8:44).

Yes . . . it is Satan who was the original liar and is the perpetrator of lying even to this day. He loves and lives on lies. That is his M.O.—his mode of operation. From the day that he managed to deceive Adam and Eve by his falsehoods—his string of lies, down to this very day—his entire system—his evil kingdom—it's <u>all</u> based on falsehoods. We cannot depend on anything that the Evil One says or promotes—and we can be certain that he will not change his course of action. Why not? <u>Because, it works so well with his potential targets</u>! And who might be his favorite targets? Sad to say, they are God's chosen people, then and now—including you and me!

Indeed, *"Why change?"*, the Evil One concludes. *"My mode of operation works perfectly well with those standing at the foot of Sinai. As a matter of fact, my sly method works very well on every one of God's children in their everyday lives."* We've got to admit it—Satan is telling the truth (of all things)! Why is that true? <u>Because he has a natural ally in every one of us</u>. Do we need to be reminded of what that natural ally is? Well, in case we've forgotten, it is our sin-corrupted nature. So you see, his job becomes rather easy. Our sinful self often enjoys telling half-truths or outright "digging up dirt" about someone. It makes us feel so superior, doesn't it?

But our gracious LORD doesn't see it that way. He wishes for us to realize that defaming someone with lies can have a devastating effect upon their well-being—it can <u>cripple them</u> in many ways and, without question, it can <u>negatively affect how others view us</u>! More importantly, <u>it is not in keeping with God's Word and will</u>. But, of course, it is right up Satan's alley!

In order to make this point very clearly, the Biblical book of James uses various illustrations to summarize the power of the tongue, which is generally used very effectively in lying. James was inspired to say it like this: **Indeed, we put bits in horses' mouths that they may obey us, and we turn their whole body. Look also at ships: although they are so large and are driven by fierce winds, they are turned by a very small rudder wherever the pilot desires. Even so the tongue is a little member and boasts great things. See how great a forest a little fire kindles! And the tongue is a fire, a world of iniquity** (James 3:3–6a).

Contrariwise, God expects His children to be shining examples of people who love and care for each other. They were and are to love as God loved them. Indeed, what are God's words spoken to us through His mouthpiece, the Apostle John? **In this the love of God was manifested toward us, that God has sent His only begotten Son** (the Seed of the woman), **into the world that we might live through Him. In this is love, not that we loved God, but that He loved us and sent His Son to be the propitiation for our sins. Beloved, <u>if</u> God so loved us, we also ought to love one another** (I John 4:9–11).

Yes, God had certainly proved His love to the children of Israel in every way imaginable. Besides, they were entrusted with the grandest treasure ever to be held by any people—the forgiving gospel of God's love for all humanity in the promised Messiah. Slandering and telling lies about their neighbor would be a gross contradiction to godliness. For after all, the good name of their neighbor, (their neighbor's reputation), was to be regarded as precious and protected in every way possible.

Things can be replaced, but one's reputation can easily be damaged for life by lying words and accusations. Indeed, <u>jumping</u> to conclusions about the words and ways of others is a "sport" that can be practiced quite easily. God's people were and are called upon to carefully weigh their judgments, words, and actions. After all, they were and are to be a light of godliness in the midst of a world filled with satanic lies and falsehoods. God's dear souls will want to counter Satan's falsehoods with truth and love. As Martin Luther put it in this paraphrase of his words:

> *"Bear no false witness nor defame*
> *Your neighbor and destroy his name,*
> *But view him in the kindest way;*
> *Speak truth and love in all you say."*
> *Have mercy, LORD!*

PRAYER

LORD, my ever-living, loving, and forgiving Savior, I come before You with a repentant heart. You have been so gracious to me, drawing me into Your kingdom of love, forgiving my sins and sending Your Spirit to strengthen me through Your words of grace and mercy. Yet time and again I find myself being judgmental and unforgiving toward my fellowman. LORD, it is my prayer that You will work in me with Your Spirit and move me to cast aside snap judgments of others. Help me always to put the best construction on things that I don't fully understand. It is my earnest prayer that You will steadfastly work in me that I may always forgive as You have forgiven me, for the sake of Your Son—the Seed of the woman—my Savior, Jesus the Christ. Lord God, I pray that You will be with me every day, guiding my tongue that You have given to me. May it always be used for the welfare of my fellow man and to the praise of Your holy name. Amen.

You shall not covet.
(Exodus 20:17)

GOD FORBIDS COVETING OUR NEIGHBOR'S POSSESSIONS

Without intermission God's words continued to thunder from Mount Sinai while God's people stood in awe at the foot of the mountain. One last exhortation penetrated down into the very heart and soul of each of God's children and uncovered a spiritual cancer that lurks within the heart and mind of every individual: It is the sin of COVETING!

This spiritual disease hides within the sinful soul of all humanity and reveals itself through such attitudes as jealousy, envy, dissatisfaction, discontent, greed, and lust—to name a few. Ever since the fall of man into sin, human beings have been encumbered with this terrible, soul-destroying affliction. It manifests itself in covetous desires to possess what others have. When permitted to have free course, the sinful desire to obtain what God has given to others will work hand-in-glove with stealing!

If the sinful flesh of mankind is permitted to run rampant, no one is safe from this plague that dominates the natural heart of man. Satan knows this. He does everything in his power to lead humanity away from the guiding hand of God. His constant theme might be described like this: *"You only go around once in life, so have at it! If you*

413

desire someone else's wife, try to lure her into your covetous net—and call it love! If your neighbor has possessions that you want, figure out a way to snatch them. If you can obtain them only by cheating, lying, or some other underhanded method—go for it!" Satan loves it! He continually ruins lives by convincing people that coveting, avarice, and acting upon one's sinful desires are totally acceptable.

God, however, says, *"No! That is not acceptable! Rather, listen to My words to you. Whether your neighbor recognizes it or not, the fact is, I have provided him or her with everything that he or she has. Besides, I continue to give you what you have and need. I will never let you down. So please— please do not covet what your neighbor is using. Come to me. I will hear, and I will answer."* It shall ever be true, as King David sings: **The LORD is near to all who call upon Him, to all who call upon Him in truth. He will fulfill the desire of those who fear Him** (Psalm 145:18–19).

Now, we must clarify: We ought not confuse "interest" with coveting. Personal curiosity, learning about recent inventions and cultivating understanding about what God has permitted us to discover is healthy. If our neighbor possesses a given item that we think would be helpful in our life, let us pray about it. Our ever-caring LORD will hear and will answer. After all, we can't do better than going directly to the Maker and Preserver of all things . . . can we? And, as you remember very well, He continually invites us: **"Ask, and it will be given to you; seek, and you will find; knock, and it will be opened to you. For everyone who asks receives, and he who seeks finds, and to him who knocks it will be opened"** (Matthew 7:7–8).

Without question, the 17th-century hymn writer has it exactly right:

> *Well He knows what best to grant me;*
> *All the longing hopes that haunt me,*
> *Joy and sorrow, have their day.*
> *I shall doubt His wisdom never—*

> *As God wills, so be it ever—*
> *I to Him commit my way. (CW 421:4)*

That's it! The giving of God's eternal, moral Law to His people was all over. What a day it was! The happenings of that encounter with God were, without a doubt, indelibly imprinted upon the heart and mind of every individual standing at the foot of Mount Sinai. They must have told and retold, again and again, their vivid recollections of that one incredible day: The deafening thunder, the blinding lightning flashes, the piercing blare of the trumpet, and the entire mountain smoking like a giant furnace! And in the midst of it all, the LORD God Himself descending upon the mountain and directly speaking to them as they stood at the foot of Mount Sinai.

Yes, our forefathers and mothers in the faith were there! They witnessed it all. They stood spellbound as the Almighty LORD God of heaven and earth proclaimed in His own words—His moral code for all people for all time. Did they fully realize what they had just witnessed? Maybe not. But this we know: with trembling hearts and voices, the people of God had just one request of Moses: **"You speak with us, and we will hear; but let not God speak with us, lest we die"** (Exodus 20:18).

The whole event was so overpowering—so overwhelming that we can well understand that they were utterly shaken to the core. Imagine: sinful people as we all are, hearing the LORD God of heaven and earth speaking His will clearly and unequivocally. Well, their immediate reaction was to plead with their God-given leader to continue to be the middle-man: *"You talk with God and relay His words to us. This direct approach is more than we can bear."*

But Moses reassured them that this was a test administered by God Himself. He only hoped, during their spiritual education in this God-designed "Academy," that they would fully realize their position in God's plan for all the world. God's intentions were clear: As His people they were to remember His words to them and hold them as precious, guiding them all the days of their lives in the paths of righteousness. **Do not fear; for God has come to test you, and that His fear may be before you, so that you may not sin** (Exodus 20:20).

Remember, they were to be God's saving beacon in the midst of a dark and godless world. As such, they were to take God's words of godly life and light into their hearts by faith and become constant reflectors of that light to others.

What about you and me? Does the Law of God as delivered on Mount Sinai apply to us and to all humanity today? That's an easy question, isn't it? We have said it before and we repeat: The answer is YES! ABSOLUTELY! In fact, this brief summary of spiritual righteousness is the only standard acceptable to the Almighty. To put it another way: These commandments are God's course entitled: Morality 101. Further, that outline for life will never change because God will never change. They are as applicable to us in this 21st century as they were for God's people thousands of years ago.

However, God also knows that sinful humans are incapable of walking perfectly according to this faultless standard. God fully realizes that **the imagination of man's heart is evil from his youth** (Genesis 8:21)—so where does that leave us all? Answer: It leaves us at the foot of the cross. The Apostle Paul, inspired by the Holy Spirit, spells it all out for us: **<u>The law was our tutor to bring us to Christ</u>, that we might be justified by faith . . . And if you are Christ's, then you are Abraham's seed, and heirs according to the promise** (Galatians 3:24, 29).

Because the Law of God is perfect, but we are imperfect, there is a huge gulf between us and God. The promise in the Garden of Eden, given by God immediately after the fall into sin, bridges that division with the Seed of the woman—the Lord Jesus Christ. As our substitute,

He came to fulfill God's Law perfectly for us. Listen to the words of our Savior: **"Do not think that I came to destroy the Law or the Prophets. I did not come to destroy but to fulfill. For assuredly, I say to you, till heaven and earth pass away, one jot or one tittle** [*the smallest stroke in the Hebrew alphabet*] **will by no means pass from the law till all is fulfilled"** Matthew 5:17–18).

Yes, our Savior, the Seed of the woman, lived for us and thus fulfilled the Law of God perfectly for each and every one of us. But since **the wages of sin is death** (Romans 6:23a), our Savior also sacrificed Himself on the cross and paid the **wages of sin** for each and every one of us. The result, **the gift of God is eternal life in Christ Jesus our LORD** (Romans 6:23b). So when we put it all together, we arrive at this God-given conclusion: **The wages of sin is death, but the gift of God is eternal life in Christ Jesus our Lord** (Romans 6:23).

But maybe we are puzzled a bit. Maybe we still have some questions.

Question 1: *"How about those poor souls, our brothers and sisters in the Old Testament times—before Christ came? How could they be assured of God's forgiving love?"*

That's a good question and shows a loving and healthy concern! So here's the answer from God Himself: Since it has always been true that **the wages of sin is death**, and since it is clearly pointed out by God that **without shedding of blood there is no remission** (Hebrews 9:22), the LORD God established an elaborate system of substitutionary shedding of blood and death in His Ceremonial Laws.

In accordance with these Laws/regulations, various animals and birds were brought to the place of worship by the individual as substitutes for their sins and for their comfort. These animals or birds were killed, and their blood was sprinkled on the altar as a substitutionary death of the sinner. This was done for the immediate comfort of His children. It was also a forecast of the once-and-for-all shedding of the blood of the Seed of the woman and His substitutionary atonement for the sins of the whole world.

But make no mistake about it—the Moral Law of God stands absolutely firm and is applicable to every generation and for all time. It stands as a solid and sure rock of God's moral standards in the midst of a decadent, corrupt, and sin-filled world. Its purpose is and always will be, to teach everyone of the righteousness which God demands of everyone.

That is where the Seed of the woman comes in. <u>By faith</u> in the LORD's Christ, the Seed of the woman, who lived perfectly for us and gave His life a ransom for us, God transfers the righteousness of Christ to us. **For by grace you have been saved through faith, and that not of yourselves; it is a gift of God** (Ephesians 2:8). Yes, praise the LORD, the believing children of God are free from the condemnation of the law. **For the law of the Spirit of life in Christ Jesus has made me free from the law of sin and death** (Romans 8:2). How do we respond? We joyfully sing and praise our merciful LORD God:

> *Praise to the LORD, the Almighty, the King of creation!*
> *O my soul, praise Him, for He is thy Health and Salvation!*
> *Join the full throng;*
> *Wake, harp and psalter and song;*
> *Sound forth in glad adoration!*
>
> *Praise to the LORD! Oh, let all that is in me adore Him!*
> *All that has life and breath, come now with praises before Him!*
> *Let the Amen*
> *Sound from His people again;*
> *Gladly for aye we adore Him. (TLH 39:1&4)*

Question 2: *Since the holy Law of God is totally fulfilled in the Christ, do those holy precepts delivered by God on Mount Sinai serve any good purpose for God's faithful people today?*

Another good question! And here is God's answer: The Law of God is very important to us, for there we see God's holy and perfect will for humanity. Though we are free from the condemnation of the Law by faith in Christ Jesus, we as God's loving children continually use God's Law as a <u>curb</u> against sin and a <u>guide</u> in our lives. Of course, by reason of our sinful nature we regularly miss the mark of perfectly walking in His ways. That is why we regularly flee for refuge to God's infinite mercy, seeking and <u>imploring His grace for the sake of our Lord Jesus Christ</u>.

The Apostle Paul, moved by the Spirit, used himself as an example and put it this way: **I know that in me (that is, in my flesh) nothing good dwells; for to will is present with me, but how to perform what is good I do not find. For the good that I will to do, I do not do; but the evil I will not to do, that I practice. . . . O wretched man that I am! Who will deliver me from this body of death? <u>I thank God—through Jesus Christ our Lord!</u>** (Romans 7:18–19, 24)

Yes, my friends in Christ, it's a long way from Eden to Bethlehem. The preparation for the Savior's birth was thousands of years in the making, but absolutely necessary. God was preparing His people for the most important task on earth—namely, to give to the world the Child of Hope in the midst of a hopeless world held in the grip of sin and Satan. For that reason God's faithful people have never faltered but faithfully continue to sing:

By grace God's Son, our only Savior,
Came down to earth to bear our sin.
Was it because of your own merit
That Jesus died your soul to win?
No, it was grace, and grace alone,
That brought him from his heav'nly thone.

By grace! Oh, mark this word of promise
When we are by our sins oppressed,
When Satan plagues our troubled conscience,

And when our heart is seeking rest.
What reason cannot comprehend
God by His grace to us does send.

By grace to timid hearts that tremble,
In tribulation's furnace tried—
By grace, despite all fear and trouble,
The Father's heart is open wide.
Where could we help and strength secure
If grace were not our anchor sure? (CW 384:2,3,4 adapted)

PRAYER

O LORD my God, as I review Your commandments, I too recognize my utter inability to faultlessly walk in them. My sinful flesh continually rears its ugly head, and I find myself frustrated as was the Apostle Paul when he cried out, **"I delight in the law of God, in my inner being, but I see in my members another law waging war against the law of my mind and making me captive to the law of sin that dwells in my members."** Therefore I also realize with the Apostle Paul: **Wretched man that I am! Who will deliver me from this body of death? Thanks be to God—through Jesus Christ our Lord!** (Romans 7:22–25 ESV) Indeed, I too continually flee for refuge to Your forgiving, saving grace and love for me in my Savior, Jesus Christ. What would I do without my Lord and Savior? What would I do without Your blessing of forgiveness in Your Son? LORD, help me by Your Spirit never to take this gift of Your forgiveness for granted. Rather, I pray, fill me with Your Spirit that I may continually fight the good fight of faith— constantly putting down the urges of my flesh and the evil ways of Satan and continually clinging alone to Your forgiving love. In the gracious name of my Savior I pray. Amen.

INI

"Then the LORD said to him, "This is the land of which I swore to give Abraham, Isaac, and Jacob, saying, 'I will give it to your descendants.' I have caused you to see it with your eyes, but you shall not cross over there" (Deuteronomy 34:4).